[A PLACE FOR DIALOGUE]

AMERICAN LAND & LIFE SERIES

Wayne Franklin, series editor

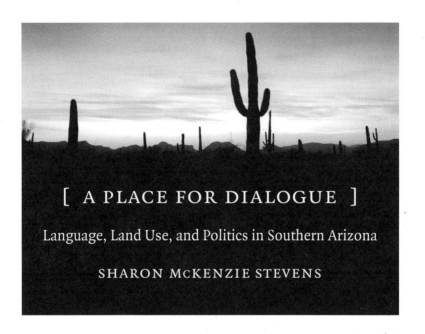

[A PLACE FOR DIALOGUE]

Language, Land Use, and Politics in Southern Arizona

SHARON McKENZIE STEVENS

FOREWORD BY WAYNE FRANKLIN

University of Iowa Press, Iowa City

University of Iowa Press, Iowa City 52242

Copyright © 2007 by the University of Iowa Press

www.uiowapress.org

The University of Iowa Press is a member of Green Press Initiative
and is committed to preserving natural resources.

Printed on acid-free paper

ISBN-10: 1-58729-534-2 cloth

ISBN-13: 978-1-58729-534-8 cloth

LCCN: 2006935964

07 08 09 10 11 C 5 4 3 2 1

For desert grasslands and watersheds,

and for Tilly Warnock

[CONTENTS]

Foreword by *Wayne Franklin*, ix

Acknowledgments, xiii

Prologue, 1

1. The Range of Rhetoric, 7

2. Open Space, Conservation, and Endangerment, 38

3. From Battle Lines to Collaborative Space, 72

4. Socioecology and the Future of the Land, 105

5. From Identity Politics to Dialogic Identities, 137

Epilogue, 171

Methodological Appendix, 183

Notes, 189

Works Cited, 199

Index, 215

[FOREWORD]
Wayne Franklin

What do we talk about when we talk about land? Sharon Stevens deftly answers this question by redirecting it. She attends to what we say about land, to be sure; but more than that, she attends to *how* we say it. Not that she is interested in the literary "style" of environmental discourse. What attracts her far more than that is the social rhetoric by which we constitute the environment as a subject, by which in the process we also form ourselves into a community.

We are all familiar with the polarization that often seems to rule discussions of the world around us. People are presumed to hold a priori positions that sharpen their individual arguments at the same time that they limit the freedom with which they can talk about what are at bottom shared problems. Without denying that people do indeed take such rigid stances, both as a matter of practice and as a matter of ideology, Stevens insists that we should not therefore jump to conclusions. Suspending for a while the urge to pin people down to the implied or stated positions they occupy is common courtesy. It is also a very useful strategy if what we really value is effective (meaning effect-bearing) discussion.

Problems with the environment seem so pressing at this point in the twenty-first century that it is easy to become impatient with the endless talk that environmental issues generate. If the insights offered by Stevens appear to be productive of yet more talk and little action, one might reflect that human action in many cases has been a big part of the problem. Had we attended more to the world and less to our own imperatives, the world (and we) might be in better shape today. But I do not want to divide action from language, for language is, as it were, a precursor of action—that which both disposes us to and serves to rationalize certain courses of action. Part of the lesson Stevens gives is that discourse is itself part of the problem. We know that is so if we observe how people in modern industrial cultures tend to speak about nature. It is usually the object of our verbs, the plastic recipient of our meanings and purposes. Of course it is much more than these things; but that is how we talk about it, where we position it in our discourse about the world. Because we assign it such narrow, passive roles in our language, we rarely see beyond those roles to the booming, buzzing realities of the world-as-such. Our sentences are imperially self-centered. An acquaintance in a well-settled part of metropolitan Boston, talking on the phone the other day, blurted out, "There is a moose in my backyard!" That was, as one might say, an utterly natural response to an unusual occurrence. Yet one might perceive the intrusion quite differently if one viewed nature as something more than a collection of yards and fields and roads and parking lots. An ecological language might de-center the sentence, replacing the presumption of human control with something like a web of syntactic crossings. In many ways, we cannot imagine the world as science tells us it is because our everyday language is inherently possessive.

The limits placed on nature by our discourse about it have the tendency to suppress our recognition of the dissonance between statement and actuality—and to worsen the bad effects of our "doing" on and in the world. Nature writers since Gilbert White of Selborne and Henry Thoreau of Concord at times have managed to crack open the hazy, shellacked surface of our talk about nature and let some light and air and actual things through. In *Walden*, Thoreau erases our terms while endeavoring to listen for those the world might be thought to offer. At the end of his chapter "Sounds" (which is a mélange of human and nonhuman noise, from locomotive whistles to the "dismal screams" of the screech owl), he thus imagines the human house as a natural object, with "No yard! but unfenced Nature" reaching up to its sills, so that an intrusive suburban moose could be no surprise at all in *his* Concord.

Such flips of terminology and perspective are salutary and sanative. But for the most part even nature writers do not often allow nature to take over human language. They deal in talk, not things. Thoreau himself verges perilously close to mere wit. Still, this gross distinction between talk and things may be part of the problem Sharon Stevens wishes to solve. Since language is one large cognitive environment outside of which it is very hard for us to venture, it may be better to acknowledge its constraints and endeavor to have the best sorts of talk we can. For Stevens, whose methodology is rooted partly in rhetoric and partly in dialogical theory, talk constitutes us as both individual human subjects and as a community. Discourse about anything is first of all a negotiation between people. Her fieldwork in the Sonoran desert of Pima County, Arizona, stimulated by the complexities of a collaborative conservation plan initiated there, leads her to offer stunningly humane observations about how people by and large do (or might) talk about the world they collectively inhabit, use, love, exploit, and . . . talk about.

The application of her insights to that situation and others like it is merely one part of what she offers. We all would learn a great deal if we could begin to listen as she does with such consummate civility to the concerns of people with whom she may or may not share core assumptions. If language is a prison, it is also an immensely useful tool, an innately human construction, that can domesticate us in the here and now if only we have the wit to let it.

[ACKNOWLEDGMENTS]

I owe first thanks to those men and women who allowed me to interview them for this study. They shared their time, their words, and often their homes with me; they welcomed me into their world of concerns and ideas and hopes; and they allowed me to be a student learning about qualitative research, about rhetoric, and about Arizona. I additionally thank Nicole Fyffe from the Pima County Administrator's Office, who generously pointed me in the right direction for Sonoran Desert Conservation Plan documents and who supplied me with web archives on disk for easier access.

Though now significantly revised, this project began as a dissertation funded by two Dean Charles Tatum Awards and a Patrick Dissertation Award. I am grateful for this financial support as well as for the more general support of the University of Arizona's English Department. I especially thank the faculty and graduate students in the University of Arizona's program in Rhetoric, Composition, and the Teaching of English, from whom I learned the intellectual tools necessary for this book. Special thanks go to Tilly Warnock, who encouraged and inspired me as a dissertation director and a friend; to Tom Miller, who commented tirelessly on my dissertation chapters, pushing me to develop my intellectual rigor and to clarify and humanize my prose style; to Roxanne Mountford, who first mentored me in qualitative methods; and to Ed White, who generously gave advice. Jen Croissant also served on my dissertation committee, generously contributing her enthusiasm, her useful critique, and her understanding of science studies. I also thank Sarah Soule, who introduced me to social movement studies, which have shaped my approach to this field site more than may be evident from the final product. Still others, including Paul Anderson and Joan Fujimura, have given me key assistance at conferences. Jason Thompson, Jillian Toomey, and McKenzie have helped with my approach to Kenneth Burke's work.

In the process of this work, I have found several people invaluable for a combination of intellectual stimulation and holistic support. Chief among these is my husband, Phil Stevens, who argued grazing politics with me, pointed me in the right direction for more information, fixed my computer, web-designed my first images of stasis and skew for conference presentations, gave me advice on word choice, comforted and prodded me, married me in the midst of it all, changed diapers, cooked, allowed me to publicly characterize him, made me stop for Tucson sunsets, and assisted in a million other ways to keep me writing and to keep me enjoying my writing. To my parents, who have cheered (and sometimes funded) me as I studied, I am also grateful. Thanks are due to Patty Malesh, Kat McLellan, and Leslie Dupont, among others, for intelligent companionship. And, just by making life that much better, my young daughter, Rain, has also helped me write.

Throughout the creation of this book, the editors and staff of the University of Iowa Press have been consistently helpful, including Arnold Friedman, Allison Thomas, and Charlotte Wright. In particular, Wayne Franklin and Holly Carver have been as supportive as any writer could hope for. Thank you.

[A PLACE FOR DIALOGUE]

SUMMER 2001

Early morning, somewhere near the U.S.-Mexico border, sitting on a bench on the wood porch of a near-permanently boarded-up general store. We are surrounded by desert floor, by dry state lands, but around us we can see the National Forest Service's "sky islands," mountain forests that mark Arizona by suddenly rising into cooler air. An employee of a government agency has chosen to meet me here before moving off to his work for the day, and we are discussing the contentious politics of ranching. "I don't know who's winning," he tells me. "My opinion is the land use is almost forgotten in the process."

Our discussion ranges from the government agent's personal involvement in range management to his perspective on the larger field of decision-making. He traces his choice of a career to an agricultural background and a love for working with the land, but also to the idealism, social movements, and environmentalism of the 1960s, which led him to seek a public career where he could do some good in natural resource management. He opines that the current regulatory climate complicates practical decision-making, but he still believes he has seen improvements, such as increased grass cover and soil stability, in "allotments," in public lands leased to ranchers for grazing under government management. As an example of his daily work, he discusses working with a rancher to maintain check-dams, which slow the rush of water through a wash and help watersheds recharge.

Water is the most obvious limit on land use, and it is one of the key inputs into the shape of the landscape in these desert grasslands of southern Arizona. When winter rains are good, gold Mexican poppies, pastel globe mallow, and owl clover draw photographers to the public lands of Arizona ranches. When the summer rains are poor, ranchers find themselves selling down their herd or buying hay as supplemental feed for their cattle. Yet, as the check-dam example indicates, rain is not the only factor affecting watershed recharge and the landscape more generally. Direct and indirect human activity—some beneficial, much harmful, as when devegetation leads to accelerated erosion—is also a significant contributing factor.

Practical everyday management decisions, such as building check-dams or laying fences, are, at least on their face, simple but crucial decisions people make about the land. More complex scenes of deliberative land use planning are ubiquitous throughout the American West. As a concept, the West serves as a national placeholder for untamed nature, open space, and extensive resources, and, in an even more undefined way, for the future and for possibility. At the heart of these meanings are frequently contradictory hopes and desires that symbolically mark the Western landscape and intersect with the material reality of the American West, influencing what gets interpreted as beneficial, what gets interpreted as harmful, and by whom.

In this book, I sketch a webbed interaction where human agency is a response to the land, and vice versa. What I have just called "material reality" is the living integration of the land with both human practices and natural systems, a reality that varies both geographically and temporally, shaped by human choices and the land's responsiveness to those choices. Human choices, in turn, are constructed within a web of social, political, and ecological relationships—a "socioecological" web where every strand reverberates in response to the movement of any other strand, as with passing breezes or insects on spider webs.[1]

These interactions are system-specific: I choose to focus on land use conflicts in southern Arizona. In particular, I examine conflicts between cattle ranchers and environmentalists, although I refer to others, such as developers and recreationists. These diverse stakeholders seek different outcomes, often through political channels, thereby deciding what is in fact possible for ranching, for environmental conservation and preservation, and for other uses of the land. As I examine resulting political conflicts, I analytically foreground language. That is, I use the way that socioecological relationships are discussed and debated as a lens for understanding human practices toward the land.

Why language? One answer to this question is disciplinary. My training is in rhetoric. While this term has multiple meanings—its popular use in the phrase "mere rhetoric," for example, connotes both moral and material emptiness—its disciplinary uses point as far back as Aristotle's concern not only with persuasion but also with deliberation, with political but nonetheless collaborative decision-making (*On Rhetoric*). More contemporary sources of my understanding of "rhetoric" are Kenneth Burke's interest in the relationship between human symbol use and human action (*Language*) and historian of rhetoric James Berlin's claim that rhetoric is a form of social epistemic, which means that language and socially learned patterns of language use shape how people view the world. I also look beyond the discipline of rhetoric to the broad field of science studies, emphasizing Bruno Latour's concern with the way a material referent, such as soil in a single field at the edge of a Brazilian rainforest, becomes inscribed within language so that it can be used as delocalized scientific knowledge (*Pandora's* 24–79). By connecting language to materiality, especially when examining science-based claims, I approach language as a participant in relationships that extend beyond language.

A final significant influence is the Soviet-period linguist Mikhail Bakhtin, who emphasizes the social nature of language use. "I live in a world of others' words," writes Bakhtin, "and my entire life is an orientation in this world, a reaction to others' words (an infinitely diverse reaction) beginning with my assimilation of them" ("From Notes" 143). Bakhtin argues that language is always learned through conversation, spoken to an intended listener, or written for an intended audience, and, therefore, thoroughly oriented toward dialogue. Meaning is dynamic rather than static because words are inflected by different speakers within the specific context of their use. However, Bakhtin also notes that while "understanding is always dialogic to some degree," it can become, to a greater or lesser degree, monologic, decontextualized from dialogue, without expecting a response, without expecting to itself change in response to others' voices ("The Problem" 111). The tension between language's inherent dialogism and its potential monologic use is a central concern of this book, as actors move between attempts to collaborate and the reification of arguments in polarized political debates. Together with other disciplinary and interdisciplinary influences, Bakhtin's concern for the social consequences of particular forms of language use shapes my understanding of language as a site where socioecological relationships become bound together and fixed, at least momentarily, into specific cultural meanings that shape human decision and action.

My second reason for focusing on language points beyond this academic response to my concerns and values for the land. I have lived with—indeed, when I consider my work from an ethnographic perspective,[2] I think of myself as having lived in—debates over how to act toward southern Arizona's land since I moved to Tucson in 1997. I have lived in western lands and in debates over western lands all my life, as I hiked and ran rivers with my parents as a child, as I visited my uncle's ranch in southern Oregon, as I overheard political arguments (often taking the form of jokes and personal stories at holiday dinners) about what it means to live well with the land. I have lived in these debates as I read regional news, and my environmental and economic consciousness has been formed by the stories and arguments told to the general public. In the process of this living, I have learned to love the land, and learned to love people, in ways that often are contradictory. In my more formal research—a series of interviews with ranchers, environmentalists, scientists, and land managers, combined with an analysis of public texts—these contradictions have become acute as I have confronted the potential incompatibility between my desire to respect diverse viewpoints, lifestyles, and values while simultaneously promoting diverse and healthy ecosystems, economies, and cultures. Not surprisingly, then, I have developed an admiration for those who have successfully learned to create productive dialogue in the face of difference and conflict. I now focus on language also so that I can understand the rhetorical practices of those who take the tensions of conflict and use them to propose creative responses to land use. On another level, I am interested in participatory democracy more generally and in the rhetorical practices that sustain it.

In my first chapter, I begin to sketch some of the more prominent lines of conflict over grazing on public lands. At the same time, I examine competing historical narratives and representations of land use to provide an overview of the contradictions within debates over the cultural, economic, and environmental value of grazing on the public lands of southern Arizona. One story traces public lands ranching to the inadequacies of the Homestead Act of 1862 when applied to arid lands. In this story, the 1934 Taylor Grazing Act, with its system of leases, formally recognizes the necessity of using public lands for grazing. Another story instead sees public lands grazing as a system of appropriation and privatization of the commons. These competing narratives structure the way different debaters understand current rights to the land and how they justify prioritizing different land uses, such as grazing, recreation, or species preservation. However, these arguments about the history of Arizona lands—and about their present use, as well—disguise desires and decisions oriented toward the future of land use. When histories are taken for granted, they become a source of misunderstanding and friction. Rhetorical analysis is eminently suited to a more reflexive approach to language, and in this first chapter (which, incidentally, shares the title "The Range of Rhetoric" with part 1 of Kenneth Burke's foundational A Rhetoric of Motives) I introduce key approaches to rhetorical analysis to illustrate what rhetoric adds to study of the western range.

My second chapter focuses on one key arena of current politics by considering the Sonoran Desert Conservation Plan initiated by Pima County, Arizona, in 1998.[3] Through this plan, the county hopes to create consensus-based managed growth that can curb its current pattern of rapid and sprawling development. By working with scientific and cultural experts, with property owners, nongovernmental organizations, and other stakeholders, and with the interested public, the county government hopes to create, pass, and act on legislation that preserves open space for such uses as recreation, ranching, and species and habitat conservation. The inclusiveness of a process that must balance multiple goals and enact them in specific zoning and conservation purchase practices has turned the SDCP, hailed in 1999 by Interior Secretary Bruce Babbitt as "the most exciting event of its kind anywhere in the United States,"[4] into a much longer process than originally hoped, with the last word yet to be written. The plan has led to some remarkable advances, such as the passage of a May 2004 open space bond that allows the county to raise money for more than one hundred million dollars worth of conservation purchases. But it also has highlighted the contentiousness of issues that seamlessly traverse social and ecological boundaries. In this chapter, I analyze key reports, draft plans, and public comment, considering how language used by different actors points to different assumptions about conservation and land use.

In chapters 3, 4, and 5, I turn to a microlevel analysis, one focused on specific habits of language use. My core sources for this analysis are private interviews with ranchers, environmentalists, and those who work with them as government agents or advisors, all speaking as individuals with experience directly related to grazing politics. Chapters 3 and 4 focus on science-based arguments. At the heart of much of the debate over land use in southern Arizona is a concern for the impacts of grazing on biodiversity and ecosystem health. I identify three competing arguments about these impacts: that cattle break up crusted-over earth, fertilize soil, and thereby help restore desert grasslands; cattle erode topsoil and spread "invasive exotics" (aggressive introduced plants) and thereby destroy desert grasslands; and cattle do not benefit grasslands in substantive ways but still can be managed to avoid substantive harm.

Because of the popular status of science as a truth-based form of knowledge beyond interpretation, it is typical for adherents to any one of these arguments to be derisive of proponents of competing arguments, attributing disagreements to self-interested lies or delusions and thereby shutting down dialogue. In chapter 3, I use stasis theory to analyze rhetorical practices that contribute to this dynamic, and I suggest an alternative approach, "skew" rhetoric, that creates space for dialogue. In chapter 4, I look more closely at the content of these competing ecology-based truth claims, suggesting how they might each have validity if grounded in different desired futures.

My fifth chapter turns from the way my informants talk about the land and ecological relationships to the way they talk about themselves and others. Despite the shift in focus, I maintain an analysis that focuses on relationships, discussing how identities shape both human relationships and human-land relationships. I begin by examining the politics of antagonistically positioned rancher and environmentalist identities. In spite of the challenges created by the ubiquity of identity politics, however, many of my informants find ways to play with the meaning and behaviors associated with these identities, either by bridging the two identities, by acknowledging diversity within each identity, or by proposing alternate identities, such as "applied ecologist," that altogether circumvent the oppositional use of the terms rancher and environmentalist. This identity-shifting is key to the ability of many of those I interviewed to create dialogue that develops mutual understanding and respect, as well as changes in ranch management and conservation. Many have successfully worked through conflict and different ways of understanding the land to collaborate with past antagonists. Their work points the way to more productive forms of problem solving.

I do recognize that dialogue between environmentalists and ranchers is possible, in part because of historic antagonisms that have created a social motive—a rhetorical exigence—for finding new ways to manage the land. Traditional approaches have become encumbered by routinized power struggles carried out in legislatures and the courts. There are limits to collaboration as well as to conflict, and there are limits to rhetorical analyses that focus on inclusive politics rather than margins, movements, and agonistic strategies. I briefly consider these limits in my epilogue. Nonetheless, while I recognize the importance of agonism to the overall debate, I still consider visionary those who respond to this embittered situation by deciding it is time to cooperate. These persons have taught me something about deliberation, about participatory democracy, and about using differences to solve, rather than to aggravate, entrenched problems that bridge land and language. This book is about what I have learned.

[1]

THE RANGE OF RHETORIC

Once a year, my maternal uncle allowed my parents to hunt on the southern Oregon ranch that had once belonged to my great-grandfather, who had bought the land as an investment. My parents' hunting trips were my autumn vacation, my opportunity to know firsthand a landscape of my mother's childhood. While my mother and father hunted, I would run through cattle chutes, ride horses, and wander oak woods. As my uncle and father inter-acted, I internalized the basics of ranchland etiquette: get permission to use the land, wave at drivers of passing pickups, and, most crucially, leave gates and everything else as you find them. When I visited my cousins who lived on the lower portion of the ranch, I helped herd sheep, collected eggs, and failed trying to milk with the small hands of a bookworm.

In these and other family visits, I overheard—in the way that a child hears the talk of adults and only later tries to make sense of it—a narrative of ranch life. I was struck by the romance of my uncle harnessing Team, a single Shire, when winter snows required him to cart hay to cattle on roads impassable to motorized vehicles. I wondered at my uncle's disappoint-ment in having no sons, especially as I was in awe of my cousins for their long hours of physical labor, a daily summer routine of stamina and strength I felt was beyond me. I noticed the ranch household's limited cash flow, but also its plentiful food and expansive property, which extended beyond my ability to walk in a day. Such an economy did not fit into my American habit of routine consumption or my developing distinctions between rich and poor.

At home, I overheard my mother as she worried about my uncle's choice to take a dangerous summer job as a flagger to help pay property taxes, working long hours for the road construction company while still tending the ranch. The challenge of making ends meet became even clearer to me as I grew older. Once, my father and I stopped to visit with my uncle as he supervised work at a new gravel pit. Somehow I got the impression that this mining was a secret, though to this day I am not sure my impression was accurate. Perhaps my uncle was dissatisfied with the compromise of mining, just as he was dissatisfied with my parents' hunting; perhaps he only wanted to avoid meddling from neighbors, from the "rich Californian environmentalists" he increasingly railed against, who bought up adjacent lands, built large homes on ridge tops, and then tried to put him out of business. My uncle understood that the motive of the suit filed against him was the desire to improve the view from a newcomer's trophy summer home. He defended himself successfully, and by the time I was in high school, he had painted on the roof of his barn an image of one of the green circular creatures from the cover of *A Hitchhiker's Guide to the Galaxy*, its red tongue wagging derisively at the neighbor up the hill. The only reason my uncle flew a Confederate flag, I was told in response to my criticism, was to irritate these same neighbors, though the complex of issues coalescing around private property, states' rights, and federal regulation, banner issues for sagebrush rebels, must have had something to do with my uncle's decision to see the flag as an appropriate symbol of his resistance.

When I was in eighth grade, my science teacher encouraged me to apply for an Oregon Museum of Science and Industry scholarship to its science summer camp. When I received it, my father helped me earn the remaining money I needed by selling wood from trees on our lot. My father came from a farming family, and while he himself was a millworker in pulp and paper, he had turned much of our backyard into a large vegetable garden that dwarfed the majority of urban gardens. My father liked the work and loved the corn and tomatoes; I preferred the climbing trees with their broad shade- and privacy-granting leaves that ringed our property. My father could count on me to actively protest every time he felled a tree to let in more sunlight. I made signs to expose his duplicity and wrote poems to denounce his rapaciousness, poems that had the unintended consequence of making him laugh, although today he does call me to let me know when he has instead planted trees. For the sake of science camp, however, I chose to accept my father's assistance and profit from the felled trees.

My favorite counselor was an energetic graduate student in botany who led my friends and me wading through streams to identify plants and to discuss their habitat. I was nervous about violating property rights the first time this counselor bent down barbed wire for us to squeeze through, but she explained to me that the fence was intended to manage cattle, not to keep us off public land. This was my first conscious introduction to public lands ranching, and it messed with my sense of exclusive property rights and clear divisions between private and public, imbibed from mainstream culture. This botanist's explicit interest, however, was not in the range but in the riparian area beyond it. She was concerned about the way my friends and I walked along the streambed, discouraging us from stepping near its edges, teaching us to minimize our footprint on the plants and erosion-prone banks. When we returned from the stream through dry grass fields back to camp, this botanist showed us charts of flower parts almost as an afterthought, but the message that drew my heart to botany was not her talk of stamens and stigma but her commonsense coupling of respect for nature and scientific ways of knowing.

From another counselor, I learned that ecology could have a politics and that the scientific gaze might support a public imperative. This counselor, a wildlife biologist, I remember only on the ground: kneeling to show us black widow nests, squatting to poke through coyote scat, bending to point to the meristems—the growth cells—of bunch grasses. Spiders and scat failed to capture my imagination, but on subsequent family vacations in eastern Oregon, I railed against overgrazing whenever I saw bunch grasses grazed below their meristems. Gradually I became convinced that ecological botany was my life's work, and I maintained this conviction until my final undergraduate year, when I acknowledged to myself that, regardless of my attraction to botany as a system of knowledge, I nonetheless preferred my work as a writing tutor to my internship in a field-based science lab. I graduated in English. When I decided to return to graduate school, my interest in writing led me to the discipline of rhetoric and composition, to studies focused on the relationships among language use, understanding, persuasion, and deliberation, and back to the environment as a particularly fraught site of public debate in the West. At this point, I lived in Tucson, Arizona, where the politics of public lands grazing is a particularly salient environmental issue. Arizona's biodiversity and aridity only exacerbates the more general contention over western ranching that I had first encountered in Oregon.

Despite some specific differences in ecology and legislation, however, many of the issues evident in my experiences in Oregon are also central to debates about grazing in southern Arizona and throughout the West. Debate frequently turns on topics that appear even in my short narrative, such as the role of scientific knowledge, habitat conservation, the ecology of grazing, predator control, the distribution of different grass species, the relationship between ranching and housing development, watershed restoration, landscape aesthetics, extractive uses of the land, rural lifestyles, ranch economics, property rights, the meaning and management of public lands, litigation, the role and value of fencing, and recreation. Other topics central to the debate include wildlife management, fire management, the protection of endangered species, the distribution of power in the courts and legislatures, the role of bureaucratic management, the culture of ranching, and archaeological preservation (particularly because many ranchlands are historic homes and hunting grounds of Native Americans).

These specific topics are regularly invoked in grazing debates, although the approach to these topics differs depending on speaker or writer, context, purpose, and audience. These topics point to what is at stake in arguments about whether, and how, cattle should be grazed in the West. In this book, I focus on contention over grazing in the desert grasslands of southern Arizona, but much of my analysis is broadly applicable to—and certainly informed by, implicated within, and saturated by—debate about grazing that ranges more generally throughout the western United States. Any decisions made about who gets to manage western public lands—and how—may have significant impacts on the lives of ranchers and recreationists, and on western economies traditionally founded on agriculture and resource extraction, though now increasingly oriented toward development and tourism. These decisions also impact the ecosystems and watersheds[1] that are intimately caught up in human land use, as well as the myriad species that depend on them. How many cattle should be allowed in which areas, and in which seasons? How much should the Arizona State Lands Department, the National Forest Service, and the Bureau of Land Management charge ranchers for grazing their cattle on these public lands? Are the grazing leases granted by these public agencies similar to private property (ranchers use them as collateral on loans and sell them when they sell their ranches), or are they privileges that can be revoked? How should ecological information be gathered and used to determine whether public lands grazing allotments should be renewed, increased, decreased, or withdrawn? Should environmental groups be allowed to bid competitively for grazing leases for the explicit purpose of resting the land? Should state and federal legislatures designate some public lands, such as federal wilderness areas, as cattle free? Or should all lands be off limits to cattle, as called for in the now dated Earth First! slogan "Cattle Free by '93"? Would de-cowing any public lands be an ecological disaster, as suggested by the controversial guru of Holistic Range Management, Allan Savory? Even if cattle are ecologically damaging, how should their impacts be weighed against the contributions of ranches to rural economies? Do ranches contribute to rural economies? Are ranches instead an economic drain, a form of welfare to the rich? Are ranches and ranch lifestyles a significant part of western culture with intrinsic worth? How is their worth measured against the worth of endangered species? Is it even appropriate to pit ranching against preservation, as in the preceding question, or must one first inquire into ways that ranchers are adapting to the demands of ecosystem management? How might models of sustainable ranching be developed and implemented? Can there even be such a thing as sustainable ranching in the arid West?

I analyze the debate surrounding these questions, but not with a view toward answering any of them in a way that could provide a prescription for land management. Instead, I examine how these questions are raised, how persons involved in the debate try to persuade others of their views, and to what effect. I analyze how different persons draw on topical resources, address anticipated counterarguments, and contribute to the dynamic political scene. I address, as a crucial aspect of these deliberations, the acquisition and deployment of power, power that is exercised in legislatures, law courts, bureaucracies, and on the ground in the rural and wild landscapes of the West.

I especially attend to how these deliberations participate in constructing the communal future of western residents—human, plant, and animal. The interactions among these residents form a dynamic system of response and counter-response, an integrated social and ecological web that varies by place and shifts over time. Both human and nonhuman residents act within this socioecology. Squat mesquite trees drop their sweet blonde beans and spread upland as cattle and birds eat them; chain fruit cholla drink from precious rains; remaining moisture soaks down into the water table or races swiftly through arroyos during summer monsoons; Lehmann lovegrass spreads along roadsides and grasslands burned in summer fires. The actions of these and other nonhuman residents shape the landscapes of southern Arizona. With these residents, humans codetermine ecosystem dynamics. Unlike nonhumans, however, humans may act with the agency that comes from reflexive symbol use.

The use of symbols to shape the socioecology of land use systems is my central topic, a topic I approach through the lens of political rhetoric. The central concerns of political rhetoric are outlined in Barry Brummett's "Communities, Identities, and Politics":

> When we say political rhetoric, we are speaking of discourse, of symbolic and significant behavior, that creates, maintains, challenges, and overthrows power; of discourse that creates community in all its complexity, of discourse that creates identity; and of discourse that creates shared definitions of reality, even if increasingly fragmented and parochial communities congeal around those definitions. (295–96)

Inquiry into political rhetoric, then, will investigate the role of symbols in negotiating power, constituting communities and identities, and defining reality. It will address the interactive nature of symbol use, the processes of identification and differentiation that occur as humans dialogue with one another.

These concerns bridge cultural and structural analyses. Popular uses of the term "rhetoric" tend to focus on language that is strategically targeted at structural changes (electoral or legislative politics). Disciplinary definitions, however, tend to additionally foreground rhetoric's importance to the meanings and practices that constitute culture, to the role of language in shaping community, identity, and, especially, what James Berlin has called social epistemic—the way humans understand reality as a result of their interactions with one another and with the material world. Culture and structure interact (Polletta "Culture"; "Snarls"). Both are key to understanding political action. Throughout this book, then, I examine cultural constructs as well as official politics as a way to understand the political rhetoric of debate over grazing in Arizona.

Popular representations of this debate suggest it is an intractable conflict. CBS's 60 Minutes episode "Wild Wolves," aired on March 5, 2001, is an example. Much of this episode flips back and forth between close-ups of a rancher and of Kieran Suckling, who was then the head of Tucson's Southwest Center for Biological Diversity, an environmental nonprofit focused on the preservation of endangered species and their habitats. The episode frames Suckling as a spokesperson for wolves. CBS's online archive begins with the comment: "There's a war over wild wolves in the American West. It pits traditional enemies against each other in a feud that has already claimed casualties." These casualties are later revealed to be wolves that have been deliberately shot. As the television episode approaches its finale, it provides a close-up of a rancher who makes an us-or-them statement suggesting that ranching and wolf introduction are fundamentally opposed. While 60 Minutes is infamous for its antagonistic either/or issue framings, this episode is in many ways typical of mainstream journalistic representations that understand public lands grazing to be a two-sided issue of ranchers versus environmentalists. These representations accurately reflect—and at the same time, help to constitute—a polarization that is common among many, but not all, participants in grazing debates.

At the same, time, however, an increasing number of political actors are working to disrupt two-sided representations of grazing conflict through collaborations among environmentalists, scientists, and ranchers. Examples of these collaborations are the Quivira Coalition in New Mexico and the Malpai Borderlands Group that straddles the border of Arizona and New Mexico. Also relevant are the Nature Conservancy's cooperative Muleshoe Ranch in southern Arizona and the Udall Center Common Ground Roundtable, a mediated dialogue not tied to any one ranch. To these nongovernmental alliances might be added the Pima County-sponsored Sonoran Desert Conservation Plan, a collaborative land planning process aimed at habitat and cultural conservation with the intention of reconciling the diverse values brought to bear on these issues.

Despite my interest in political cooperation, however, I wish also to attend to the (frequently more extreme) viewpoints that might be left out of these newly crafted places for dialogue. Conflictual and cooperative rhetorics interact. With this in mind, I ask several questions. How are arenas that enable face-to-face deliberation created? What are the limits of that deliberation? How do these de facto rhetorical communities create a place for dialogue that helps build cooperative management communities? How are those cooperative communities shaped by the conflicts they externalize, and how do they interact with continuing critiques of the managed ranching practices they promote? How are debate and dialogue linked to place in mutually constitutive relationships?

Contemporary environmental studies tend to focus unevenly on dialogue and divisive political practices. In *Image Politics*, for example, Kevin DeLuca examines how environmental groups craft images that challenge the dominant hegemony as a means to create social change. His work draws on studies of social movements that are concerned with how persons are mobilized around conflict, as do the (otherwise different) studies of

Timothy Ingalsbee and Robert Brown and Carl Herndl. Another area of environmental scholarship focuses on participatory democracy at the local level. Examples include *Bringing Society Back In*, Edward Weber's analysis of three Northwest cases of grassroots ecosystem management; "Landscape, Drama, and Dissensus," Zita Ingham's study on mediated community building; and *Finding Common Ground*, a collection edited by Robert D. Brunner et al. that addresses collaborative land management. These studies frequently acknowledge a backdrop of conflict to which local collaborations respond, and my study is more closely aligned with them than with those that foreground agonistic mobilization. I will also address how polarization and collaboration interact across the western range. Precedents for such a move include Marilyn Cooper's "Environmental Rhetoric in the Age of Hegemonic Politics," which argues that Earth First! and The Nature Conservancy have complementary functions, even though the rhetoric of the former constitutes conflict with industry while that of the latter works for conciliation. Another precedent is Craig Thomas's analysis of interagency environmental cooperation, which examines cases of cooperative failure as well as success. These studies point to the importance of understanding how conflict and cooperation dialogically influence one another in an interconnected system of meaning, persuasion, and action. When scholars examine language use in an interactive and relational context, they can make more apparent the broad range of rhetoric.

The Western Range as a Storied Place

I begin my exploration of political grazing rhetoric with a focus on texts that, by virtue of their audience, appear to most immediately target culture. In this section and the next, I examine stories that people tell to understand how they—and cattle—might belong in Arizona's politics of place. These stories create an identity for public ranchlands and the people who use them, and, at the same time, they judge whether that identity is appropriate to the future of Arizona. By evaluating the present and suggesting needed changes, these stories complement arguments aimed directly at legal and management action.

While there are many possible approaches to narrative analysis,[2] a rhetorical approach should focus explicitly on the ways that narrative shape belief and influence action. Rhetoric asks of narrative, as does Carolyn Ellis about her personal accounts, "What are the consequences my story produces?" (quoted in Ellis and Bochner 746). This question orients analysis toward the future. Yet narratives, on their face, point to the past, recalling events in meaningful tellings that shape how humans experience the world. In the individual and the collective present, past and future interact in "tension," as Stephen Crites puns in "Storytime" (165). Crites argues: "The apparent necessity by which [narrative] episodes unfold in this fictive temporality [narrative time, as opposed to phenomenological time] can beguile me into thinking that the later episodes are causally related to the earlier" (168). This beguilement occurs even though, from a temporally prior vantage point, the contingency of events was once readily apparent. Narratives replace this contingency with causality, endowing time with a logical structure. They thereby extend the experience of the past as a limiting influence on the still indeterminate future.

Crites's comments depend on one of the more commonly noted features of narrative, which is that their coherence depends on the selective emplotment of events. Narrative not only recollects but also orders. With respect to personal narrative, Colette Dauite and Cynthia Lightfoot write: "Narrative discourse organizes life—social relations, interpretations of the past, and plans for the future" (x–xi). Hayden White, addressing historical narrative, similarly argues that narrative tropes pull events from a temporal series into a meaningful whole, endowing them with "a structure, an order of meaning, that they do not possess as mere [chronological] sequence" ("The Value" 5; "Literary" 21). These plots give meaning and direction to the passing of time. Going one step further, some theorists, such as Crites, suggest that storytelling is key to turning perception into experience and to taking ownership of events as part of one's identity (160–61). Crites writes: "the subject secures its experience by digging out, archaeologically, its past in pursuit of its future pro-ject" (167). Theorist David Carr similarly locates the perceiving subject in a bidirectional timeline: "Our very capacity to experience, to be aware of what is . . . spans future and past" (12, Carr's emphasis). The narrative structure of human experience locates identity in meaningfully directed activity, as if a plot were being fashioned out of human lives.

By orienting memory toward the future, narrative takes on a rhetorical character. There is persuasion inherent in the representation, even to oneself, of a life experienced through story. Though the future remains still an unsettled object of hope and of agency, as Crites celebrates, the urge for an integrated self to act in the creation of a life story means that the past, as it is experienced and narrated, influences the shape of the future. This point has its analogue in the way a historical narrative crafts an identity for a collective, such as a nation, a culture, or a place. Sociologist Margaret Somers, who offers the concept of "narrative identity" as a corrective to structural and essentializing identity categories such as class, race, or sex, distinguishes between the "ontological narratives" of individuals and the "public, cultural, and institutional narratives" of groups and networks ("Narrativity" 604). Yet she applies to both ontological and public narratives[3] the comment: "Social identities are constituted by narrativity, social action is guided by narrativity, and social processes and interaction—both institutional and interpersonal—are narratively mediated" ("Narrativity" 606). Narrative structure, and its generic function in shaping identity, applies equally to multiple varieties of narrative.

This point applies to historical narrative as well. Hayden White, an early and leading proponent of the idea that historical interpretation is fundamentally shaped by its narrative structure, identifies several features of narratives that shape their meanings and help create social identities. These features include emplotment, ranking the importance of events and selecting among them, and the construction of narrative closure to give coherence to temporal events.[4] An individual must selectively recollect from the wide range of perception to craft personal experience. Analogously, historians must choose what to include and exclude in their histories. To do this, they need to rank events according to their cultural importance ("The Value" 10). This ranking, in turn, depends on what White calls a "social center," or type of social order, that governs the narrative. In narratives relevant to grazing debates, nonhuman actors (cattle, grasses, rains) frequently figure within this social center, creating a socioecological order that acts as a coherent identity at the center of narrative. Within this socioecological order, the agents of history act toward other humans and toward the land in ways that advance the narrative's plot.

These narrative plots achieve closure, White argues, when agents successfully shift an original order to create a new one. This is the drive of politics—to actively work to take one configuration of socioecological relationships and to shift them into new, desired relationships (or, in contrast, to actively sustain existing relationships against pressures for change). By basing closure in the establishment of (or failure to establish) a new social order, narratives inscribe a "moralizing impulse," as White puts it, and thereby give evaluative meanings to socioecological relationships and to the actors that constitute them ("The Value" 24).

White's approach complements the concept "chronotope," often used in literary analyses of narrative. This term, adopted by Mikhail Bakhtin, "expresses the inseparability" of the two components of its literal meaning, time and space ("Forms of Time" 84). Bakhtin argues that, as space and time merge in narrative, "Time thickens . . . [and] becomes . . . visible; likewise, space becomes charged and responsive to the movements of time, plot and history" ("Forms of Time" 84). He continues: "[Chronotopes] are the organizing centers for the fundamental narrative events of the novel. The chronotope is the place where knots of narrative are tied and untied. It can be said without qualification that to them belongs the meaning that shapes narrative" ("Forms of Time" 250). For Bakhtin, then, chronotopes function in the same way that a social center does for White. These similarities add to the analyst's tools the argument that chronotopes imply socioecological relationships. Shifts in chronotope indicate plot development and, ultimately, closure around a new socioecological order, an order whose moral goodness the narrative itself evaluates.

Writers' choices of chronotope, plot, and socioecological order depend on their cultural and interactional context. "People are meaning-generating organisms," explain Amia Lieblich, Rivka Tuval-Maschiach, and Tamar Zilber; "they construct their identities and self-narratives from building blocks available in their common culture, above and beyond their individual experience" (9). Mary Gergen and Kenneth Gergen concur: "Accounts of 'experience' seem more adequately understood as the outcome of a particular textual/cultural history in which people learn to tell stories of their lives to themselves and others. Such narratives are embedded within the sense-making processes of historically and culturally situated communities" (1027). This culture is not just "out there" like an atmosphere through which we move, but it is instead something that we interact with, like the air we breathe in and out, changing it in the process. Culture is a process or, better, a set of dynamic relationships. This approach to culture leads Somers to argue that the social order that gives coherence to narrative is a "relational setting" ("The Narrative Constitution" 626). Storytelling is interactive.

For example, the narrative with which I opened this chapter is a response to a broad set of relationships, not only with the other persons directly represented in my story, but also with many others. My use of the term "footprint" in a context of learning streamside manners (as in "minimize your ecological footprint") is not the term I would have chosen as an eighth-grader, or even before doing research for this book. My under-standing of my own experience has changed as a consequence of my inter-actions with ranchers, scientists, environmentalists, government agents, and the others whom I have interviewed and observed, as well as my inter-actions with print sources. As another example, during my first interview with a rancher, I suddenly "remembered" having heard many of his argu-ments before, including an appeal to the economic challenges of his lifestyle, a theme now in my opening narrative. In the process of this remembering, I took an "overheard" narrative of my uncle's ranch life, renarrated it, and came to experience it as having something to say about who I am and where I come from, identifications with the ranching culture that I did not have when I first planned this project.

Like my vocabulary, the structure of my personal narrative also indicates my intersubjective positioning in broader cultural narratives. My story has three clear parts, one whose socioecological center is located at my uncle's ranch, another that keeps its focus on science education, and a final one that achieves narrative closure by privileging rhetorical study. The first two parts create a division between ranching and rural economies, on one hand, and science and environmentalism, on the other. By the end of this book, I will challenge this bipartite division of paired topics by the presentation and analysis of multiple other ways of talking and writing about the worth of cattle grazing. The cultural ubiquity of the division inscribed by my nar-rative, however, makes it easier for me to discuss my uncle's road work as (economically) related to ranching, just as a typical but by no means univer-sal antagonism between ranchers and coyotes makes it seem natural for me to talk about coyote scat and bunchgrass meristems in the same sentence.

Each part of my narrative depends on a different chronotope. I introduce the ranch in a multigenerational temporal context that contains timeless, place-sensitive activities: "I would run through cattle chutes"; "I was struck by the romance of my uncle harnessing Team." The seduction of this time-lessness is such that I ambiguously write, "I failed trying to milk," obscuring the fact that I made this attempt only once. My narrative participates in a widely available cultural chronotope that associates ranching with tradition, crafting ranching as a cultural lifestyle that withstands the pressures of modernization. The political importance of this chronotope is underlined by a ubiquitous argument that pits ranching against development, seeing in cultural preservation a means to resist the fragmentation of western land-scapes.[5] As my narrative develops, the chronotope of timeless ranchlands give way to an ecosystem-based chronotope. This chronotope is bound not to an enclosed ranch space but instead to an ecosystem characterized by its plant and animal life. Its plot develops by accumulating knowledge until political action (or a child's complaints, at least) becomes imperative. This chronotope depends in part on a progressive narrative of science, and its activist outcome makes it a generic story of environmentalism.

These rhetorical choices reflect my immersion in grazing debates and the cultural drag of its typical features. The events I select and the way I emplot them, originally quite uncritically, says even more about this culture. It matters that I chose to include as a narrative subplot my arguments with my millworker father about felling trees for his garden. Inclusion suggests relevance, and in the interpretive act of deciding why the event is relevant, some readers are likely to see a resonance between my story and scenes of environmental activism against timber harvesting, scenes that were common news items in western Oregon as I was growing up in the seventies and eighties. Others readers—or perhaps many of the same ones—might make connections between cattle and timber industries, especially as these are frequently grouped together as extractive or agricultural industries. Readers who attend to this theme might note that my story shifts from one characterization of a relationship (disagreement between my father and me) to another (my dependent cooperation on him), and they may understand this story as providing moral support for the popular argument that environmentalism (which my narrative elides with science) is a luxury dependent on industry (which my narrative associates with ranching).

It does not matter, necessarily, that I am troubled by the way my narrative might suggest to readers that I believe that preservation-oriented approaches to the land ride on the back of resource-oriented approaches that they ironically (or so goes this cultural story) attempt to undermine. I would rather read this story as pointing to my limited resourcefulness in seeking alternative ways to fund my activities. Yet my preferred reading, I predict, occurred to far fewer readers than did the reading that troubles me, both because my preferences are less culturally resonant and because the plot itself, by linking one event (attending camp) to an earlier event (felling a tree), tends to suggest a natural causal relationship. The contingencies of my past, and of the experiences I choose to narrate as important to my sense of self, are obscured by narrative and by the ways it guides interpretation in ways that also might limit visions of a contingent future. Both the writing and reading of narratives are culturally shaped, so that resistant interpretations (that alternatives exist) are possible, but more difficult to access than culturally mainstream stories.

This short example demonstrates how easily narratives can make associations natural by grounding them in the reality of experience. Indeed, the naturalization of the past (and the present, by extension) is one of narrative's primary rhetorical effects. Compare my personal narrative to the two paragraphs following it, which rely on non-narrative genres. The first of these is a list of topics that are important to grazing politics, such as landscape aesthetics, rural lifestyles, and predator control. This type of debate-specific topic listing is a traditional form of rhetorical analysis, taught by Aristotle, for example, as an invention strategy to generate culturally-relevant arguments about an issue, as well as a means to anticipate probable counterarguments (*On Rhetoric*). Rhetorical critics have since adopted topic analysis as a convenient way to map the contours of debate, but its original purpose (taking stock of argumentative resources) was meant to make analysis available for participating in a debate without constraining the perspective a debater chose to speak from. While narrative genres are distinguished by their causal emplotment of events, their constitution of communal and personal identities, their moralizing impulses, and their projection toward the future, topic analyses are distinguished instead by their apparent nonpartisan value for teachers, participants, and critics of debate. Further, a list of topics suggests inclusion, because adding one more item to a list does not change its structure. The necessity of ending at some point, however, requires deciding which topics are significant enough to include, and which are marginal. By not adding "Hinduism" to my topic analysis, for example, I am judging as less central, less public, and less significant to contemporary land use decision-making a Tennessee pastor's online complaint, embedded within a site on Christian prophecy, that the Nature Conservancy established a cattle-free sanctuary in the Canelo Hills south of Tucson primarily because the Conservancy members are Hindus and/or Mafia (Van Nattan). I also ignore parts of Jeremy Rifkin's popular environmental polemic, *Beyond Beef*, which, unlike the Christian prophecy web site, is not a marginal text in grazing politics, though it similarly links environmentalism to Hinduism by suggesting that Hindu reverence toward cows indicates a better relationship to nature than does American exploitation of cattle (39). Such inclusions and exclusions are an inevitable aspect of topic analysis, and they contribute to arguments that Aristotelian rhetoric ignores marginalized voices.[6]

The questions I raise in the paragraph following my topic analysis, how-ever, are even more clearly non-neutral. Sustainability, for example, has become a shared debate topic by virtue of the cultural salience of the term following the United Nations's Brundtland Commission Report. The prac-tical meaning of this term is not shared, however. As I interviewed people for this book, I asked questions that I hoped would demonstrate some of the variability in how they define sustainability: "What in current ranching would you call sustainable? What would you call unsustainable?" Just by asking my informants to discriminate between sustainable and unsustain-able practices, however, I was already asking a leading question from the viewpoint of my informants who believe current ranching is already sus-tainable and, from the opposite end of the spectrum, those who think desert grasslands ranching can never be sustainable. Similarly, the ques-tions that I raised in the first pages of this chapter also make presumptions. The questions—"How should ecological information be gathered and used?" and "How much should [agencies] charge ranchers?"—presume, respectively, that ecological criteria are significant enough to be relevant and that some type of payment is due from ranchers. The presumptions behind these questions are not universally shared. In fact, the concept of a leading question is a tautology made meaningful only by the way it points to the possibility that some questions accommodate shared assumptions and others violate them.

The interestedness of rhetorical choices arises inevitably with language. As the above examples demonstrate, a choice of genre already circum-scribes action, whether the choice be for narratives, topic analyses, or ques-tions.[7] Questions involve assumptions; inventories of topics involve inclusions and exclusions; and narratives can make their associations and causal implications seem more natural not only to their listeners and read-ers but also to their narrators. A foundation of rhetorical analyses of genre is Carolyn Miller's claim that genres "represent typified rhetorical action" (151). Miller argues that rhetorical actors (speakers and writers) decide appropriate responses in part based on their knowledge of genres used in similar situations. For example, environmental organizations are likely to respond to what they consider to be faulty Environmental Impact State-ments (EIS) with a combination of written comments, press releases, and lawsuits. These previously used responses are habit-forming. Additionally, each response genre fulfills a different function: creating a public record of dissent, raising awareness and public pressure, and attempting to legally force a deferral of a management decision until after more in-depth scientific studies. These purposes arise together with genre, an insight that extends back to Aristotle ("The Poetics").

In the following section I return my focus to narrative genres, though I also discuss how the narrative texts I analyze draw on multiple genres to become hybrids serving complex rhetorical ends. These narratives take the landscapes of the West—its wilderness areas, open spaces, ranches, and public lands—and fuse them with temporal plots to make judgments about the socioecological relations that provide structure to their telling. In the process, they construct a range of identities, differently characterizing ranchers, activists, and bureaucrats. They interpret the past meanings of these identities and project their importance into the future. In the process, they work to subtly persuade both their narrators and their listeners about how to participate in socioecological relationships and in the political interactions that craft those relationships. These narratives, then, are not simply about the identities of their human characters, but about the identity of the West itself.

Rhetorical Fencing: Hybrid Narratives and Political Matter

In this section, I focus on a single historical event, the 1934 Taylor Grazing Act, as it is narrated in three contemporary books aimed at broad popular audiences. The Taylor Grazing Act is one of the pivotal events in range history. It is widely understood as a response to the "tragedy of the commons" on the open range. As the West became increasingly settled in the mid-to-late nineteenth century, few limits were placed on who could run cattle on public lands, or in what quantities. This led to widespread overgrazing and, especially in the late nineteenth century, to large die-offs as poorly managed cattle starved during drought years. In 1906, the Forest Service began charging grazing fees, albeit in an unsystematic manner. Most grazing land, however, did not fall under the Forest Service's jurisdiction. Not until the Dust Bowl did Congress extend the fee and allotment system to remaining public lands. As Table 1.1[8] illustrates, the Taylor Grazing Act served a pivotal role in the history of federal regulation of grazing. It is temporally located between earlier homestead acts, which encouraged westward expansion, and later acts that legislated increasing federal involvement in public lands management. The Taylor Grazing Act signified, and constituted, the end of the open range. At the same time, it helped create a system of proprietary use of public land associated with the fee-for-grazing system.[9]

TABLE 1.
Key Federal Legistative Acts Affecting West Public Lands Grazing

1785	General Land Ordinance	Grants land to new states. Unlike many other states, Arizona keeps much of its land.
1862	Homestead Act	Grants to western settlers 160 acres of land after five years of residence.
1891	Forest Reserves Act	Sets aside forests for timber. Allows grazing.
1897	Organic Act	Authorizes the Forest Service to administer forests for timber and watershed protection.
1909	Enlarged Homestead Act	Allows settlers 320 acres instead of 160, if one quarter is cultivated. Leads to the cultivation of unsuitable land.
1916	Stockraising Homestead Act	Grants 640 acres to ranchers running at least 50 cows. Leads to overgrazing because, in many western areas, 640 acres cannot support 50 cows.
1934	Taylor Grazing Act	Establishes a grazing permit and fee system for lands administered by the Grazing Service. Also creates grazing advisory boards, which tend to be dominated by more established ranchers. In 1946, Grazing Service functions are taken on by the Bureau of Land Management (BLM), which is created by merging the Service with the General Land Office.
1960	Multiple Use and Sustained Yield Act	Officially institutes the Forest Service's multiuse philosophy, thereby validating the agency's choice to manage not only for timber, watersheds, and grazing but also for alternative uses, such as game and recreation.

TABLE 1.
(Continued)

1964	Classification and Multiple Use Act	Gives the BLM a limited-time authorization to follow a multiuse philosophy.
1964	Wilderness Act	Allows Congress to designate wilderness areas. The act permits grazing in areas grazed prior to their designation as wilderness.
1969	National Environmental Policy Act (NEPA)	Requires the preparation of environmental impact statements before making federal land management decisions. Also mandates opportunities for public participation in management decisions.
1973	Endangered Species Act	Requires the protection of species listed as threatened or endangered.
1976	Federal Land Policy and Management Act	Permanently makes the BLM a multiuse agency.
1978	Public Rangelands Improvement Act (PRIA)	Establishes that a percentage of grazing fee receipts will go to range projects.

These changes were controversial in 1934. Seventy years later, they continue to be interpreted differently by different parties to contemporary grazing conflict. In this section, I analyze the interpretations implicit in three different narratives of this event, narratives chosen to serve as a metonymic representation of the broader field of contemporary grazing debate. Throughout this book, I will frequently begin my analysis by dividing arguments into three general categories: arguments that support the status quo, arguments that urge the abolition of public lands grazing, and arguments that promote increased cooperation between ranchers and environmentalists. Categories are always reductive, and mine are no exception. Nonetheless, they provide a workable first orientation toward the debate. The texts I choose to illustrate these positions are: Judge Sandra Day O'Connor and her brother H. Alan Day's memoir *Lazy B: Growing Up on a Cattle Ranch in the American Southwest*, which romanticizes traditional ranching culture; Jeremy Rifkin's *Beyond Beef: The Rise and Fall of the Cattle Culture*, which, as already noted, is an environmental polemic that critiques beef production and consumption from numerous angles; and Thomas Sheridan's *Arizona*, a state history that complexly judges the historical role of cattle ranching, arguing that ranching has had mixed socioecological effects in the past but that it holds particular promise for the future of a dry state.[10] Each of these texts is a narrative, but each also all draws on multiple other genres that shape the meanings each gives to events in the history of ranching, including the Taylor Grazing Act.

Sheridan's history begins with an introduction that evokes the conventions of nature writing. This hybridization draws upon the moralizing impulse Hayden White's historiography predicts, but at the same time locates readers within the scene of nature, as is typical of nature writing. Nature writing, as H. Lewis Ulman argues, is a reflective and ethical discourse produced "when self and scene dynamically blend" in response to a felt need to fix the perception that society has become alienated from nature (47, 48).[11] One of the generic actions of nature writing is to create an ethical imperative for restoring harmony between self, society, and the natural world. Sheridan's introduction draws on these generic functions through a narrative that locates his personal devotion to wilderness in his experiences of the Mazatzal Mountains, in the geographic center of Arizona. This narrative, which is reminiscent of many of the concepts, motifs, and turns of phrases used by conservationists Aldo Leopold and Wallace Stegner in some of their most famous writings—particularly "Thinking Like a Mountain" and "The Wilderness Letter," respectively—culminates in an ethical appeal for humility, an argument based on the contention that the Mazatzals are a timeless place that will pre- and postdate human constructs, such as the state of Arizona.

This nature writing quickly recedes to make room for a conventional historical narrative, but its presence imprints that subsequent history. The Mazatzals, for example, recur in several places, providing a reminder of the reflection that opened the book. More significantly, generic features of nature writing recur again in the book's concluding chapter, but there they are seamlessly hybridized with conventional features of historical narrative.

This chapter draws on typical features of nature writing, especially a propensity to sermonic jeremiad that urges reform to prevent retribution (Slovic). In Sheridan's case, retribution is threatened by a desert that will stand only so much human manipulation and alienation (alienation packaged as a consumer good in irrigation canals, air conditioners, and urban denial): "Will nature rebel? Will the Colorado burst its dams? . . . Or will we ourselves rebel for spiritual and aesthetic reasons and put a brake on growth?" (362–63). Sheridan's history builds toward this imperative for change, using nature writing to locate us readers directly within the historically crafted identity of the West. Nature writing helps Sheridan defer historical closure to the future, creating an ethical imperative for readers to act to establish preferred socioecological relations. The way they should act, and the ideal future Sheridan proposes, is suggested throughout his history. The Taylor Grazing Act provides one example.

Sheridan introduces the act in the context of a power struggle between environmental preservationists and conservationists. He writes that, in 1896, preservationist John Muir convinced the Forest Committee of the Department of the Interior to prohibit grazing in forest reserves, so that eventually sheep and cattle raisers turned their anger to alliance building and lobbying (259). A member of the 1896 Forest Committee, Gifford Pinchot, was persuaded to study grazing's impact on forests (260). His report, which concluded that "properly managed grazing did not harm the forests," was suppressed within the still-preservationist Interior Department. However, Pinchot's friend, President Theodore Roosevelt, placed the reserves under the new Bureau of Forestry, headed by Pinchot (260). Sheridan emphasizes that Pinchot's tolerance of managed ranching aligned him with conservationists rather than preservationists. It was Pinchot who first established federal regulation of grazing, using the system of allotments and fees that, thirty years later, the Taylor Grazing Act would extend in response to the simultaneous drought and depression that faced ranchers in the 1930s. Sheridan's choice to rhetorically construct continuity between the turn-of-the-century ascendance of Pinchot and the 1934 act inserts the legislative event firmly within the ideology of conservationism. Sheridan's subsequent positive evaluations of the act's consequences are transferred to a conservationist ethic that, ultimately, is the primary determinant of the socioecological relations that Sheridan promotes. Ranching regulated by conservationist measures, Sheridan makes clear, is a prime candidate for a future socioecology that can be "sustainable over the long haul" (309).

In an emplotment that evaluates positively the Taylor Grazing Act and, by extension, conservationism, Sheridan recounts some of the act's consequences. He notes that new fences led to herd rotation. Allotments, as well as a shift to selling beef by the pound rather than by the head, led to an emphasis on weight and quality rather than quantity. New water sources spread cattle out across the countryside (261–62). All these changes are associated with ecological health. Sheridan writes: "After more than sixty years of abuse, the range finally had a chance to restore itself" (262). However, this evaluation, narrated as though it is an established fact, is actually highly contested in current politics. While Sheridan argues that regulatory reform enhances the chance for environmental restoration, many debaters argue that only a ban on grazing could lead to substantive range restoration. However, within Sheridan's history, the value of regulative reform is a given, a past decision with demonstrable positive results.

This and similar events in Sheridan's history provide a grounding for a series of conservationist evaluations. A few pages after narrating the history of the act, Sheridan discusses the difficult choices made by rural Arizonans who have to decide between their economic livelihood and their environment. As background information meant to help readers understand this conflict, Sheridan adopts Pinchot's conservationist claims as a historically-validated truth: "When properly managed, stock raising was a sustainable enterprise. With rotation and the regulation of livestock numbers, grasses recovered and erosion could be controlled" (300). Sheridan later demonstrates that this claim is contested, pointing out: "The antiranching lobby rightly zeroed in on ranchers who overgrazed their allotments" or performed other illegal activities (309). However he criticizes these activists because:

> They never talked about the family ranchers who . . . [engaged in many beneficial activities and] ran fewer animal units than their permits allowed because they had made a long-term commitment to the land. Nor did the critics admit that ranching was one of the few extractive industries that could be sustainable over the long haul. (309)

In this statement, the possibility of sustainable ranching is assumed; antigrazing activists may tell part of the truth, but if they deny the possibility of ecologically beneficial ranching, they do not tell the whole truth. The rhetorical position of these activists stand in marked contrast to the rhetoric of Sheridan's historical narrative, which critiques overgrazing and other damaging practices but also insists that improvement is possible. For Sheridan, preservationism's chief value is its ability to temper extraction, thereby transforming the cattle industry into a conservationist culture of sustainable ranching.

Sheridan's complex perspective is in part a consequence of the multi-century and spacious scope of his historical narrative; Lazy B, in contrast, narrates the Taylor Grazing Act through the lens of a single family, allowing O'Connor and Day to more starkly evaluate the act. For these authors, broad historical trends are not the context for judgment; instead, a very personal sense of loss or gain fills that role. O'Connor and Day primarily discuss the act through a story whose features suggest an inscription of oral history, as is typical of their narrative style. One of the primary impacts of oral story-telling is that it creates an illusion of presence, drawing readers into the storied culture.[12] By incorporating numerous markers of orality—by explicitly noting that they are retelling oral stories, for example, or by allowing the narrative "I" that indicates O'Connor slip into a "we" that suggests her symbolic presence even in her physical absence—the narrators encourage readers to identify with the ranch culture at the heart of the memoir.[13]

The morality of this culture is emphasized through character sketches that arise together with these inscribed stories. These characters include family members, neighbors, ranch hands, and even horses. Those most closely associated with the Lazy B are most praised, and even eulogized. In classical rhetoric, the funeral eulogy always has a communal aspect. In Aristotle's classification of rhetorical types, eulogy is considered part of epideictic, which is concerned with praise and, to a lesser extent, with blame. It is particularly concerned with publicly recognizing strength of moral character, or virtue. Aristotle writes: "Since virtue is defined as an ability for doing good, the greatest virtues are necessarily those most useful to others" (On Rhetoric 8). This emphasis underscores the communal aspect of epideictic address. This communal function continues to inform contemporary genres of eulogy. In "The Genre Function," Anis Bawarshi claims that contemporary eulogy is intended "to assess and praise the meaning of the deceased's life and death" (356). In Lazy B, eulogy is evoked in the context of a potentially disappearing lifestyle (the memoir concludes with the family selling its ranch), allowing the memoir to function as praise for a tradition even more than it serves as an autobiography of its narrators.

As part of the Grazing Act story, readers learn that the Lazy B did quite well in leases, receiving approximately 52,000 acres in state leases and roughly 100,000 acres in federal leases (18). A neighbor, "Orville," received four square miles, which works out to a bit over 2,500 acres, less than 2 percent of the Day family's allotment (17). These differences are not so much explained as justified, using stories in which Orville serves as a foil to establish the moral character of O'Connor and Day's father, Harry Day. Orville's allotment is explained in a series of apparent non sequiturs that are only sensible within the story's character-based moral logic: "Orville . . . seldom shaved or bathed. The only money he ever spent to develop water was to drill a well on his small homestead. He was eventually allotted four square miles" (17). The juxtaposition of these sentences creates an associationist logic in which Orville's negative qualities are implicitly the cause of his smaller allotment. This character-driven moral is reinforced by subsequent events. Though Orville agrees to the divisions initially, when federal fencing crews arrive, he approaches them wearing "dirty long johns" and threatens to shoot them (17). Orville's slovenliness is associated with a contentious character: both provide supporting evidence for the justice of his smaller allocation. This associationist logic is enthymematic: while it would be impossible to argue directly that dirty clothes lead to fewer grazing rights, O'Connor and Day's detailed repetition of Orville's uncleanliness allows character development to eclipse alternative emplotments.

In contrast, Harry Day's approach to the situation is represented in a way that highlights conscientious leadership and largesse. Day, readers are told, was a member of the Taylor-created Grazing Adjudication Board. His method of dealing with the perhaps compromising situation of having authority over a neighbor with a much smaller allotment is the inverse of Orville's bad behavior. O'Connor and Day relate: "DA [Harry Day] could have forced settlement. Orville had no right to any additional land" (17). In a few background comments prior to the beginning of this story, O'Connor and Day had mentioned that the process of granting allotments had been complex and controversial. In the context of the story, however, allotments are not a matter of controversial politics, but of rights. Despite what are represented to be superior claims, however, Harry Day offers Orville three thousand acres of the Lazy B's leases. When Orville once again threatens fencing crews, Harry Day offers a total of six thousand acres of federal land, resolving the dispute. The implication of the story is that, during this period of transition, Harry Day had the ability to give away his allotment, a gift that depends upon the right of ownership.

The story is not over, though, but develops in a way to further reinforce the clustering of moral superiority and property rights around Harry Day's character. Within the same paragraph, the story shifts from the scene of federal lands to the privately-owned homestead headquarters. After the six thousand–acre grant, Orville decides he is a friend, coming to the headquarters uninvited. Once there, he would often "wolf down food [the Days's mother] had prepared and then saunter down to the barn to help himself to horseshoes" (17). Orville is shown to be a thief who is taking advantage of Day generosity. This unambiguous act of theft is easily applied by readers, retrospectively, to the debate over land, suggesting Orville had also stolen the Days's public ranchlands. Finally, Orville goes too far, interrupting uninvited a family evening, putting dirty shoes on the coffee table, and spitting tobacco in the living room. The narrator's mother "stood up immediately—all five foot, four inches of her—and asked Orville to leave" (18). The power relation is reversed, providing the opportunity for narrative closure. Orville reduces his infringements on Day property. In the process, the narrative pushes legal distinctions between public and private land into the distant background of the story: Orville has implicitly been kicked off the public land as well. The rhetorical logic governing these stories treats all lands within the ranch boundaries, public or private, as family owned.

This inscribed oral history points to a sore point in contemporary conflicts over grazing: disagreement over the property rights associated with grazing leases. In *Public Lands and Political Meaning*, Karen Merrill argues that these disagreements are rooted in historical ambiguities and contradictions in governmental practices, together with long-standing interpretations of those practices by ranchers. The cultural implications of O'Connor and Day's story is that ranchers have public lands grazing rights that might be considered at least partially analogous to private property rights.

In direct contrast, Rifkin's discussion of the Taylor Grazing Act emphasizes public aspects of the land. Rifkin introduces the act by writing:

> The cattlemen's associations' final triumph came in 1934 when President Franklin D. Roosevelt signed the Taylor Grazing Act into law. Ostensibly, the law was supposed to allow for the improvement of public land by leasing it to ranchers who would take collective responsibility for its management and improvement. In reality, the act succeeded in transferring tens of millions of acres of public lands to private leases in return for a token permit or lease fee. (105)

This account is fully consistent with—and derives part of its meaning from—the rest of *Beyond Beef*, a narrative historical in scope but primarily inflected as an environmental polemic. *Beyond Beef* shares a number of characteristics with Rachel Carson's earlier, highly influential *Silent Spring*, so many as to suggest that the later book might be consciously modeled on the earlier one. Both have generically unusual first chapters. Both are polemics that demonstrate how the acts of evil institutions cause wide-scale public harm through a combination of ignorance and, more often, the blindness of self-interest. By raising consciousness/interpreting events as dire public threats, both books attempt to create a collective response to a perceived environmental problem. Finally, both bring closure to their jeremiad rhetoric with a more rhapsodic chapter that provides hope, one that shows the benefits of exercising agency on behalf of social change.[14] These features work to mobilize readers to specific actions on behalf of the environment. In Rifkin's case, environmental salvation comes through refusing to eat beef, with the implication that decowing public lands will be one of the positive consequences.

By the time Rifkin's narrative arrives at the Taylor Grazing Act, it is clear to readers that cattlemen's associations must be unmitigated villains in the same way that Carson's pesticide producers are evil chemists. This is not the rhetoric of conflicting interests that was reflected in Sheridan's more complex history, in which the land and larger ranchers could win where many small ranchers lost. Instead, this is the rhetoric of the good versus the bad, the public versus those who would take advantage of it. Rifkin's apparent intent (or his culturally conditioned decisions) to mimic Carson's success at creating a collective movement is indicated by his choice to emphasize that the cattlemen, who might have been acceptable had they chosen to act collectively for the greater good as the public act intended, instead acted for their private interests while only apparently advocating responsibility to the land, to each other, and to the public. The narrative calls on readers to identify with this representation of the public as victim and to take personal offense, thereby constituting a collective that is willing to rise up against Rifkin's interpretation of injustice.

This point is even more evident in the larger narrative context. Unlike in *Lazy B* or even *Arizona*, ranchers in *Beyond Beef* are never personified. They are not even "ranchers," who are too easily romanticized; they are "cattlemen." By paying attention to the deeds of depersonalized associations and corporations, Rifkin entirely erases the character sketch that is so important to O'Connor and Day's moral memoir. To the extent that cattlemen are given character at all, it is the character of colonizers and unjust rulers. Rifkin emphasizes that many cattle associations are run on behalf of British investors, thereby further demonstrating the distance between cattlemen and the public Rifkin hopes to simultaneously appeal to and rhetorically constitute. Rifkin summarizes his story of how the West was won by writing: "Behind the facade of frontier heroism and cowboy bravado, of civilizing forces and homespun values, lies . . . a saga of ecocide and genocide, of forced enclosures of land and people, and the expropriation of an entire subcontinent for the exclusive benefit of a privileged few" (107). Even the title of his Taylor Grazing Act chapter, "Barbed Wire and Land Scams," helps to take potentially ambiguous events and lock them into a narrative that clearly indicates the wholesale injustice of ranching (100–109). In Sheridan's narrative, barbed wire—which is both legally and commonly called an "improvement"—figures as a tool for ecological restoration. In Rifkin's narrative, barbed wire is transformed by emplotment into the negative scar of private interest traced across the landscape. In O'Connor and Day's narrative, the boundaries of ranches instead are enforced by moral authority and property rights.

As these three contrasting narratives illustrate, historical events such as the Taylor Grazing Act do not arrive with their meanings ready-made. Instead, they are given meaning by the very narratives that bring those events to present memory. In consequence, narratives are not just about past conflicts, but also present ones. They also indicate different desired socioecological relationships, and consequently persuade readers to different actions.

The three stories analyzed above point to different broad categories of positions. First, O'Connor and Day's stories celebrate a conservative stance in favor of the ranched status quo. Sheridan's history promotes a conservation or sustainable ranching perspective that is pro-ranching but that expects ranchers to change when necessary to ecological sustainability. Rifkin's narrative urges a preservation-oriented environmental perspective that understands grazing to be socially unnecessary and ecologically damaging. Around each of these positions is clustered a set of associated values. Conservative ranchers speak from a moral authority tied to a labor-intensive and under-appreciated lifestyle. They speak for property rights, for tradition, and for the intrinsic worth of ranching culture. Conservation ranchers and their supporters instead take a stand for the reform of ranching practices, while arguing that ranches are necessary to maintain open space against wildcat development. They promote a vision of human society in harmonious relationship to nature, and frequently use the goal of sustainable agriculture as a keystone emblem of this idealized socioecology. Finally, preservation-oriented environmentalists champion habitat and ecosystem restoration, endangered species preservation, and the value of wildness. They assert that public lands are a shared and non-commercial heritage, and they refuse to make what they consider to be a false choice between ranching and development.

These three categorical positions are useful to begin sketching a rhetorical map of contemporary grazing debates. In the next and final section of this chapter, I discuss more explicitly what I mean by rhetorical mapping, addressing in the process the chronotope of my own writing.

History, Geography, and the Ethnography of Debate

Return to Table 1, which summarizes Federal legislation that has been key to shaping grazing practices and politics in western states. From one angle, the passage of each law is a historic event. From another perspective, each of these events is a response to deliberative rhetoric and a spur to subsequent interpretation. While this legislation continues to shape land management, it is now also a set of symbolic meanings that are inserted into a dynamic system of language use, just as the Taylor Grazing Act becomes incorporated into contemporary narratives that are as much about current as historical range politics. When contemporary arguments about these acts are historicized, those arguments provide an index of changing cultural consciousness. One such history is Karen Merrill's *Public Lands and Political Meanings*, which examines deliberations in stockmen's associations and their newsletters, public meetings called by representatives of the United States Forest Service and Bureau of Land Management, and congressional hearings. Stories told by ranchers in these arenas have, over time, represented ranchers as homesteaders, stewards of the land, and owners of limited property rights. Each of these representations continues to exert some influence on contemporary debates, but the salience of any given representation has changed over time.

I am most interested in historical events as they are used currently. Unlike Merrill, then, I do not turn to historical archives in order to craft a narrative of political meaning. My interest in even such a key cultural figure as the cowboy of Hollywood and western novels is limited to its local appearance in debate over the management of public grazing land.[15] The voices of well-known grazing critics Bernard DeVoto and, more recently, Edward Abbey also appear only through the resonance of their voices with those that are more local and contemporary, in the same way that Aldo Leopold and Wallace Stegner weave their way into my earlier discussion of Sheridan's *Arizona*.

I deliberately avoid, then, a historical approach to grazing debates, opting for a localized mapping of a system of arguments. Bakhtin's chronotope, however, points to the impossibility of creating too fine a separation between history and geography ("Forms of Time"). The different audiences and political possibilities of different spaces—of public hearings as opposed to grazing advisory board meetings, for example—are key to many of the dynamics of Merrill's political story.[16] Just as space is necessary to history, time is necessary to a dynamic understanding of cultural systems. The traditional tendency to portray cultures as static is a frequently noted problem, well described, for example, by anthropologist Renato Rosaldo in *Culture and Truth*. Rosaldo promotes a contrasting project, one that "attempts to understand human conduct as it unfolds through time and in relation to its meanings for actors" (37). Such a reorientation is particularly salient to an anthropology-inspired rhetorician such as myself, as my understanding of rhetoric as meaning in action requires a more dynamic approach to cultural meanings. Rhetoric implies persuasion, action, and change. In part because my sources—interviews, observations, recent texts—are qualitative and contemporary, however, my temporal orientation tends toward the rhetorically-constituted, imagined past, on one hand, and, especially, the projected future. This approach limits the development of a theoretical approach centered on causation, substituting instead attention to how desire is shaped by language and enacted in the politics of land management.

Ralph Cintron's concept of the "snap," advanced in his response essay "The Timidities of Ethnography," provides a good metaphor for the ethnographic chronotope.[17] The term "snap," Cintron writes, "emphasizes an exact, unique present but, simultaneously, how the present is constituted by the past" (935). Cintron also includes in this metaphor synchronous connections to the social institutions and cultural practices that provide formative forces on any given action. Though ethnography is oriented to a chronotope of "right here"/"right now," explaining that multidimensional present requires tracing links that extend outward in space and time.

The persuasive components of this "snap" point also to the future, a point that becomes especially evident when analysis is directed also at structural elements of society. As an example, each of the previously analyzed stories is aligned with the political actions of their narrators. Sandra

Day O'Connor was, of course, a conservative Supreme Court justice, but what is less widely known is that members of her family, such as her cousin Ann Day of the Pima County Board of Supervisors, continue to be active in regional politics and to uphold the properties of ranch families however they can. Thomas Sheridan, the historian author of *Arizona*, also chairs the Ranch Conservation Technical Advisory Team of the Sonoran Desert Conservation Plan, and in that capacity he acts to integrate conservation ranching into Pima County's plans to curb wildcat development. Jeremy Rifkin's explicit target is consumption, an appeal to demolish the cattle industry through aggregate choice. As these cases demonstrate, an analysis of cultural texts is incomplete without a discussion of their possible effects that snaps together future and past. Though a snap implies a moment, it points away from itself, stretching out temporally like a fence across a landscape.

There are contingencies, however, in the writing of this snap. Switching metaphors, in writing I draw a rhetorical map shaped by the links I choose to follow. Just as my own and other narratives draw contingently on perception and are rhetorical in their effects, despite their bases in reality, the ethnographic mapping of debate also draws from the unlimited field of argument in consequential ways. The consequences of such maps are teased out, again by Cintron, in his ethnography of a Chicago suburb, *Angels' Town*. Cintron argues that maps are rhetorical because they abstract and select details to provide focus. They confer power "after real space overwhelms the eye," transforming chaotic details into something that can be more easily interpreted (29). A map, for example, allows those new to a region to move purposefully, rather than wander without direction. In the process of flattening multidimensional reality, maps confer increased ability to act. This agency comes at the price of selectively ignoring details.

One late morning, after a summer rain had cleared some of the oppressive monsoon mugginess, a rancher and his retired father invited me to travel their ranch and observe a working meeting with agents from the Arizona State Land Department (ASLD) and the Bureau of Land Management (BLM). A birder had recently reported a southwestern willow flycatcher nest in one of the ranch's riparian areas, and the men had gathered to investigate the report and decide whether they should change management to accommodate the habitat of this endangered species. The young birds had already fledged, however, and the group redirected to discuss whether and where to lay fence. Since the ranchlands were public, the fences required agency approval.

While we were driving, the rancher explained to me that a new fence would help him force cows to eat sacaton rather than overgrazing tastier upland grasses. The group conferred together on the design of fences, making sure they had a shared understanding of regulations, created in consultation with wildlife biologists, that are meant to protect deer and pronghorn by stringing wires a certain distance from the ground and each other and by disallowing barbs on the lower two wires. Upon reaching a sacaton field, the five of us slid off the bench seats of the rancher's large pickup, and the Australian shepherds riding in the pickup's bed launched themselves to scamper down the road.

As the rancher indicated how an already staked-out fenceline fit the contours of the land, the ASLD agent spread his map over the truck's nose. At first, the agent had difficulty locating the map's representation of the scene in which we all stood. When the BLM agent's assistance proved inadequate, the rancher joined the consultation and, together, the three men found the spot. It appeared that the proposed fence, which was primarily located on BLM land, might actually traverse a small portion of state land. The BLM agent, somewhat surprised, unfolded his own map to check, and the two agents conferred to find how their maps aligned. They finally agreed that the proposed fence did cross both types of land—which meant that it required approval from both agencies. An application had already been made to BLM, but not to Arizona.

One agent suggested that the fenceline be redesigned to fit into one jurisdiction only, thereby subordinating the rancher's landscape-based concerns to a desire to more easily navigate the bureaucratic process. The rancher, who knew his land by its sight but not by its legal classification, rejected the suggestion, snapping back, "I go by contours." Besides, he pointed out, he had already had an archaeologist examine the fenceline, a legal requirement to protect valuable sites from cows pacing along fences. Changing the fenceline would require yet another consultation, yet another interpretation of the rancher's actions through the disciplinary lens of applied archaeology. The group instead agreed to rush the neglected state lands application.

For the rancher and agents simply to agree to what was at stake in this fencing decision required aligning three maps—the rancher's mental image of the land's contours with the two agents' paper representations. The negotiation this alignment required illustrates the rhetorical significance of maps, literal and symbolic, to the way humans relate to the land. It also illustrates that this mapping is interactive. As the three men tried to make a fenceline decision together, they put their own abstractions of the situation into dialogue with one another's, altering their own understanding of the situation in the process. The outcome of this dialogue was a shift in meaning. For the state lands agent, the role of the bureaucratic process in shaping decisions was subordinated to the rancher's "contours." For the BLM agent, land that he had once understood to be under his jurisdiction was shifted to the ASLD. For the rancher, compliance had become noncompliance, a translation problematic enough that he requested (and received) my promise to temporarily not write about the event. As the meanings of the fence shifted for each of the men, so did their understanding of management decisions, so that in the dialogic realignment of their maps they came to an agreed-upon plan of action intended to bring the landscape back into harmony with newly crafted social meanings.

In the next chapter, I begin to more systematically map the dynamic interactions of argument by focusing on how grazing debate is incorporated into the Sonoran Desert Conservation Plan, a land management planning process sponsored by the Pima County government. Pima stretches northward from the central portion of the Arizona-Mexico border to encompass Tucson, Arizona's second-largest and rapidly growing metropolitan area. Voices in the Sonoran Desert Conservation Plan share traces of the conservative ranching, conservationist, and activist-preservationist perspectives I have metonymically represented through the narratives of O'Connor and Day, Sheridan, and Rifkin. In the symbolic space of the Sonoran Desert Conservation Plan, those voices interact directly with one another, calling on their political others to reinterpret beliefs and shift values in the process of dialogue.

Ultimately, the Sonoran Desert Conservation Plan is oriented to the construction of a consequential zoning map that will help order management actions across the landscape of Pima County.[18] The exigence created by this government-sponsored planning process has called forth a broad range of public responses, in part because of the evident political impact of drawing this particular map. By directing human action in ways that are responsive to and consequential for the ecosystems in which humans are embedded, the Sonoran Desert Conservation Plan map is one important constitutive symbol that is pivotal to how humans participate in the socioecology of the southern Arizona landscape.

[2]

OPEN SPACE, CONSERVATION, & ENDANGERMENT

Early one January, my partner, Phil, and I took advantage of a rare overcast day and drove into the Sierrita Mountains looking for a small but still vital 1895 settlement, the McGee Ranch. The community is currently home to around 350 inhabitants, many of whom work in construction, mining, or, more irregularly, as ranch hands ("Our Common" 3). In October 1998, Pima County Administrator Chuck Huckleberry submitted a proposal to the County Board of Supervisors to turn the mountains around McGee Ranch into a park as a core component of a habitat conservation system for the county. A map accompanying the proposal outlined park boundaries that encompass 10,904 acres of state land, 5,870 acres of federal (Bureau of Land Management), and 4,348 acres of private (Pima County "Draft SDCP" Fig. 20). I glanced at this map before Phil and I left Tucson for our south-ward drive, but then left it at home, knowing that we had all day to find our bearings in the mountain region.

As a map primarily intended to indicate boundaries, the GIS image shows relatively little of the area surrounding the proposed Sierrita Moun-tain Park. Topo lines are overlaid with Arizona's typical checkerboard pat-tern of land ownership, a legacy of old railroad grants. The map highlights the park at its center and minimizes connections to surrounding regions, although a few unlabeled roads visibly snake into the area. A couple of south/southeast-flowing washes are drawn in beige to emphasize their importance as wildlife corridors that link the park to the other proposed core reserve areas in Huckleberry's Draft Sonoran Desert Conservation Plan. Between the map's limited connection to other regions, the town's obscurity (which kept both a rancher with long roots in the area and the owner of a crossroads watering hole from being able to give us directions), and my own habit of not putting much thought into locating myself geo-graphically, Phil and I spent nearly half the day circling the mountains on jeep trails before taking a road that dead-ended into Phelps-Dodge's Sier-rita Mine. As we back-tracked at dusk, we finally saw McGee Road stretch-ing westward and up into the mountains.

Climbing the road, we passed a couple of real estate signs and a single new home under construction. The road twisted through miles of mistle-toe-draped scrub catclaw, whose gray winter limbs created a waist-high desert thicket of bush and thorns. Further up the road, we increasingly came across manufactured homes, mobile trailers, and historic adobes, while the gray scrub started alternating with lawns turned blonde with dry winter grass. Near the center of the community, we saw homes spaced at comfortable shouting distances from each other. The town's apparent cen-ter is formed by a loop near the end of the road, well into the Sierrita foothills, a loop lined with a cluster of thirty-seven mailboxes.

In December 1998, many of these mailboxes held outgoing mail addressed to Chuck Huckleberry. Although individually inflected, these letters shared common concerns. The handwritten letter of Janette Awtrey is in many ways typical. Awtrey, a resident of the town and employee of the town's primary employer, the Sierrita Mining and Ranching Co., a construction and cattle business, writes that she fears a new park might bring visitors, leading to an increase in pollution and a loss of safety. Alarmed, she wonders if the park will mean an end to her land-based way of life and work. After a formal opening, Awtrey introduces herself as a lifelong resident of McGee Ranch and contin-ues: "It is the only home I have known." She adds that all the town's residents, regardless of whether they work for Sierrita Mining and Ranching, "all have one thing in common. The fear of the unknown. The fear of losing our home."

Awtrey's letter is one of 170 received by Huckleberry during the two-month public comment period on the Draft Sonoran Desert Conservation Plan, and one of 48 received from the McGee Ranch area and the Sierrita Min-ing and Ranch Co. ("Re: Correspondence"). A family member, Lora Awtrey, writes also, discussing her grandfather's life on the land and her own experi-ences watching grandchildren grow up in the community. She tells her read-ers: "We have kept the land free from litter. . . . We are very afraid that if this land is opened up . . . danger will move in. . . . Our forefathers have been buried here. . . . *WE LOVE THIS LAND!*" She is joined by additional Awtreys and other members of the community. More formal and less pathos-driven letters echo similar themes, though there is a tendency for those primarily identifying first as workers (often men, but not always) to subsume the child safety theme in generalized references to a "way of life" while instead developing arguments about land stewardship. A letter from the managing partners of the Sierrita Ranching and Mining Co., written on company letterhead, is typical of the stewardship approach. Partners Lynn Harris, Gary Fox, and David Harris argue that the plan for Sierrita Park is unnecessary because the company and six generations of McGee Ranch residents are good caretakers. They explain that watering holes developed for cattle have also supported and attracted wildlife, and they conclude that, "Overall, our rangeland is in excellent condition." They argue that there is no need to create a park in order to curb development or create public access: "As long as the State Trust Land we lease for grazing is left in that category, there will be no development on it. . . . We share our ranch property with others: hikers, birdwatchers, picnickers, hunters, and others." These partners, like working rancher Fred Depper and others from the region, also argue that the proposed mountain park is a waste of taxpayer funds, as the community and company are independently able to maintain the good associated with the park (land stewardship and access) without its ills (purchase costs and the pollution and crime associated with an increase in urban recreationists).

The letters highlight a significant difference between the community's and the county's understanding of a mountain park. In addition to upholding rural land stewardship, the community's letters are filled with references to a feared increase in litter, pollution, and crime—problems associated with urbanization. The county's intention in setting the area aside as a park, in contrast, is to create a core reserve for wildlife and a limit to development: a nonnegotiable barrier *against* urbanization. The urbanization rejected by the community is slightly different than that rejected by the county, however; while the county's report measures urban areas in terms of the desert scraping and habitat destruction that are typical of housing developments, the community members' letters indicate fear of a mobile urbanization introjected by a transient population of tourists and others who view land as recreation. In his February 1999 Sonoran Desert Conservation Update, which includes a report on public comment, Huckleberry refers to the community's concerns as a "misunderstanding" of the park designation (Pima County "Draft Sonoran Desert Conservation Concepts" 19). My tendency is to agree, but as Phil and I drove our Toyota Land Cruiser back down McGee Road, past a small group of youths heading down the road from the cemetery on foot, past a pair of Dalmatians running eagerly up the mountain slope and, notably, *not* past any other vehicular traffic, I had to acknowledge the community is not inaccurate to claim it will have to deal with more traffic simply as a consequence of being on the map.

In response to the forty-eight letters of concern written by members of the McGee Ranch community and the Sierrita Mine and Cattle Co., Huckleberry includes in his March 2 update the recommendation that the name of the proposed Sierrita conservation area be changed from "Sierrita Mountain Park" to "Sierrita Ranch Conservation Area" ("Report" 3), in accord with the community's reported consensus request (Pima County "Draft Sonoran Desert Conservation Concepts" 19). While ratifying Huckleberry's draft plan "in concept," the Board of Supervisors accepted this change and several others that shifted boundaries and/or designations but that did not substantially undermine the basic plan. The draft, renamed the Concept Sonoran Desert Conservation Plan, has become the primary basis for further deliberative planning about the details of county land use, including zoning, boundaries, incentive structures, fees, funding, and ongoing monitoring and management arrangements. The name change for the Sierritas does not necessarily entail any change in the proposed status of the land—later reports in the planning process continue to categorize the Sierrita Ranch Conservation Area as one of the plan's fifteen (past, present, and future) mountain parks projects instead of as one of the eleven proposed ranch conservation projects—but the name change nonetheless tempers some of the concerns of the McGee Ranch community (Pima County "Draft Sonoran Desert Conservation Concepts" 19). This chapter explores what's in a name by looking more closely at the idea of ranch conservation as it is used within the Sonoran Desert Conservation Plan and by examining why the designation of ranch conservation area is both easily embraced within the plan and highly controversial.

As the McGee Ranch example suggests, this controversy hinges on the ambiguous status of ranch lands in relation to environmental conservation (Huckleberry's version of a park) and to urbanization (the McGee Ranch community's version). To further explore this ambiguity, I turn to a brief discussion of how the immediate cause of the Sonoran Desert Conservation Plan has framed Pima County's talk about land use as an opposition between wildlife and development, creating an uncertain place for ranching in the process.

What's in a Name? The Uncertain Status of Ranch Conservation

On March 10, 1997, the U.S. Fish and Wildlife Service listed the cactus ferruginous pygmy owl as a federally endangered species (see table 2). The
listing surprised no one, as surveys conducted earlier that year could confirm sightings of only twelve of these barred owls (Pima County "The Cactus Ferruginous"). The owls can be difficult to spot. They are tiny enough
that one can rest comfortably in the palm of a hand or make a spacious nest
for itself within one of the small holes drilled by a Gila woodpecker high in
the tall sides of columnar cacti. Yet even if one grants that the inconspicu-
ous birds are significantly undercounted, the survey provides persuasive
evidence that the species is imperiled. As an additional incentive for taking
this dwindling population seriously, many in the environmental and scientific community consider the owl to be an indicator species, a canary in a
coal mine that can help ecologists know when habitat degradation has
reached a critical point that suggests a threat to an entire ecosystem.

To many members of the building community, however, the owl's 1997
listing is a threat to business. The listing has led to alarmist projections that
suburban development will be severely disrupted. It has been especially
controversial because the owl's primary known range is in one of Pima
County's fastest-growing sites of urban development—the Tucson-Marana
urban corridor that stretches through an opening between the Catalina,
Tucson, and Tortolita mountains that otherwise border the Tucson metrop-
olis. In response to the listing, the Southern Arizona Home Builders Association (SAHBA) commissioned an economic report from Phoenix economist
Elliott Pollack, which projects that critical habitat designations for the owl
will cost millions of dollars in decreased development and lowered values
for undeveloped land (Pollack, cited in McKenney). These forecasts have
been discredited by a retrospective analysis (McKenney), but the report
nonetheless validates the concerns of already galvanized developers. In an
economy largely driven by new home construction and the service industry,
a threat to development is often interpreted as a threat to the economy at
large. It is not unusual to hear locals quip that the traditional three C's of
Arizona's economy (copper, cotton, cattle) have been surpassed by a new,
integrated pair: climate and condos.

As if this basic conflict does not create drama enough, almost immediately after the listing, a proposed site for a new high school became the focal
point of contention over habitat conservation. A January 1998 public meet-

TABLE 2.

Important events in the development of the Sonoran Desert Conservation Plan, including USFWS and court decisions regarding the cactus ferruginous pygmy owl's endangered species listing, key reports of the Sonoran Desert Conservation Plan, and key political enactments of aspects of the plan.

December 28, 1973	Congress passes the Endangered Species Act
October 13, 1982	Congress amends the Endangered Species Act to allow applications for incidental take permits (Section 10 permits). These permit incidental take (indirect harm, harassment, death) of threatened and endangered species that is caused by otherwise legal activities. Permit applications must be accompanied by a mitigation plan documented in a habitat conservation plan.
March 10, 1997	The United States Fish and Wildlife Service lists the cactus ferruginous pygmy owl as a federally endangered species.
October 21, 1998	Pima County Administrator Chuck Huckleberry presents a draft of the Sonoran Desert Conservation Plan to the County Board of Supervisors.
October 27, 1998	Pima County officially launches the Sonoran Desert Conservation Plan planning process.
October 27, 1998– January 15, 1999	Official public comment period for the Draft Sonoran Desert Conservation Plan, extended in practice until the March approval of the plan in concept.
March 2, 1999	The Pima County Board of Supervisors approves the Draft Sonoran Desert Conservation Plan in concept, and establishes a Steering Committee and four technical advisory teams, including the Science Technical Advisory Team and the Ranch Technical Advisory Team.
June 30, 1999	The Fish and Wildlife Service designates 731,712 acres of critical habitat to protect the owl.

TABLE 2.
(Continued)

November 23, 1999	The U.S. Court of Appeals for the Ninth Circuit approves the construction of a new high school for the Amphitheater School District within designated cactus ferruginous pygmy owl habitat.
September 26, 2000	The Pima County Board of Supervisors accepts a Preliminary Sonoran Desert Conservation Plan, which includes zoning recommendations.
June 9, 2000	President Bill Clinton establishes the Ironwood National Monument, furthering conservation measures included within the Sonoran Desert Conservation Plan.
September 19, 2001	In a ruling on a suit filed by the Southern Arizona Home Builders Association and two other builders' groups, United States District Court Judge Susan Bolton upholds the pygmy owl's endangered species listing but vacates its designated critical habitat.
December 18, 2001	Pima County Board of Supervisors adopts a Comprehensive Land Use Planning Update to its 1992 plan, incorporating principles of the Sonoran Desert Conservation Plan in a Conservation Lands System.
April 16, 2002	The Sonoran Desert Conservation Plan receives the American Planning Association's annual Outstanding Planning Award.
August 19, 2003	The Ninth Circuit Court calls the Fish and Wildlife Service listing of the pygmy owl "arbitrary and capricious" and remands the case back to Judge Bolton to issue a new opinion.
January 15, 2004	Huckleberry submits to the Board of Supervisors a Draft Multi-Species Habitat Conservation Plan, written by Paul Fromer of the consultant firm RECON.
June 25, 2004	Judge Bolton requires the Fish and Wildlife Service to review its pygmy owl listing and to submit a progress report to the court by the end of January, 2005, leaving the listing intact in the interim.

TABLE 2.

(Continued)

May 18, 2004	The Pima County Open Space Bond passes with 66 percent of the vote.
February 3, 2005	Huckleberry releases Draft II of the Multi-Species Habitat Conservation Plan.
January 3, 2006	Huckleberry releases Draft III of the Multi-Species Habitat Conservation Plan. The goal is to finalize the application for a federal Section 10 permit application in 2006. The draft cover memo also notes the likelihood of the pygmy owl's delisting within the year, and gives conservation- and science-based reasons for the plan covering only thirty-five species rather than the fifty-six considered earlier.

ing facilitated by Congressman Jim Kolbe aired the conflict without attempting to resolve it.[1] Some claimed that pygmy owls have been seen at or near the proposed school site; others argued that they are unlikely to return because great horned owls had moved in. Several claimed that there are both less expensive and less controversial school sites available—the Southwest Center for Biological Diversity had even hired a certified pygmy owl biologist to locate these sites—but Amphi School Board Vice President Gary Woodard expressed skepticism about alternatives. Many made a call for better, region-wide planning to try to balance needs and also to create clarity so that property owners will not be surprised by changes in the listings of their land. Bill Shaw, for example, chair of the Department of Wildlife and Fisheries Sciences at the University of Arizona, spoke moderately about the effects of the proposed school development, arguing that no single development would in itself threaten the bird, but that the ongoing fragmentation of its habitat would. Shaw added that uncertainties about the owls—such as their relationship to apparently more abundant populations in northern Mexico—indicate a need for further research and slower growth within ironwood forests until more becomes known. Shaw saved his most forceful argument for the end of his portion of the presentation, as paraphrased in a meeting report:

We *do* know, Shaw emphasized, that the confrontational, piecemeal, liti-gious approach to land use planning that has characterized this commu-nity for so long, is no substitute for comprehensive long-term land use planning. Good planning will also help maintain the quality of this envi-ronment which fuels the economic growth that attracts people and new residents to this community, especially if we adopt a far-sighted, long-range planning strategy to preserve the quality of this environment. (Udall Center for Studies in Public Policy 15)

Shaw's call for planning is particularly forceful but not unique. Kieran Suckling, executive director of the Southwest Center for Biological Diver-sity, expressed hope that the owl would motivate long-term planning (9); Alan Lurie, executive vice president of the Southern Arizona Home Builders Association complained about lack of clarity on rules and regulations and called for better decision making (9–10); Craig Miller, Southwest represen-tative of the Defenders of Wildlife argued that the "short pause" in growth necessary for regional planning would hurt no one and would only lead to a better future for all (11). During the forum's question and answer period, these calls were picked up as a major topic of discussion, with a specific focus on species recovery plans mandated by the original Endangered Species Act and on habitat conservation plans. Attendance was estimated at well over four hundred people (2).

The attention to habitat conservation plans illustrates the powerful incentive for urban planning that is provided by a 1982 amendment to the Endangered Species Act. More than any other Arizona county, Pima (with the state's second-largest population) already has a history of making attempts to control the shape of its urban development; yet none of its prior actions have been as comprehensive as the Sonoran Desert Conservation Plan is intended to be. The Endangered Species Act amendment allows gov-ernments to use habitat conservation plans in order to apply for what is known as a Section 10 permit. This permit protects against penalties for incidental take, which is harm, harassment, or death of an endangered species caused indirectly by human activity, typically habitat destruction. Protection is conditional on the permittee developing and implementing an approved habitat conservation plan that the Fish and Wildlife Service has judged effective for minimizing take overall.

On a small scale, this might mean that ranchers make sure that any stock ponds used by reproducing Chiricahua leopard frogs are left alone during breeding periods, receiving in return immunity from the incidental take of the frog as a result of livestock-induced habitat degradation. On a larger scale, the owl is providing an exigence to involve landowners in comprehensive county planning. To integrate planned growth with species and habitat protection, Pima County intends to develop a core reserve linked together by biological corridors (washes, typically) in exchange for development in other areas deemed less critical for wildlife habitat. In the process, the county has not stopped at trying to protect the pygmy owl and eight others species (including the leopard frog) that are listed as threatened or endangered. Taking a more comprehensive approach, Pima County has worked instead to create a Multi-Species Habitat Conservation Plan intended to protect the region's biodiversity on a broad scale. The Draft Multi-Species Habitat Conservation Plan responds to the habitat requirements of fifty-five "Priority Vulnerable Species."[2] These chosen species have been culled from a longer list of vulnerable species provided by the federal government on the basis of their potential to benefit from conservation planning and on their usefulness for making distinctions between more and less important habitat areas (Pima County "Draft Pima County Multiple Species" 12).

The pygmy owl's listing has motivated widespread participation in the Sonoran Desert Conservation Plan necessary to private landowner buy-in, but it also frames land use planning in terms of a conflict between wildlife and development. The major purpose of the Sonoran Desert Conservation Plan is to refashion the antagonism between these two poles by creating a plan comprehensive enough to contain them both, but the challenge of this goal is inherent in its framework. The 1998 Concept Plan explains its overall purpose in terms that assume a distinction between natural and urban environments even while attempting to bind them together: "The Sonoran Desert Conservation Plan combines short-term actions to protect and enhance the natural environment with long-range planning to ensure that our natural and urban environments not only coexist but develop an interdependent relationship, where one enhances the other" ("Draft SDCP" 5). This rhetoric, inherited from the exigence for the plan, creates a deliberative space in which two environments whose identities depend on their opposition are nonetheless meant to coexist harmoniously. Such a deliberative space might invite the refashioning of the two concepts; yet the goal of the plan has been instead to map the boundaries between them.

This goal has contributed significantly to the troubled place of ranching within the SDCP. The neat bifurcation along natural and urban lines, together with its implied opposition between humans on one hand and plants and animals on the other is destabilized by rural activities, especially ranching. The dichotomous framing invites the question: Is ranching part of the conservation efforts that will help conserve critical habitat for listed species, or is ranching, like urban development, a threat to nature? Past patterns of land use give credence to these either-or questions because, over the last decades, many prime privately-held ranch lands near population centers have been sold off to developers for subdivision. In Pima's neighboring Santa Cruz County, for example, the town of Sonoita has swollen with newcomers, many of whom work in Tucson or are retirees rather than traditional rural residents. As Tucson becomes more congested with homes and people and traffic, the option of moving out of primarily urban areas becomes more appealing, perhaps especially to westerners who already are accustomed to their daily dependence on automobiles. One of my colleagues claims that his commute to the University of Arizona on the uncrowded highway outside Sonoita is no longer than a rush hour commute into the sprawling Northwest Tucson, but by living on a ranchette just outside of Sonoita he can watch desert pronghorn from his living room window. His ranchette, like the majority of those in the region, is built upon a subdivided parcel of what was once the core private land of a working ranch.

Many ranched state lands near population centers are as likely to be sold for development as are private lands. The 1910 Enabling Act, which paved the way for Arizona's statehood, and the Arizona State Constitution together set aside land to be managed for a group of public beneficiaries, with public schools the chief among them. As urban areas have grown, the Arizona State Lands Department's primary focus for revenue growth has shifted to selling land for urban development, according to the agency's 2004 annual report. In particular, the 1981 Urban Land Act has given the department more flexibility in working with local governments on zoning and planning in order to increase the value of state lands. When state lands are not used for development or commercial purposes, however, they are most frequently leased for grazing. Because of past patterns of state land sales, as well as private, the dominant regional tendency is to rhetorically position ranching against development, thereby aligning it with conservation.

This is not the only tendency, however. For many involved in the Sonoran Desert Conservation Plan, the fear of a future that looks like Phoenix or Los Angeles is, indeed, the driving force of conservation, but for others the dream of preserving as much as possible of a disappearing past habitat is the hope that depends on a successful plan. These motivations may appear to be two sides of the same copper penny, but they are not, at least not entirely. The hope for ecological preservation is most clearly institutionalized in the Sonoran Desert Conservation Plan's Science Technical Advisory Team, the group responsible for ecological research, advising on species protection and habitat preservation, and creating the Multi-Species Conservation Plan that will support the county's Section 10 permit application. When this or other groups use ecological preservation as the benchmark for decision making, ranching moves toward the other end of the urban-nature pole by being cast as anti-species instead of as anti-development.

This point was dramatically enacted when the Science Technical Advisory Team released one of its early reports at a public meeting, walking into a naming quagmire comparable to the Sierrita Mountain Park controversy. The team created a list of plant and animal species that have been introduced into the region (i.e., introduced after the arrival of Europeans, changing the ecosystem as originally encountered by settlers). This species list is intended to help define the nature that requires conservation by defining what should be excluded from it. As if the goal were not politically charged enough, the team neglected to use a standard, accepted designator for external species such as the common terms "exotic," "introduced," and "non-native." Instead, the team chose to name its ecological others "pests." These pest species include cattle. In an interview, a participant in the planning process recounted this story to me and added the comment: "You can imagine if your livelihood depends upon cattle that having cattle labeled a pest is going to raise a red flag." Moves such as this one help keep the different constituents of the Sonoran Desert Conservation Plan in opposition to one another.

Distrust developed still further in response to some of the actions of RECON, a consulting team hired by the county to make ecological recommendations. When RECON released a report in July 2001, it appeared to prohibit ranching in the core, according to the interpretations of one of my informants. He told me:

The core reserves encompass most of the Altar Valley, for example, which is the largest undeveloped block of land in Eastern Pima County. That generated a tremendous amount of concern because nobody is really sure what activities will be allowed . . . in the core reserve: what activities would be prohibited or even more regulated than they are now? And then, at a meeting in July, RECON provided a land use matrix by all of these different land use designations—multiple use, core reserve—and, again, with no key, no explanation. . . . In the matrix there were a series of little n's, and big N's . . . apparently meaning [that ranching is] absolutely prohibited. But again, this thing was just dropped by RECON on the Science Team and the ranchers. All these meetings are open meetings and so . . . people got hold of [the matrix and] this engendered tremendous concern among the ranchers. The Science Team and RECON were very apologetic, saying "Look at, we didn't really mean—this was just a draft—we didn't mean to say that we were going to prohibit [ranching], just that it would have to be regulated." They did a lot of backtracking but by then the damage had been done.

The informant telling this story is a member of the Sonoran Desert Conservation Plan's Ranch Technical Advisory Team (also known as the Ranch Conservation Team), a group that represents a public view that is frequently in tension or at odds with the perspective taken by the Science Technical Advisory Team. The separation of these two teams into different consultancy purposes has helped to institutionalize the conceptual opposition of nature and ranching culture. Within the original two-sided exigence of the Sonoran Desert Conservation Plan, this opposition can suggest inadvertently that ranching is anti-habitat, counteracting the tendency to frame it as anti-development.

In short, ranching's place within a polar framework is easily unsettled. One obvious response is to recognize ranching's legitimacy as a unique third alternative. The Draft, or Concept, Sonoran Desert Conservation Plan does this by promoting historical and cultural conservation, though it implies these goals remain subordinate to habitat conservation. A typical statement of cultural goals reads: "Where possible, operating western ranches should be conserved. Through their conservation, the metropolitan urban boundary is better defined and the heritage and culture of the West is preserved" (5). The priority in the second sentence, and in the ensuing discussion, gives more weight to defining the urban boundary than to cultural tradition. Yet cultural tradition is nonetheless an acknowledged good. Treating ranching as a full third option in its own right shifts the rhetorical challenge from locating ranching within an oppositional binary to evaluating its worth within an increasingly complex plan.

This refashioned, triangulated rhetorical situation has created almost as much antagonism as did the situation when framed as a binary, despite many participants' apparent hope that the three concepts of urban, rural, and natural can coexist or even become interdependent. The keystone report of the Ranch Conservation Advisory Team and its reception by members of the environmental community illustrate how attention to ranching can easily extend the drama, rather than resolve it. The county report, *Our Common Ground: Ranch Lands in Pima County*, clearly attempts to locate ranching as a conservation force within the urban-nature dichotomy and, simultaneously, to place a high value on ranching as an independent third term. The report's subtitle is *A Conservation Objective of the Sonoran Desert Conservation Plan*, suggesting the elision between ecological and cultural goals. The introductory paragraph of the executive summary reinforces this elision:

> By virtue of its extensiveness as a land use and the ongoing land stewardship provided by ranchers, ranching in Pima County is uniquely suited to preserve natural, unfragmented open space, habitat, and the land's natural and cultural resource values. Consequently, ranch conservation was identified . . . as a conservation element of the Sonoran Desert Conservation Plan. (1)

As the report develops this argument, it continues to foreground land stewardship and depict ranching as a sustainable and "extensive rather than intensive use of the landscape" (2). In explaining how ranching fits into the Sonoran Desert Conservation Plan, the report gives first priority to "defining the metropolitan urban boundary" (3) and, later, stresses its role in preserving open space and in conserving Arizona's limited water supplies, which are overtaxed by development. These rhetorical moves make the most of the Sonoran Desert Conservation Plan's dichotomous framing in order to underscore the importance of ranching to the conservation (anti-urbanization) goals of the region.

As the report discusses some of ranching's other contributions to the Sonoran Desert Conservation Plan, however, it focuses more directly on ranching as a third term by stressing ranching's cultural role. The report defines culture, in part, as "practices that reinforce [social and community] values and inform members of that society about themselves, how to conduct themselves, and how to interact with their environment" (3). The report argues that the embodied knowledge of ranchers is unique, irreplaceable, and important because of "intimacy with the land that grows out of first-hand experiences" and "wisdom passed on from previous generations" (3–4). By helping ranching to remain a viable cultural tradition, the authors argue, not only is history preserved "but the entire cultural land-scape is preserved to provide meaning and context" (4). Ranching is further credited with contributing substantially to the rural economy. This high evaluation of ranching supports an action plan that calls for considerable financial incentives to keep ranchers from selling to developers. These incentives include government and land trust purchase of development rights or conservation easements that pay ranchers to continue using their private property for all purposes other than intensive development. Another proposed incentive is for land management agencies to issue long-term leasing rights to allow ranchers to make long-term decisions with secure knowledge that they will be able to continue grazing on government lands (136–37). As the cost of these measures will be carried by taxpayers, the public relations challenge for ranchers and their supporters is to raise the salience of ranching's cultural cache within the planning process, empha-sizing the importance of preserving ranching and valuing it for its own sake rather than simply for its role in containing development.

Those who oppose ranching on ecological grounds also stand to benefit rhetorically by treating ranching as a full third option, perhaps even more than do ranchers and ranching sympathizers. For these, turning ranching into a third term helps counteract its subsumption into nature in response to anti-development positioning. This enables environmental organiza-tions to fight against both development and ranching, and to avoid having to support ranching as a result of opposing development. During inter-views, two activists explained to me that the either-or framing of land plan-ning decisions strikes them as an indication that the public is ignoring many possible alternatives, thereby abdicating the agency to frame the debate and to choose preservation over either of two poor alternatives.

To this end, a coalition of nongovernmental environmental organiza-tions that formed specifically to play a role in the Sonoran Desert Conserva-tion Plan has developed a counter-report that challenges some of the basic assumptions of *Our Common Ground* while seeking even more clearly to keep ranching a third entity separate from both urbanization and conservation. In *Livestock Grazing and the Sonoran Desert Conservation Plan: A Conservation Per-spective*, the Coalition for Sonoran Desert Protection argues:

> Most of the peer-reviewed scientific literature available does not support conservation benefits of livestock grazing. The draft preliminary Plan, for example, emphasizes the use of ranch land as a boundary for urban

growth. Ranches may well provide valuable open space. But where live-stock grazing contributes to the degradation of native ecological conditions and imperilment of species, other means of urban growth control must be utilized, and grazing must be eliminated from the most ecologically sensitive areas. (1)

Throughout the report, the Coalition rebuts the claims of the Ranch Conservation Team, primarily by means of a review of scientific literature. Its primary argument is that ranching should be disassociated from ecological conservation. While ranching can clearly counteract development, the Coalition argues, this does not mean that ranching serves the habitat conservation purposes of the Sonoran Desert Conservation Plan. Only by creating ranching as a third term, and then by devaluing it, can the Coalition effectively oppose both development and ranching simultaneously.

For the discipline of rhetoric, one of the implications of this case is that adding options does not necessarily ease opposition: three-way opposition can be every bit as contentious as two-way. It is not uncommon for teachers of rhetoric—college composition instructors, for example—to urge their students to move away from framing their arguments in two-sided terms that ignore complexities and tend to recycle already defined arguments. The complexities of ranching, however, suggest that what keeps disagreements from moving forward is not two-sidedness per se but the reification of alternative positions, regardless of whether those positions are wildlife versus urbanization or wildlife versus urbanization versus ranching. In fact, in one of his lessons on persuasion, Aristotle suggests to his tutees that one way to persuade others to adopt a position is to use the strategy of division, that is to claim that there are three possible explanations and then show why two of these are unreasonable, leaving the debater's preferred option as the only remaining evident choice (On Rhetoric 196). This rhetorical strategy can circumvent the rhetorical need to directly support the preferred option while at the same time closing down others' ability to imagine new ones. The strategy of multiplying options, in Aristotle's lesson, is ultimately intended to make it more likely that a position is accepted unchanged by the deliberative process. Similarly, in some instances, the Ranch Conservation Team and the Coalition for Sonoran Desert Protection both act rhetorically to add a third option in order to keep their own position discrete and to hierarchically order the three different and clearly defined options. While long-standing differences remain reified in fully discrete options, the drama of western conflict over land use will continue.

This debate over the role of ranching in ecological conservation implies that "what's in a name?" matters immensely in the choice, for example, of Sierrita Ranch Conservation Area over Sierrita Mountain Park. Under either name, the plan proposes making the Sierritas a core part of the reserve that will serve as critical habitat protection in the Multi-Species Habitat Conservation Plan used for the Section 10 permit. Renaming the park does not reclassify the Sierrita's role as a core reserve, but it does validate ranching as a core reserve activity—and this validation implicitly extends to the other mountain parks that share its classification. As shown by examples in this section—which are just a few of the many examples that could have been drawn from the debate—renaming the park in the first few months of the process did not put a stop to the mistrust, contention, and differences in desire that have fueled antagonism among ranchers, environmentalists, and developers throughout the planning of the Sonoran Desert Conservation Plan. More than eight years after Huckleberry first submitted his draft plan, this process is only now reaching some closure. There have been some real reasons for optimism over progress in planning, such as the 2004 Open Space Bond, discussed in the next section. But there also have been plenty of examples of hostility. When the planning process has failed to contain this antagonism, arguments have moved out of deliberative arenas and into the courts: homebuilders' associations, for example, have challenged the owl's endangered species listing, leading to a constant possibility of delisting as the case has moved from District Court to Court of Appeals, and back again. (See Table 2). As for ranching's role in the core reserve and corridor system, the argument over the naming of the Sierritas is but a microcosm of a drama that is temporally and geographically larger than the Sonoran Desert Conservation Plan and that has saturated the activities of a county heroic enough to address this drama in public forums.

Open Space, Urban Boundaries, Cores, and Corridors: Beyond Drama

Drama, fortunately, is not the only approach to deliberation, and not the only approach taken within the Sonoran Desert Conservation Plan. I turn now to a different method for multiplying options, one that does not depend as fully as does drama on separately characterizing those options. I borrow this method, in large, from the new rhetorics as laid out by Kenneth Burke. Burke calls this method "dialectic"—a choice of term informed by its use by Socrates/Plato, Marx, Hegel and others. Burke, however, gives dialectic a unique, language-centered spin. In general, dialectic refers to the use of opposing theses to probe, try, and develop each other until one of them is proven false. Classically—in Plato and Aristotle, for example—dialectic and rhetoric are hierarchically ordered in dialectic's favor: dialectic, associated with philosophy, is the preferred route for discovering truth, whereas rhetoric, at least in the first part of Aristotle's *On Rhetoric*, is primarily valued as a way to persuade others of truths that are arrived at independently.[3] Burke, in contrast, considers rhetoric to be the superordinate concept and central to human understanding as well as to action. Burke treats dialectic as but one of many possible approaches to rhetoric, though he sees it as a particularly valuable form of rhetoric because of its capacity to generate new ideas from the tension among differing concepts.

While Burke discusses rhetorical dialectic in much of his writing, my primary focus is on Burke's essays "Four Master Tropes" and "I, Eye, Aye." The former is considered to be a pivotal essay in Burkean thought. I include the latter, less frequently cited essay in my reading because of Burke's assertion that his claims within it apply not only to the central object of his critique, Ralph Waldo Emerson's essay "Nature," but to "symbolic action in general" ("I, Eye, Ay" 186). The focus on Emerson also provides a welcome fringe benefit because it generates claims about how humans relate to nature and about how language serves an important role in figuring and forming those relationships. While Emersonian transcendence does not substantively inform the Sonoran Desert Conservation Plan, the topical overlap between many of Emerson's basic concerns and those underlying County deliberation indicates how questions raised by the Sonoran Desert Conservation Plan are as old as American nature writing, and older.

In "Nature," Emerson performs an idealistic rhapsody that moves from a contemplation of nature to an argument that what nature actually reveals is the poet's self, and then to the claim that the self can construct its own world (including its own nature) on the basis of what is revealed through perception. This final development most fully reveals Emerson's idealism. In his conclusion, Emerson writes: "So shall we come to look at the world with new eyes. . . . Then shall come to pass what my poet said: 'Nature is not fixed but fluid. Spirit alters, moulds, makes it.'. . . Build therefore your own world" (42). This claim is consistent with the teleology of Emerson's essay and Emerson's assertion that all nature serves a unitary purpose. Emerson argues that, in order to realize their own intentions, men must first apprehend a supernatural purpose that is revealed through nature. In the process of making this argument, Emerson raises questions about humanity's role in constructing future social-natural relationships, and foregrounds the importance of thoughts and ideas to this work.

Burke, in a fashion consistent with his earlier work, treats Emerson's idealism as a predilection for writing about ideas that originate in the speaker's self. In *A Grammar of Motives*, Burke argues that idealism's chief characteristic is that it foregrounds the thinking agent. He continues:

> [Idealism's] close connection with epistemology, or the problem of knowledge, is due to this same bias [its stress upon agent]. For to approach the universe by asking ourselves how knowledge is possible is to ground our speculations psychologistically, in the nature of the *knower*. (172, emphasis in the original)

By arguing that the referent of what is known is actually the knower, Burke plays with the foundation of Emersonian transcendence. Unlike Emerson, who believes that nature reveals the supernatural, Burke sees transcendence as a normal function of language and especially as a function of language's potential to move from the particular to the general. Elsewhere, in "The Four Master Tropes," Burke discusses this "upwards" or "transcendent" movement from particular to general in terms of synecdoche. He argues that this trope is basic to understanding being and motivation because recognizing that language is always partial and that it does not fully represent reality is essential to moving beyond the limits of a single perspective. David Tell explains that "The Four Master Tropes" indicates that Burke believes that synecdoche in particular and rhetoric in general are essential to developing an understanding of the truth, because rhetoric can induce an audience to understand more than is literally stated, thereby helping to overcome some of language's limitations. In other words, rhetoric's historic association with persuasion is preserved in Burkean epistemology, but revalued to suggest that persuasion is essential to move beyond the limited literalism of terminology in order to fully grasp reality.[4]

While Burke values rhetoric in general and synecdoche in particular, he concludes "The Four Master Tropes" by arguing that irony is a particularly sure route to knowledge, because irony self-consciously recognizes its limitations and points beyond itself (Burke 514; Tell 47). For irony he also substitutes dialectic, for the tension in dialectic oppositions perform this self-critiquing function (Burke 513; Tell 48). The rhetorical usefulness of dialectic brings me to my primary interest in "I, Eye, Ay." This essay makes an explicit and succinct opposition between drama and dialectic by arguing that while drama reifies concepts by identifying them with particular characters, dialectic instead allows the disentanglement of concepts from identities. Dialectic thereby makes a virtue out of the partiality of language, for it provides a way for thinkers to shift positions and avoid the limits of a single perspective.

The limits of identity politics, including identity politics within the Sonoran Desert Conservation Plan, indicate the problems caused by too closely identifying concepts with persons. Drama, Burke argues, is like dialectic in that both "exemplify the competitive cooperation" where conflict leads to a "unitary view transcending the partial views of the participants" ("I, Eye, Ay" 188). In drama alone, however, different ideas require a "formal division into cooperatively competing voices" or separate characters (188). So, for example, the third term, "ranching," is brought into the political dynamics of the Sonoran Desert Conservation Plan through the addition of a new cast of characters: ranchers, the letter writers from McGee Ranch, the county's Ranch Conservation Advisory Team, and others who are identified with ranching or formally responsible for voicing the concerns of ranchers. In drama, new terms and new concepts are added through the identification of new stakeholders. To take this multiplication of voices and create unity, Burke argues, the cast of characters needs to find either scapegoats or other "imaginative devices . . . whereby members of rival factions can weep together" (186). In the Sonoran Desert Conservation Plan, the obvious choice for scapegoat is unplanned urbanization. By pointing to evils that can be avoided through centralized decision-making, temporary coalitions have been able to form among various stakeholders to the plan.

These coalitions easily fragment, however. An informant who has worked with environmentalists and ranchers in conjunction with legislation to promote statewide land use planning (Arizona's Growing Smarter Initiatives) argues that participants often fail to sustain working relationships after meeting concrete goals because they do not distinguish coalition-building from collaboration. Coalition-building is directed at getting a majority of votes, she explains. Burke likely would argue that successfully passing legislation is a moment of dramatic resolution. In contrast, my informant continued, "When you're working as a collaboration you're trying to get all the information into the mix so that you understand what's created a problem and how solutions might be constructed that will not lead to unintended consequences." When coalition-building, she continued, "you don't surface differences" because you are trying to create unity of purpose, but collaboration instead requires addressing "deep-seated conflict." Burkean dialectic is a route to addressing this conflict, because it requires participants to hold opposing viewpoints in tension.

Burkean dialectic does not, however, require the fixed identification of concept with speaker, which opens up a new path to resolving difference. Unlike drama, whose primary action occurs through characters interacting to change a scene, dialectic occurs through concepts interacting to change an agent. In dialectic, the agent needs to view all perspectives as contributions to understanding. This does not require (or even allow) relativism, but only a deliberate decision to try to understand multiple others. When thinkers, alone or in dialogue, attempt to resolve the opposition between two ideas, between thesis and antithesis, the conflict between them will cause a transformation that generates new, third terms. These thirds are not the same as the multiplication of stakeholders and stakeholder-identified options seen previously, but rather transformations that subsume the previous ideas within broader terms. In "I, Eye, Ay," Burke explains this dialectic development of new concepts by consciously playing with the rhetorical functions of Emersonian "transcendence." Burke claims that transcendence simply requires treating a "here and now . . . in terms of a 'beyond'" (190). Burke even coins the verb "beyonding," or bridging, as a synonym (200). Emersonian supernaturalism disappears, and what is revealed in its place is a method for thinking in ways that link disparate ideas, changing them in the process and generating new perspectives. It is this conceptual flexibility that I am after.

To maintain focus in my analysis, I wish to create a dialectical interchange between just a few key terms of the Sonoran Desert Conservation Plan, which I will read as metaphors. Burke suggests that the first of his four master tropes, metaphor, is basic to the workings of language. Classically, a metaphor is defined as something that draws together two different objects in order to associate their qualities. In "The Poetics," for example, Aristotle defines metaphor as "the application of an alien name by transference," as when old age is referred to as evening ("Poetics" 77, 79). Currently, building on a Nietzschean turn, many rhetorical scholars argue that there is a metaphoric component to all language (Foss 358–59). In her primer on rhetorical criticism, for example, Sonja K. Foss reviews theories that attribute both the discovery and the structure of ideas to metaphoric thought. She concludes that "Phenomena in the world become objects of reality or knowledge only because of the symbols/metaphors that make them accessible to us" (358). Burke claims that metaphor is ubiquitous in language because terms can never be identical to what they refer to. Understanding, then, requires transferring perception into concept. In this respect, metaphors are not ornament, but necessity. Language is always a vehicle for knowing its tenor, the world we participate in and constitute. Metaphor, consequently, overlaps with Burke's remaining three master tropes, including dialectic, because all the rhetorical tropes depend fundamentally on the nonidentity of concept and referent.

Burke's understanding of metaphor thereby creates a foundation for an epistemic approach to rhetoric. More recently, James Berlin and other rhetorical scholars have extended this attention by arguing that rhetoric is not simply epistemic, but social epistemic, because conversations and linguistic conventions shared by a community condition the knowledge and values of that community. Drawing on linguistic sign theory, Berlin argues that language is always positioned in a series of relationships. These relationships are between a speaker (or writer) and the listeners (or readers) to whom words are addressed. Additionally, they are between these persons and the world referred to in those words, a world of humans and nonhumans alike (488). By inviting people into a set of symbolic relationships, language shapes the way humans respond to their world and to others. Language shapes our social habits, because it shapes our minds. Because the assumptions embedded in language are socially validated, however, there is a tendency to forget the rhetoricity and the contingency of relationships, even to forget that many claims are basically metaphors. Berlin argues, and I concur, that one of the roles of the analyst is to remember this rhetoricity so that we all become more aware of choices, of how choices are influenced by social and therefore power-laden relationships, and of how relationships might be refigured. Because this rhetoricity extends to the analysts' own words, as a whole generation of anthropologists discovered in the wake of what George Marcus and Michael Fischer call "a crisis of representation in the human sciences" (7), Burkean irony comes in handy as a way to hold the analytic viewpoint in tension with other perspectives.

At this point, I wish to turn directly to the metaphoric qualities of a couple of common and frequently paired terms in western land use planning, "open space" and "urban boundary," followed by a second pair that is less popularly ubiquitous but still central to the Sonoran Desert Conservation Plan, "core reserve system" and "corridors." Though these terms are not habitually thought of as metaphors, even in their everyday uses they are recognized as generalized concepts whose application to specific referents requires a deliberate process of matching term to landscape. In these deliberations, the devil is certainly in the details: Burke recognizes that rhetorical transcendence is achieved by moving away from detail and toward generalities. While the details take most of the blame for contention, I argue that deliberations also are hampered when the clash of contradictory metaphors is obscured through their everyday use. At the core of these terms are different understandings of the basic social and natural relationships that deliberation is meant to decide. These terms thereby shortchange constitutive features of the deliberative process. By attending to these terms through the lens of metaphor, I hope to dialectically engage their assumptions with the intention of generating alternative ways to use language, alternative ways to think about how humans should relate to one another and to the world.

I begin with the idea of open space, not only because this concept shapes the imagination crafting the Sonoran Desert Conservation Plan but because open space is a ubiquitous signifier of the West. Especially from a distance, the West is frequently imagined as a cowboy riding across a wide open desert, his solitary presence reinforcing the absence in the area. To those who live around here, open space may instead be populated with hillsides of saguaro cactus or with mesquite and ironwood forests, but even so Pima's denizens will admit the possibility of gazing romantically across an open view after only a short drive, such as a ten-minute wind out of the City of Tucson into the Tucson Mountains to watch the sun set over a desert expanse from Gates Pass. And, unlike in the dense deciduous forest of my native Western Oregon, here it is possible to walk across land that lacks paths or development without entanglement. One can easily get lost in the desert's expanse and more than a little thirsty if not experienced and prepared. Such experiences give the dry feel of reality to the idea of open space.

The apparent appropriateness of the term open space can draw attention away from its metaphoric qualities. More essential to open space than its physical characteristics is its long association with the essence of western identity. Peter R. Decker, a western rancher and writer, expresses the psychological importance of open space by claiming that it is an especially "important quality of the West . . . a physical characteristic that influences our behavior." He continues: "The sheer size of this space—all 100,000 square miles of it—affects our psyche. As westerners, we carry within our mental geography a different, larger sense of space, distinct from New

Englanders and certainly from city residents" (70). For Decker—in a way not totally unlike Emerson—the physical characteristics of the landscape, of nature, leave an indelible imprint on the soul of the westerner.

Decker's claim that the space of the West shapes western identity is far from unique; it is of a species with Frederick Jackson Turner's famous 1893 paper advancing his frontier hypothesis to argue that not only western but all of American identity—an identity of rugged individualism and demo- cratic tendencies—is determined by the experience of inhabiting vast and unshaped open spaces.[5] According to Turner, American history is substan- tively shaped by frontiersmen who at first followed the paths of Native Americans ("savages") but eventually created a new society on a partial pat- tern of previously developed eastern society. By enabling this evolution in space and time, the frontier ultimately promotes the construction of a new and better society. The frontier hypothesis in this way follows the same development pattern as Emersonian transcendence: nature shapes the human, and in response the human becomes the person who creates an ideal society.[6] This "transcendence" is not supernatural for Turner, though, but the materialistic "beyonding" of moving westward. Throughout Ameri- can history, Turner continues, this frontier has always renewed itself by westward movement. As a result, the West has come to signify America's ability to reach its democratic ideals through an inexhaustible inventive- ness. Open space has come to signify the promise of a better future.

Turner further argues that the process of moving to the open spaces beyond the frontier fosters a type of rugged individualism that is necessary to survive in the wilderness beyond the civilized East. This individualism in turn feeds into democracy as frontiersmen engage in creating a new society. These identifications account for the continued emotional power of the idea of open space, for individualism and democracy continue to be key social values within the United States. These values are at work, for exam- ple, in O'Connor and Day's memoir, reviewed in chapter 1, and through them moral authority is ascribed to the ranched landscape and ranching culture. These associations, conscious or not, have become a part of Ameri- can culture and create a positive rhetorical valence to the use of the term open space.

The idea of open space, however, also has always been associated with the anxiety of its own disappearance. Already in his frontier hypothesis, Turner raises questions about how American society will respond to the imminent end of westward movement. He declares that the frontier has closed, and claims that its closing marks an end to an era of American history and its particular form of nationalism (38). After the closing of the frontier, the open range also closed in stages, beginning with the 1891 Forest Reserve Act and reaching its culmination in the 1934 Taylor Grazing Act, discussed in the last chapter. Current invocations of open space, situated as they are within this anxiety of disappearance, almost always have a protectionist motive. In the Sonoran Desert Conservation Plan, certainly, open space is figured as a precious resource that will disappear without human intervention.

The cause of open space's imminent disappearance is, of course, urbanization. The threat is that developers might look at open space and see only vacant or undeveloped land, as Robert Gardner and his collaborators suggest in their study of Colorado land disputes (356). Ironically, however, open space only holds together as a coherent identity by just this type of opposition from urbanization. Turner's open space depends on the concept of the frontier between the civilized East and the wild West. Contemporary open space depends upon the urban boundary. This is evident in the earlier quote from Decker. Decker draws on environmental determinism to argue that the West, elided with open space, creates a way of seeing the world that is "distinct from New Englanders, and certainly from city residents" (70). When the West is associated with open space, then the city, even more than the East, becomes the West's other, and in one swoop not only residents of Los Angeles and the western seaboard but also Boise, Boulder, Tucson, and other western cities are excised from the essence of the West.

Defining open space by its difference from city preserves its association with Turnerian possibility without requiring much specificity in terms of the social and natural relationships taking place within that space. In consequence, open space is a politically useful concept for coalition building. Pima County has a history of passing open space bonds: in 1974, 1986, and 1997. The county's best funded open space bond, however, is the Sonoran Desert Conservation Plan's cornerstone piece of legislation, surpassing President Bill Clinton's June 2000 creation of the Ironwood Forest National Monument in terms of significance to the plan. In May 2004, in a special bond election, the county passed several bonds. The most expensive and most publicized bond measure, "Sonoran Desert Open Space and Habitat Protection; Preventing Urban Encroachment of Davis-Monthan Air Force Base," allows the county to raise $174.3 million. The bond passed with 66 percent approval. The bond's title, which conjoins biological habitat and military operations, points to the odd coalitions that open space enables. The bond allows ranches and mountain parks and other types of conservation to share space through their shared opposition to urban development. Open space is neither wild nor rural nor military; it is only non-city.

This very potential for coalition-building across disparate interest groups points to why the Coalition for Sonoran Desert Protection chose to protest framing the Sonoran Desert Conservation Plan solely in terms of open space. By erasing all differences except that of urbanization, open space also erases the habitat differences that are at the root of the deep-seated contention over the ecological impacts of ranching. When someone attempts to create a pictorial image of open space, the contingencies embedded within it become more evident. A pre-election mailing from another coalition of conservation organizations features a wide-angle shot of the Tucson Mountains, a saguaro in the foreground. In the background, more saguaros share hillsides of brown and red dirt, hills that fold up toward the rocky mountain tops. The tall cacti and their understory of barrels, cholla, and bursage are interrupted only by rocky escarpments, too steep to hold even a thin layer of dusty desert soil (Friends of the Sonoran Desert). The picture is of Saguaro West, a national park that disallows ranching. The bond itself, however, allows funds to be used to support ranchers who put legal easements on their properties to prohibit development. The image privileges a particular view of open space that is not upheld by the practical application of the term, pointing already to potential fault lines among supporters of the bond.

Within the Sonoran Desert Conservation Plan, the most common metaphoric alternative to the tensions inherent in the open space/urban boundary concept is a second pair of terms: core reserve and biological corridors. These concepts are central to the development of the habitat conservation plan that is to accompany the county's Section 10 permit application. By developing a core reserve system, with different core areas connected by biological corridors intended to enable species dispersal, the county plans to mitigate against the effects of incidental take elsewhere, as required by the permit guidelines.

Read metaphorically, the paired terms "core" and "corridor" have strikingly different implications than does "open space." Defined by the absence of city, open space is, at base, an anthropocentric concept. A core, in contrast, is a biocentric concept defined by the presence of biodiversity, critical habitat, and desirable species. Cores have a dense and populated identity, unlike open space. Because presence rather than absence defines the core, the metaphor admits the possibility that even "pest" species—species that are not central to the core's identity—might be incidentally present alongside defining inhabitants, so long as their presence does not degrade the core itself (which is, of course, the sticking point in the debate over cattle).

Further, cores imply their margins (or buffers, the more common term in habitat conservation plans). The difference between a core and its buffer is one of degree, one of distance from a dense center, rather than a non-negotiable boundary. "Core" thereby implies dispersal rather than containment. This implication is enhanced by the pairing of cores with biological corridors. Corridors allow species to move from core area to core area while cutting through human areas. The overall image created by the paired concepts of core reserve and corridor is a sense of intense centers of wildness fading out to margins, but with vital systems of movement through those margins. This biocentric image pushes human activity, and especially urban development, into the far physical margins of the core and corridor system. The metaphor additionally pushes humans into the conceptual margins, for the idea of cores and corridors makes human activity incidental rather than integral to the plan.

Embedding the contradictions between anthropocentric and biocentric metaphors within the planning process can make for contested map drawing. To paraphrase Decker in unintended ways, the physical geography signified by a map that is drawn using both concepts will embed within it a conflicted mental geography. On one hand, the map will suggest an inviolable boundary between a crowded urban space and its opposite, the absence of city; on the other, it will suggest a geography based upon dense centers of diversity ranging out from and between those centers. The maps drawn from these two approaches are difficult to align. Yet, every time people with these contrasting mental geographies meet in deliberation, they must attempt this alignment.

While a dramatic approach to deliberation, as we have seen, will attempt a resolution either through the conquest of one method of mapping or by building a coalition by discovering a shared enemy—both of which seem rather short-term approaches to a long-term conflict—a dialectic approach tries to move through the tension between opposing conceptual geographies and to use that tension to create something that moves beyond either of them. This goal is embedded in the purpose of deliberations of the Sonoran Desert Conservation Plan, which brings together on the Steering

Committee developers, property owners, recreationists, government representatives, ranchers, scientists, and others. The plan thereby validates the tensions that structure its key concepts by shaping deliberative spaces able to bring together diverse voices in face-to-face settings. Thus, it requires a deliberative dialogue created out of the social and ecological concerns of the two metaphoric pairs.[7] For the remainder of this chapter, I will refer to the creation of this dialogic space and the material practices that accompany that dialogue as a socioecology.

The term "socioecology" has precedents. The most direct is a branch of primatology that examines the adaptivity of primate social behavior in its ecological context. While the primate focus is irrelevant here, primate socioecology's concern with adaptation and its insistence on a relationship between social behaviors and ecological issues is an analogous analytic interest. However, I am equally concerned with ecological and social change, and with the relationships between the two, in a way that eschews making ecology the context for social behaviors except as a temporary heuristic that calls for a shift in figure and ground as a complementary analysis.

Another precedent is social ecology, preeminently associated with Murray Bookchin. The key questions of Bookchin's own approach to dialectic, which he calls "dialectic naturalism," refuse to take for granted either nature, humanity, or the relationship between the two: "What is nature? What is humanity's place in nature? And what is the relationship of society to the natural world?" (7). Bookchin accompanies his dialectical method with a social program, developed from the synergy of his anarchist and ecological commitments, that emphasizes direct democracy and local control. Another, less programmatic approach to social ecology (alternatively ecohumanism) is identified with Aldo Leopold, Rachel Carson, and others, according to Jimmie Killingsworth and Jacqueline Palmer. Killingsworth and Palmer argue that writers in this social ecological tradition are united by a common view that environmental problems require significant social and cultural change, not just technical and bureaucratic fixes (2). The issue, for social ecologists, is whether humans will change to improve their fit with the environment.

Like Killingsworth and Palmer, I am particularly sympathetic to the social ecological approach to human and nonhuman relationships. My adoption of socioecology as an overarching concept, however, is primarily analytic. Certain premises do arise together with this choice, such as the presumption that society and ecology can be thought about and constructed

in an integrative manner, but the affinity between this view and certain attitudes underlying the social ecological program does not ultimately require
an endorsement of any particular program for environmental policy or
social change, as is clear from socioecology's usefulness to describe relationships between competing programs.

Admittedly, socioecology's comprehensiveness is related to its general-
ity, which is in turn a consequence of transcending anthropocentric and
biocentric approaches. It is also simply a metaphor, one that serves as a
heuristic, but it cannot in itself resolve the details of the desert plan. Where
Emerson transcended toward the supernatural and Turner moved beyond
history to a more democratic future, this socioecology takes urban and natural environments and crosses them with one another, so that the "beyonding" of the wild points to the city and vice versa. Like the constituent
metaphor of corridors, the metaphor of socioecology implies a mobile
interpenetration, but, unlike corridors, this mobility is not limited to the
wild; it also includes what is human: animals and plants dispersing not only
through the city but humans dispersing through the wild. Indeed, we have
left behind the wild, just as we have left behind the urban boundary, and
replaced both of these with relationships shaped through movements and
reactions to others (on the part of nonhumans) and reflexive, deliberative
actions and responses to others (on the part of humans). Socioecology
implies a set of human and nonhuman corridors, a set of pathways complete with diverse habits and relationships. Unlike a map, a socioecology
implies a dynamic system of responses and relationships that will change
with time, partially in response to the reflexivity of humans, exercised in
language, tried by deliberation, and enacted through management.

I recognize that socioecology does not settle the needs of the planning
process, but it does have the potential to transform the way deliberative
actors approach public arenas. Socioecology points to the need to always
account for humans and nonhumans in relation to one another, without
ever letting one obscure the other. Untransformed, open space separates
the human and nonhuman into opposing sides, only allowing the human
into nature through a deterministic, one-sided relationship in which open
space crafts a rugged individual, a stalwart of democracy who nonetheless
somehow remains separate from the demos. A transformed open space
requires accounting for a more interactive set of relationships. How does
the rancher transform the ranchland? (This in itself is a question not
allowed within the metaphor of open space.) How does ranch work create a

culture? How does the urban center relate to its rural and wild surrounds, and what are the pathways among the three that keep them from being clearly distinct and separately mappable entities? How do the monitoring of the scientist and the policies of the bureaucratic manager create the wild? How do the aesthetic sensibilities of the recreationist create the wild? How does the wild create the manager, the scientist, the rancher, the recreationist, the urban dweller? These broad questions settle nothing, but they reframe the old questions about open space versus urban area in a way that creates new pathways for inquiry and accountability, new possibilities for decision and for interaction.

Similarly, socioecology transforms questions about the core reserve and corridor system in a way that points less to preserving a threatened, ecological past than to the dynamics of constructing a vital future. Socioecology is a broad enough concept to contain the goal of replenishing and dispersing biodiversity. Yet it opens more routes to attaining that goal because it draws attention to the human in the midst of the natural world, and acknowledges that goal-oriented, agency-inflected monitoring and management decisions are a part of the ecosystem that participants in the deliberative process hope to create.

To illustrate, I turn for a moment from the Sonoran Desert Conservation Plan to a smaller-scale incident wrapped around similar themes of threatened and endangered species, permits, and the movements of humans and nonhumans in relation to one another. On January 12, 2004, the Fish and Wildlife Service put on administrative leave Wayne A. Shifflett, manager of the Buenos Aires National Wildlife Refuge.[8] Shifflett had moved 400 tadpoles of the Chiricahua leopard frog, a protected species, allegedly without legal authority to do so.

Despite the questionable legality of Shifflett's procedures, his actions are generally recognized to be true to the spirit of biological conservation. In 2002, University of Arizona biologist Cecil Schwalbe had moved water used by Chiricahua leopard frogs from a drying stock pond on the refuge to a pond in his backyard, where he began a captive breeding program. The population soon outgrew Schwalbe's ponds, and Shifflett sought permission to return some of the tadpoles to the refuge. When he failed to receive the requested Safe Harbor permits, he chose to move the tadpoles anyway to prevent their cannibalization by adult frogs. This move led to the charges against him. Shifflett ultimately accepted early retirement and paid a $3,500 fine rather than face criminal charges filed by the Department of Justice.

Speculation was rampant, but denied and untried, that Arizona State Commissioner of Game and Fish Sue Chilton, who with her husband Jim owns a ranch adjacent to the Buenos Aires, had deliberately blocked attempts to obtain appropriate permits. Several dynamics contributed to the speculation. First, the environmentalist community is by and large opposed to Sue Chilton's appointment as commissioner. This antagonism, which is much more broadly based than frustration over the Buenos Aires incident, has assisted in the creation of what Scott Hunt, Robert Benford, and David Snow have called antagonist identity fields, rhetorical resources that stand ready with "constellations of [negative] identity attributions" that are drawn upon to negatively characterize others (199). That is, the Chiltons as a couple have been depicted as an enemy of the environment long before Shifflett got in trouble for crossing the line between private and public land, the line between permissible and unpermitted conservation measures. This antagonistic identity frame has made it easier for members of the environmental community to simply extend past perceptions and paint Sue Chilton as the bad guy in this situation as well.

Second, the Buenos Aires itself has a contentious history that contributes to the perception that some members of the community local to the refuge would like to see it fail. Here, I present those aspects of this history that fit with the stories of several of my informants. In 1985, the refuge was established from a combination of private and state trust lands that, until then, were part of the Buenos Aires Ranch. The lands were purchased through a congressional appropriation but, due to a difference in the rancher's asking price and the appropriation, additional negotiations were required for the Fish and Wildlife Service to obtain the entire refuge. These negotiations involved a complex land swap involving Arizona State Lands, the Bureau of Land Management, and the U.S. Forest Service. Further, additional lands were temporarily purchased by the Nature Conservancy with the intention of selling them to Fish and Wildlife as soon as the agency could secure additional funds. These land deals, which partially insulated the refuge creation from the public process, earned the scorn of those opposed to the refuge, including the majority of local residents who objected not only to the withdrawal of previously private land from the tax base but also to the displacement of ranch cowboys whose children were a significant part of small rural schools. The entire process damaged the credibility of the Nature Conservancy enough that this nonprofit has since worked to change its practices by working with local communities and building trust and consensus decisions, even at the expense of moving more slowly toward its conservation goals. The Buenos Aires National Wildlife Refuge, however, has not fully shaken its local stigma as a costly drain on the local community. This stigma has made it easier for outsiders to perceive Shifflett's retirement as just one more development in two decades of conflict, and to presume that the Chiltons, as locals, are on a different side of the conflict than is Shifflett.

Third and finally, environmental argument is saturated with the belief that ranchers and leopard frogs are in conflict, or more broadly, that natural resource users and threatened and endangered species are in conflict. This assumption informs how Shifflett's letter of explanation is likely to be read. Shifflett writes: "Each time [I tried to get a permit called a Safe Harbor agreement] I was told that Sue Chilton, local Rancher and now Chairperson for Arizona Game and Fish, would not sign a 'Safe Harbor' agreement to allow for the transfer. (Ms. Chilton has a Forest Service Lease to run cattle near the eastern boundary of the Refuge)" (2). While Shifflett does not explicitly claim that self-interest led Sue Chilton to refuse the permit, anyone familiar with the debate would read Shifflett's parenthetical remark as an implication that ranchers such as the Chiltons might believe that the movement of leopard frogs will adversely affect their leases.

The idea that endangered species populations hurt those who use land as a resource is a common trope of environmental debate, one that recurs in debates over grazing. Rather than adjudicate between stories and interpretations, I wish to explicitly leave aside the Chiltons and their inscrutable motives and focus exclusively on the perception among some segments of the population that private landowners have a motive to resist the dispersal, reproduction, and discovery of endangered species populations. I encountered this concern on the first day of my official research when I met a young man with a number of social ties to ranchers who provided me with a list of research contacts. I eventually interviewed most of these persons. One referral, however, was offered with reservation, and the young man explained his reluctance. This final rancher, a close friend of his who owned private holdings east of Tucson in the area surrounding the Rincon Mountains, was a generous and welcoming person, I was assured. However, he had grown wary about inviting people onto his property for fear of endangered species sightings that could be used to hamper his ability to manage his land. If a person entered the rancher's private land illegally, sightings could not be used against the rancher, but once the man issued invitations, for example to me as a researcher, then he could be taken to court on the basis of species evidence. The rancher had responded to this situation by limiting the movements of others on his land to prevent endangered species from becoming a tool that would hamper his own freedom to act. Thus, between the rancher, other humans, and endangered nonhuman others, freedom of movement was restricted. Not wanting to divide my loyalties as researcher and environmentalist, I declined the offer of access to the rancher and his land, self-limiting my own movements as well.

This conflict over movement is embedded within the Endangered Species Act and its focus on endangerment. Mark Moore discusses a similar scenario with regard to spotted owls in the Pacific Northwest. Environmentalists have used the threatened spotted owl as an indicator of the imperilment of the old growth forest, with the ironic result that the disappearance of the owl becomes the prod for forest preservation. Loggers and others in the wood products industry, in contrast, have taken the owl as a scapegoat for industry problems, associating the owl with the extinction of their livelihoods and the failure of the woods product industry. Owls thereby serve as a negative sign, to both groups, of the endangerment of forests, on one hand, and the endangerment of economies, on the other. Neither group stands to gain rhetorically from the growth and dispersal of the owl population. Threatened and endangered species, whether they are the spotted owl, the pygmy owl, or the Chiricahua leopard frog, figure as a threat to both an ecological world, considered distinct from humans, and an economic world, considered distinct from nonhuman life. In this way, the current possibility that the pygmy owl might be delisted, or downlisted to threatened, is perceived as a threat to the environmental community and a hindrance to the Sonoran Desert Conservation Plan rather than as a cause for celebration, even though the pygmy owl's spread is a primary goal of habitat protection.

It is a far cry from the rhetorical use of a species as a negative sign to the words of another one of my informants. This rancher invited me to share in an interagency conversation about reports of a willow flycatcher nesting site on the public land of his ranch. Recognizing that endangered species are typically framed as a problem on all sides, this man told me that some fellow ranchers would view the flycatcher's sighting as a threat. Yet, he continued, for him the sighting was a cause of celebration, and he picked the day of our interview to share with me the deliberations caused by the sighting. This rancher explained that a new species is a sign of success, a sign that he is effectively managing for habitat, a sign that approbates his management decisions and his freedoms rather than a sign that his freedoms as a manager are about to be curtailed. Notably, this rancher works closely with agency representatives and also invites public scrutiny. He is accustomed to thinking of management as a deliberative rather than as an individual practice. His ranch thereby serves as a sign of a new alternative, a material and symbolic space where successful socioecological relationships are possible. To the rancher's voice is added the bureaucrat's; to the bureaucrat's is added an Audubon member's; to the public's is added the whit and sneezy fitza-bew song of the southwestern willow flycatcher. With each new deliberative voice, the vitality of socioecological relationships expands.[9]

Socioecology leaves us not with a map, but instead with a commitment to take what already exists, and to develop out of the potential of the present a future set of human and nonhuman relationships based less in fear than in the freedom to choose. This freedom requires reflexivity. I do not mean the reflexivity of the Emersonian individual who finds a way to personally transcend contemporary social problems by standing alone in the mystery of wilderness. Nor do I mean the reflexivity of the solitary westerner, the cowboy, who develops privileged moral qualities associated with the national identity in the school of rugged individualism. Instead, I mean the reflexivity created by deliberation with human others, coupled with attentiveness to the nonhuman world our society is built in relationship to. The voices of these others will do more to call us beyond ourselves than will any solitary reflection or staked-out, stakeholder position. It is this hope that the Sonoran Desert Conservation Plan has called us to participate in, trying to transcend the limits of the political exigencies that have motivated its framing. From the narrow lens of a Section 10 permit for a single species, perhaps the Sonoran Desert Conservation Plan will take us to a place where a man carrying tadpoles on his back is a validated approach to creating a shared and vital future. We can only achieve this socioecological potential when we are open to possibilities beyond those dreamed of in the drawing of lines on maps.

[3]

FROM BATTLE LINES TO COLLABORATIVE SPACE

The concept of socioecology serves as a potential tool for renewed thinking about how our relationships to both human and nonhuman others fundamentally make up our world. Defined as a potentially dynamic and mutable set of mutually constitutive relationships between humans and nonhumans, the concept requires letting go of discrete distinctions between, for example, culture and nature,[1] instead drawing attention to how these shape one other. Sociological factors make contingent what once seemed uniquely ecological, and not simply because societies can pollute their environments; ecological factors make contingent what once seemed uniquely sociological, and not just because external environments limit and contextualize societies. Questions of what type of environment we want become questions about what type of people we want to become, and vice versa.

Traditionally, deliberative rhetoric has tested ideas about the constitution and direction of human society, while science has investigated nature and the environment. When boundaries between society and its environment no longer hold, however, then neither do boundaries between the types of discourse appropriate for making decisions about them. Developing socioecological thought requires doing away with the idea that the only appropriate sites for scientific debate are scientific forums, such as conferences and journals. The separation of nature and society and the parallel separation of politics and science shortchange public debate, as Bruno Latour also argues in *Politics of Nature: How to Bring the Sciences into Democracy*. This artificial separation fails to adequately address how humans place themselves within socioecological relationships, and it truncates human agency.

In practice, however, as Latour also notes, science-based argument frequently finds its way into political conflicts. Nonetheless, those engaging in science-based arguments often join their claims to a normative assumption that science should compel consent. While not everyone adheres to such a rigid understanding of science, many do, as I demonstrate from field notes in the next section of this chapter. Because debaters often expect scientific study, rather than deliberation, to provide solutions to problems, the failure to easily reach consensus via scientific means often leads to frustration, incredulity, and suspicion, as is frequently the case within the debate over public lands grazing.

Throughout this chapter and the next, I analyze competing claims about the impacts of cattle grazing on grasslands, claims that contradict one another in ways that appear mutually exclusive. Socioecology points to a way to give credence to differing ecology-based beliefs by highlighting how differences in human choices and values lead to the creation of what Latour calls "matters of fact": knowledge produced through the human activity of science, in collaboration with the natural world that responds to scientific observation and experimentation, knowledge that is solidified into certainties only through "a long process of negotiation and institutionalization" (*Pandora's* 307). This view suggests that different human activities can provide a sound foundation for different, even apparently contradictory, knowledge claims.

In the first section of this chapter, I illustrate the need for a dialogic approach to science. Following Bakhtin, by dialogic I mean not simply face-to-face conversation (dialogue) but a way of thinking that interpretively engages others' words, changing one's own in the process ("Toward"). A dialogic approach thereby flies in the face of attempts to fix scientific meanings once and for all. Dialogism offers a way out of rigid, and culturally common, conceptions of science that can readily shut down debate in spite of the best intentions of those who invoke them.

Then, in the final three sections of this chapter, I examine habitual differences in science-based argument that can help explain differences in positions debaters hold. Rather than explain science-based argument in terms of differing degrees of adherence to institutionally legitimate or specialist versions of scientific argument, I instead use a classical approach to argument, stasis theory, which aims to pinpoint precise issues of disagreement. I argue, however, that while stasis theory may help a third party judge the merits of warring arguments, it is less helpful for finally resolving deeply rooted conflicts. In the place of stasis, I present an alternative model of rhetoric that exposes uncertainty and opens up new space for dialogue.

By more fully accounting for difference, I prepare for chapter 4, in which I elaborate on specific ecology-based claims and discuss how they indicate different desired socioecological futures.

Invoking Science, Sometimes in Vain

On January 16, 2002, the Science Technical Advisory Team (STAT) of the Sonoran Desert Conservation Plan met in Tucson to discuss a completed draft of its recommended priorities for land and habitat conservation. In addition to STAT members themselves, who sat facing one another at an oblong table in the center of the room, about twenty persons (including myself) attended the meeting, filling chairs that lined the conference room walls. While we made up a good turnout for a STAT meeting, many more would come to a February Steering Committee meeting on the same subject, when STAT would officially present its recommendations for public comment.

Though the STAT meeting was open for observation and included a call to the audience as a final agenda item, the partial separation of STAT from the core public process taking place in the Steering Committee worked to allow its scientists—ecologists, botanists, wildlife biologists—to independently reach consensus on conservation goals. The separation serves as a pragmatic and expedient way to make full use of the scientific expertise of those participating in STAT, while still reserving deliberative space for the public to later negotiate STAT's priorities in response to cultural and economic pressures stemming from development, recreational use, property rights advocacy, and the desire to preserve archaeologically valuable sites and traditions, such as ranching.

The STAT meeting covered a variety of topics, such as reports on funding sources, the buy-in of key stakeholders to past proposals, and the successful purchase of a ranch in response to a completed scientific study. The key agenda item, which drew the uncharacteristically large audience, was the release of county-wide habitat maps. One of STAT's committee members, a representative of a county agency, walked around the walls of the room where the maps were posted, enthusiastically discussing what they showed about the biological sensitivity of different habitat areas. The demarcation of biological differences, as represented on the maps, would serve as the team's primary tool for making sound judgments about conservation priorities.

After the presentation, another member of STAT elaborated on how the decisions represented by the maps had been arrived at. He pointed out that

STAT did not have "PVAs" (Population Vulnerability Analyses) available for most of the fieldwork species. This lack of species data had prompted the committee's decision to focus on habitat. The STAT member openly discussed the disconnect between ideal knowledge—the PVAs—and the knowledge readily available for management decisions. At this, a man seated along the wall opposite me spoke up, interrupting the discussion to ask the committee why its members did not just go out and collect the missing data. He said he was concerned that STAT's recommendations had no scientific basis. In response, a STAT member discussed more fully the fieldwork and scientific process, including peer review, the team had used to create the maps, explaining that STAT had created a list of fifty-six key species to use as environmental indicators. Rather than use these to create a "species by species management plan," STAT had opted for a habitat management plan, which many perceive as a more holistic approach.

The explanation did not appease STAT's critic. He asked what the committee would do to make the indicator species "invulnerable."

Now the speaker from STAT was confused. "Invulnerable?" he queried.

The man patiently explained: If you have vulnerable species, you need to make them invulnerable. Was this not the purpose of the Sonoran Desert Conservation Plan? I surmised that the man must have extrapolated from the term "population vulnerability analysis." He was using the term "vulnerable," however, in a way that the confused STAT member would not, taking language out of its original context and giving it meanings that were incommensurate with its original use. To support his concerns, the man cited lectures he had attended and textbooks he had read. He had clearly studied the issues, but his manner of speaking—such as citing a textbook as an authority whereas academics would instead reference journal articles—suggested incomplete inclusion within the scientific community represented by STAT. Confident, however, in his ability to speak as a peer, the man made his final point: STAT needed to know how each indicator species responded to fire and termites and other stressors. He asked if the committee had that information.

This type of information is difficult to come by, explained someone from STAT.

No, countered the speaker at the wall, to the laughter of many in the room. The man did not acknowledge the negative response. He cited a textbook that included a simple process for conducting PVAs. To this, a STAT member simply repeated that the process was not as simple as it appeared, and added that it could take years to get PVAs on all the species in the study. In the meantime, decisions needed to be made. In evidently growing frustration at being rebuffed, the man asked: What if there are natural disasters? What if there are earthquakes? Certainly biotic communities are vulnerable to earthquakes?

Up to this point, STAT members had responded patiently and tried to seriously address their critic's concerns. Now, however, one young scientist exclaimed: "Earthquakes? I disagree." The chair of the committee began to deliberately keep the questioner out of the conversation, calling on other raised hands in the room and naming people at the oblong table. But the discursive boundary between those at the table and those seated along the wall had been bridged. More people joined the debate. Some comments were welcome: announcements of meetings, requests for simple clarifications. Others created conflict. At one point, the young scientist who had scoffed at the mention of earthquakes called "naive" a question that, from my marginal position in the process, sounded quite competent. Another member of the audience, who had arrived at the meeting late and who was evidently enjoying the sport, responded to a mention of the need for "management buy-in" to the scientific studies by yelling: "What about the property owner? You're forgetting the property owner." To this interruption, another person along the wall exclaimed in an incredulous tone: "But we're talking about biology!"

The conversation had clearly reached a point at which no one was listening to anyone else, let alone waiting to take turns to speak and consider what each other was saying. The face-to-face dialogue had become no more than a platform for sound-bite versions of predetermined positions. Those at the oblong table started responding in ways intended to take back control of the runaway conversation, and to bring it to closure by limiting the role of those seated along the wall. Some STAT members answered interjections and questions by saying that those along the wall had the wrong audience for their concerns, and others added that the meeting's purpose did not include anything but science. To the woman with the "naive" and critical question, a couple of team members pointed out that she had not attended all the committee's meetings and suggested that her methodological questions had once been relevant but were no longer at issue within the community of fuller participants. After all, as a STAT member emphasized, the Sonoran Desert Conservation Plan process had been ongoing for years. Whatever knowledge this woman brought with her, it did not fit within the parameters of the ongoing conversation. Finally, one STAT member who had been quiet throughout the debates summarized her colleagues' comments by reiterating the scientific purpose of STAT, pointing out that the meeting was not an appropriate forum for debate, and suggesting that all dissent be deferred until the next meeting of the Sonoran Desert Conservation Plan Steering Committee, which STAT reported to. At that point, the chair of STAT adjourned the meeting.

This meeting highlighted one of the challenges of deliberating about issues that require scientific or other specialist forms of knowledge, such as most environmental issues. While debate within scientific communities is a normal part of creating knowledge, those who are marginal to those communities typically do not share the assumptions, background knowledge, and methods of debate that are used within the inner circle, making it difficult to negotiate across discursive boundaries. This problem is not unique to science but is inherent in specialization, which presumes that some persons will dedicate significant time to developing more authority than others. Science exacerbates this common problem by accompanying its specialized vocabularies and methods with barriers to accessing the tools necessary for experimentation and knowledge production. Professional scientists have something unique and valuable to offer, and their ability to contribute is further augmented in contexts, such as the Sonoran Desert Conservation Plan, where the time they dedicate specifically to particular aspects of the planning process far outweighs that of the general public. The challenge of speaking constructively across the (literal) inner and outer circle of this meeting highlights how quickly communicative contexts requiring specialization can become unbalanced and work against competing ideals of inclusivity.[2]

The problem is not easily addressed, although groups are increasingly taking on the practical challenge, leading to new models for collaborative governance and stakeholder science (Futrell; Waddell; Walker and Daniels; Weber). The Sonoran Desert Conservation Plan is clearly one such attempt, and it is particularly challenged by the size of its planning area and scope of its process. I laud the STAT member who patiently explained the difference between population vulnerability analyses and a habitat approach, thereby making scientific decision-making processes and their effects on outcomes accessible to the public. Nonetheless, those responding used the opening to further polarize the debate, leading other STAT members to shut the door on dialogue, or at least defer it to the Steering Committee meeting. There, a public discussion of both the issues at stake in the habitat mapping and the means that STAT used to create its recommendations did take place in some depth.

Because it is challenging to communicate across unlike groups using science, debaters sometimes employ certain strategies to avoid engaging others' science-based claims. One approach is to protect the boundaries of scientific decision making, and to leave debate over science within the professionally trained and certified scientific community. This strategy is seen in the STAT sympathizer's remark, "But we're talking about biology!" as well as in STAT members' arguments that the team's scientific purpose makes the meeting the wrong place for debate. In this view, once the scientific community reaches consensus, its claims can move to the broader public—such as the Steering Committee meeting—at which point the public is given the option of acting according to the best dictates of science or of setting science aside in whole or in part for political reasons. Science itself is understood to be generally apolitical.

The use of science to bring closure to debate is deeply ingrained in western culture. In "Gorgias," Plato's early Socrates distinguishes between rhetoric, widely used in deliberative and judicial arenas, and forms of knowledge that provide certainty, such as medicine. Taking a slightly different approach, Aristotle argues that rhetoric is distinct from sciences because only specialists can speak persuasively about their particular fields (*On Rhetoric* 37). Latour summarizes this tradition of thought by noting that "Nature is the chief obstacle that has always hampered the development of public discourse" (*Politics* 9). In this tradition, both science and the nature it speaks for are rhetorically placed beyond the general public's agency, leaving little room for public debate after science has spoken. You can't change nature.

Although debaters often turn to science to know "what to do" (Szerszynski 104), the ubiquity of science in debates over environmental issues and the proliferation of competing versions of science (environmental science, industrial science, bureaucratic science, managerial science, popular science, you name it) are leading some to reactively reject science. As more and more groups claim the authority of science, some begin to discount it as they interpret the contradictions between opposing positions as an indication that science is inadequate or even untrustworthy. As an example, one man who identified himself to me as an ex-rancher, a ranching sympathizer, an environmentalist, and a proponent of community collaborations shrugged off the value of science because, he claimed, you can make it prove anything. In this young man's case, the modernist assumption that science is apolitical has morphed into disillusionment, as science and politics more blatantly overlap with one another. Science has failed, in this view, because it has not lived up to its promise of apolitical knowledge.

When debaters look to an authoritative science to provide answers for them, and when they reject it in disillusionment, they lose their ability to critically engage science-based claims. These opposite attitudes contribute equally to an atmosphere where invoking science silences dialogue. Together, they narrow possible responses to a scientific argument: one can accept a claim and its resultant mandate for human action, or one can accept the claim but reject its moral priorities, or one can dismiss the claim altogether. Each of these possibilities leaves the claim itself untouched (whether accepted or rejected), foreclosing a fuller deliberation and tending to displace the public responsibility for decisions from human agency onto objectivist truth-claims. At the very least, an objectivist model of nature upheld by science takes decisions out of the realm of probability, governed by rhetoric, and places it into a moral space where we humans can only do as we are told, or not (motivated as we are by greed, delusion, short-sightedness, or whatever), and suffer the consequences.

One particularly damaging way to refuse to deliberate is to hold one's own science-based claims as self-evident while imputing apparently contradictory claims to the self-interest of others. Antigrazing activists frequently depict the claims of ranchers as deceitful defenses of a taxpayer-supported lifestyle. These defenses, activists claim, are made to an unsuspecting general public with the intention of maintaining legislative support for ranchers' economic interests by artificially reducing the costs of grazing leases and endangered species compliance. According to this dismissal, the ecological degradation caused by livestock is blatant and undeniable to anyone who has seen grazed land, let alone studied the ecological literature; only self-interest, therefore, can account for why someone would defend ranching as ecologically beneficial or even neutral.

This commonplace dismissal of grazing has its counterpart. Two ranchers I interviewed separately explained that environmentalists who oppose grazing condemn cows because they want personal power, not because they seek environmental integrity, a comment that closely parallels a line of argument promoted by former Secretary of the Interior James Watts, a notorious adversary of the environmental movement: "[Environmentalists'] real thrust is not clean air, or clean water, or parks, or wildlife but the form of government under which America will live" (quoted in Killingsworth and Palmer 37–38). Other ranchers and government managers, in a way that resonates with yet another typical Wattsian attack (Killingsworth and Palmer 37), told me that most self-styled environmentalists who oppose grazing simply want to avoid cowpies when hiking, an aesthetic that masks itself as ecological concern even though these same people may recreate in ways that degrade the land. While the reference to cowpies is an (often conscious) reduction of the problem, its larger sense is that environmentalists want to control others' activities, regardless of whether those activities have beneficial, neutral, or negative ecological impacts. Further, the slur suggests, these environmentalists do not address their own negative impacts.

The actions of many of my informants contradict the attacks made upon them. By the end of this chapter—and, to an even fuller extent, by the end of the next—I will provide an accounting for differences that is not based in self-interest. Along the way, I will also recount stories from the field that challenge the value of self-interest as an explanation for many of my informants' actions, especially if self-interest is narrowly defined as the pursuit of short-term economic gain. A broader definition of self-interest includes the need to respond to the land in ecologically valid ways. As several told me, ranchers who wish to remain ranchers long-term require a sustainable grass resource to sustain them economically. These ranchers do not find it in their self-interest to abuse the land, though some who hope to sell land for development might. Similarly, claiming that activists primarily seek control provides no explanation for their choice to dedicate their energy to one issue rather than another. The broader self-interest of those involved in debates over grazing is frequently identified with the ecological interests of the land they argue over, invalidating the claim that self-interest implies a lack of interest in learning how to act effectively on the land. Enlightened self-interest requires integrating action into ecological processes that promote and sustain goals over time: it requires thinking of a more collective and socioecological interest.

Although self-interest cannot fully explain science-based argument, the belief nonetheless persists that it can. The imputation of self-interest to dismiss others' claims serves as a form of what sociologist Thomas Gieryn has called rhetorical boundary work. In a series of historical cases, Gieryn demonstrates that over and over the question arises: What counts as science? At stake are research funding, social policy, and the way society gets constructed throughout history. Questions about the boundaries between science and nonscience are never settled decisively, but must be rhetorically sustained or renegotiated. Gieryn's argument that the boundary between science and nonscience is delineated rhetorically suggests that, outside of the social, historical, and political context of debate, there is no universally valid standard for judging what is scientific. In the case of ecological argument over grazing, polarization in both popular and professional forums demonstrates that the standards for judging claims are no more agreed upon than the claims themselves.[3]

The imputation of self-interest is a particularly damaging form of rhetorical boundary work. In his sociological study of scientists at work, Robert Merton argues that disinterestedness is one of the key norms of science. A second norm, universalism, reinforces the importance of disinterestedness. Universalism refers to the expectation that scientific knowledge will be the same regardless of who produces it, setting a standard for scientific objectivity ("The Normative"). In other words, if what a range scientist believes is backed by substantial scientific study and proof, and a wildlife biologist has a contrasting viewpoint, then the contrasting viewpoint is unscientific by default, tainted by subjectivity, and likely motivated by self-interest or ideological bias.

In an extension of Merton's argument, rhetorical scholar Lawrence Prelli examines a case of contested primate language acquisition in which scientists have promoted their findings through counternorms of interestedness and particularity in order to blur the boundaries of what counts as science and gain legitimacy. By examining the reasons given for claims and counterclaims about the scientific validity of this case, Prelli argues that both the invocation of norms and of opposing counternorms serve as idealizations of science, neither of which grasp the full complexities or contradictions of actual scientific practice ("The Rhetorical"). Prelli's study suggests that only persuasion can establish what counts as science and what is instead mere self-interest, as this distinction is never obvious or inherent in scientific practice.

Rhetorical boundary-work reifies scientific knowledge in ways that inhibit dialogue and science-based problem-solving. While establishing boundaries around scientific knowledge sometimes protects the efforts of specialists from too easy dismissal, the authoritative invocation of science is increasingly met with skepticism, counterclaims, and disillusioned disregard for the role of science within decision-making. With respect to western environmental issues especially, institutionally legitimated experts can now anticipate that their audiences will use prior knowledge to evaluate, and perhaps reject, expert claims. In the worst-case scenario, debaters will simply choose to accept those claims that fit with their pre-formed beliefs.

To avoid the reification of understanding, and with it the stagnation of conflict, members of the public need a way to critically engage and interrogate science-based claims. They need enough uncertainty to doubt their own beliefs, as well as others'. The presence of absolute certainty produces a world of right and wrong, public and selfish interests, and winners and losers. Fortunately, not all science-based argument, even in arenas that cross levels of specialization, leads to polarization. In the remainder of this chapter, I leave behind adversarial invocations of science. Instead, I illustrate that science-based argument, like other forms of rhetoric, is fully fit for deliberation.

Stasis, or Drawing Battle Lines

Throughout my analysis, I avoid a type of boundary work that makes an ethos-based distinction between institutionally legitimated claims about ecology, those made in more popular arenas, and those articulated within my interviews. I do recognize significant differences (beyond ethos) between specialist discourses and those in non-specialist forums, but leave it to other scholars to elaborate on these. In *Ecospeak*, for example, M. Jimmie Killingsworth and Jacqueline Palmer explore how the way scientists write to others within a scientific community differs significantly from the way scientists address others who do not produce scientific data and, even more substantively, from the way others make appeals on the basis of scientific claims. Interdisciplinary scholar Dorothy Nelkin has addressed discursive differences throughout her career, using *Selling Science*, for example, to analyze causes for differences in scientific discourse and science journalism, and *Science Textbook Controversies* to similarly account for aspects of public education in science. Nelkin's work is exemplary of (though not contained by) scholarship in the public understanding of science, a subfield of science studies with particular bearing on discursive differences in science-based arguments. Another line of research aims to account for times when science is opened to debate beyond specialist communities. Aspects of Thomas Gieryn's work could be placed in this category. Massimiano Bucchi also is exemplary in this regard. It is beyond my scope, however, to productively enter into this scholarship.

More pertinently, I do not find that such differentiation helps me to examine the persistence of contradictory beliefs about ecological processes and relationships, which enter public debate from a wide range of sources. As Robert Futrell remarks in "Technical Adversarialism and Participatory Collaboration," when policymakers rely too much on scientific expertise, they encounter a public that is often resistant on the basis of knowledge and concerns that are not incorporated into technical frameworks (454). This remark points to the pervasiveness of noninstitutional knowledge that needs to be reckoned with by policymakers and analysts alike. To better understand arguments that are public and science-based, I choose not to assume a connection between the impact of beliefs and the expertise of their source, and I treat any argument about ecological processes as worthy of analytic interest.

To analyze science-based claims without adjudicating truth and falsity, I adopt a method of analysis developed by sociologist Wiebe Bijker, and David Bloor before him. In blatant disregard of the general suspicion that disagreements are reducible to self-interest, I assume that my informants speak in good faith, making ecological claims that they themselves believe within the context that they make those claims. I then examine apparently contradictory claims using what Bloor and Bijker refer to as symmetrical analysis. This method uses the same analytic framework to account for true and false beliefs (for Bloor, in the context of mathematic knowledge) and for historically successful and unsuccessful technologies (for Bijker, in three cases *Of Bicycles, Bakelites and Bulbs*). By beginning with an equal treatment of all claims, symmetrical analysis elides truth and falsity, treating this distinction as unhelpful. Instead, symmetrical analysis locates (typically social) sources that explain the tenacity or disappearance of different beliefs. As Bloor's and Bijker's disparate cases suggest, symmetrical analysis applies equally to ontological and teleological claims, a point whose pertinence I will make evident by the end of the next chapter by drawing connections between the present (ontology) and goals and desires for the future (teleology). I consider symmetrical analysis even more useful in my case than in Bijker's and Bloor's, as the claims I analyze are still current, while those of Bijker and Bloor are historically settled. By refusing to prejudge the claims I analyze, I acknowledge ongoing deliberation about these claims.

In the context of arguments over cattle grazing, I like to refer to symmetrical analysis as sitting on a fence. Debaters on all sides of the issue frequently use as evidence photographs that depict contrasting fields on either side of a fence, one of which is considered healthier than the other as a result of the differing activities of managed cattle (most typically as a result of the presence of cattle on one side of the fence and their absence on the other). At times, this evidence is simply found in the fenced landscape; at other times, it is deliberately created as an experiment, such as by fencing off a small area as a cattle exclosure in the center of an otherwise grazed field. In either case, the fence, implying human decisions, and the vegetative differences on either side of the fence, which are the whole point of the photographs, aptly point to the interaction of social and ecological relationships that form the basis of scientific claims. Additionally, the deliberative use of the photographs highlights the persuasive role of evidence that points to both social and material referents.

The ecological issues raised in regard to cattle grazing are legion. Many scientists and environmental activists associate cattle with a host of ecological evils, such as watershed destruction, rapid soil erosion, riparian habitat destruction, endangered species loss, and the accelerated spread of woody plants and imported African grasses. No one denies the legitimacy of some of these claims in some circumstances, but some maintain that these problems are not *necessary* impacts of grazing. Instead, they argue, careful management can prevent most or all of the harmful effects associated with cattle. Others, taking this argument a step further, maintain that cattle can be managed so that they *help* create healthy desert grassland ecosystems. This argument is typically based on the belief that cattle can at least partially fill historic ecological niches that have been partially vacated by fire and wild grazing animals, including elk and desert pronghorn. From this perspective, removing cattle from grasslands is potentially devastating ecologically and would lead to unhealthy matting of grasses and woody plants and to reduced establishment of new grass seedlings.

With so many issues under contention, it is easy to generalize into anti-cow, pro-cow, or a more complex middle ground, positions that roughly overlap with the three contrasting narratives analyzed in the first chapter. A classical approach to argumentation, stasis theory, advises the value of more precisely deciding the source of disagreement among different debaters. While many classical rhetoricians contribute to stasis theory, including Aristotle and Cicero, most scholars attribute its core concepts to Hermagoras of Temnos, whose lost work is reconstructed through references in other sources (Braet; J. B. Davis 693). Hermagoras raises four basic questions for debate. I illustrate these questions with examples drawn from forensics, the most common application of stasis.

1. Does an issue exist? (For example, in a murder trial, is there a body?)
2. How is the issue defined? (If there is a body, is it a case of murder, manslaughter, or suicide?)
3. What are the qualities of the issue? (If it is murder, are there extenuating circumstances, such as self-defense?)
4. Is there jurisdiction to decide the issue? (Is the appropriate court trying the case, and is it following appropriate legal procedures?)[4]

These questions are meant to determine the exact points of disagreement among debaters (fig. 1). Each point of stasis is framed so that the question will have a single definite answer. This approach is meant to move the debate toward resolution and action as each of the four points is decided, either by a judge in the typical forensic case, or by concession in a deliberative case (fig. 2).

To illustrate the effects of this form of argument, I will apply the four standard stasis questions to a specific issue about the ecological effects of grazing. My move to apply stasis to scientific questions has both Lawrence Prelli's A Rhetoric of Science and Alan Gross's The Rhetoric of Science as precedents, though with an important distinction: while Prelli and Gross examine scientific argument within disciplinary contexts, I examine the invocation of science in the public domain.[5] The issue I will focus on, both for this chapter and the next, is the impact of cattle on grass cover within desert grassland ecosystems. Using stasis theory, this issue can be divided into the following questions:

1. Has grass cover changed?
2. Are these changes grazing impacts? (Answering this question requires disassociating cattle grazing from other sources of impact, including drought, recreational use, and wildlife impacts.)
3. What are the qualities of the changes? Does grazing increase or reduce grass cover? Does it alter species composition and, if so, in what ways?
4. What types of evidence are necessary to decide the issue, and who has the authority to do so? Should responses be based on multigenerational experience or managerial experience on the land, on comparison with historical accounts of the landscape, on fenceline photographs or photoplots, on vegetation transects, on range experiments, or on some other form of evidence? Should ranchers, government agents, activists, scientists, judges,

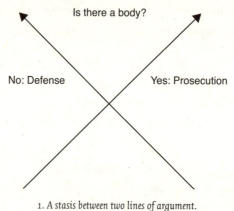

Is there a body?

No: Defense   Yes: Prosecution

1. *A stasis between two lines of argument.*

legislators, the general public, or persons in some other role decide the issue?

As deliberative (as opposed to forensic) approaches to stasis theory emphasize, reaching rational consensus (or at least a clear and stable majority agreement) on these ecological issues could substantively improve the chances of deciding the larger, complicated issue of how to respond to public lands grazing. That consensus will not be reached anytime soon.

While some hold up stasis as a dynamic means of conflict resolution (Carter; Crowley and Hawhee), its primary forensic use (and, to a lesser extent, its secondary, deliberative use, especially if contextualized by the court of public opinion) suggests that resolution is not so much about moving the conversation forward as about winning and losing. Sharon Crowley and Debra Hawhee point out that stasis is a war metaphor referring to the geographic location where two armies meet in battle (44). Rhetorical theorist Jeffrey Carroll calls stasis monologic, meaning that actors engaging in this type of debate are unlikely to change their minds (161). In a contrary interpretation, Antoine Braet calls stasis dialogic because it has "critical discussion as its object," but even Braet acknowledges that third party issues substantively alter the equation, presumably in ways that undermine its basic dialogism (90, 91). Reaching resolution through stasis does require debate, but it does not require that debaters persuade one another directly. All that is necessary is for one side to convince an authoritative third party such as a judge or, alternatively, to concede within a deliberative assembly. Third-party contexts encourage mustering additional evidence for preformed positions rather than listening and reflecting on one's own position.

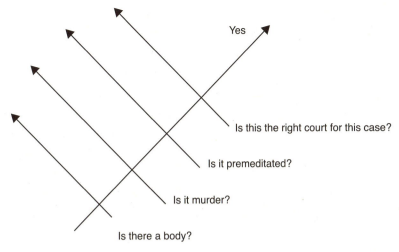

2. *Advancing the case in the prosecution's favor.*

Currently, no authority is universally accepted as a third-party judge, and there is no final forum that will allow resolution through stasis. Judges resolve particular cases, legislators pass particular laws, scientists issue their results, government agencies create reports and make management decisions, activist organizations formalize their positions. Any particular decision, however, is constantly subject to appeal, as seen with regard to the pygmy owl listing discussed in the previous chapter. Multiple routes to power exacerbate this dynamic switching of odds-on favorites within the United States democracy. The possibilities for shifting outcomes have worked to prevent closure on the public lands grazing issue while the public remains divided.

Historically, western ranchers have benefited from the status quo, as Charles Davis argues in "Politics and Public Rangeland Policy," largely because of historic and, to some extent, ongoing associations between Arizona government and ranching families (74). Yet the Endangered Species Act and the National Environmental Policy Act serve as powerful tools in the hands of environmentalists, leading them to frequent courtroom victories that help unsettle legislative and administrative setbacks. With multiple but interactive avenues to power that provide advantages to differing groups, resolution is partial, temporary, and typically based on the suppression of disagreement through the sorting of winners and losers.

When the goal is to create a generative dialogue, rather than to enable adjudication, stasis is inadequate despite its usefulness for forcing precise argument. Embedded within stasis theory, however, is a direction to turn. The fourth question of jurisdiction, which Alan Gross calls "different in character" from the first three ("Why Hermagoras" 142), is classically considered a last resort, as Braet argues:

> The presuppositional ranking [of the four questions of stasis] is seen as the order of retreat from stronger to weaker lines of defense. In this context it seems curious that the technical defense, which is nowadays in principle so powerful [as in a lawsuit based on National Environmental Policy Act procedures], should come last here. Evidently the ancients saw it as a formal refuge with which those who resorted to it heaped upon themselves the suspicion that they had no material defense. (83–84, NEPA example not in the original context)

A more positive view of the fourth question, however, sees it as the single place to defer resolving the previous questions and avoid determining a winner and loser. By raising questions about appropriate procedures and evidence, the fourth question opens up the possibility of further inquiry. By raising questions of forum, it acknowledges that the authority for adjudication is itself at stake, creating an exigence that may favor the type of mutual persuasion that arises out of sincere engagement while disfavoring appeals to third parties.

The Fourth Stasis, or the Problem of Judgment

In order to prepare the ground to illustrate how questioning standards of judgment might take us from warlike stasis to a more creative form of rhetoric, I will essay for awhile into some of the differences in evidence that contribute to disagreement over cow-plant interactions. In the process, I illustrate how differing, habitual forms of drawing on evidence keep debaters from directly addressing one another, in spite of the appearance of stasis. For the sake of focus, I primarily attend to the contested role of cattle in grass reseeding (appropriate to the second stasis question), using a symmetrical analysis to respond to differing answers to a key ecological question.

Do cows plant grass?

At the base of ecological knowledge about desert grasslands lies a fundamental uncertainty. Whether cattle help improve grassland habitat practically requires comparing land with cows to land without them; yet the historic ubiquity of cattle on the open range keeps these comparisons from achieving the idealized purity of, for example, the sterile control in a petri dish experiment. Still, approximations are possible, and debaters use both historic and geographic comparisons to make their case. A fenceline photograph is a major form of the latter; arguments about baselines serve as the primary source of temporal comparisons.

Most everyone agrees that cattle have historically contributed to ecological damage in Arizona: in the late nineteenth century, overgrazing and drought followed by heavy rains led to extreme erosion and watershed destruction (Cox 523; Sheridan *Arizona* 139–42). This agreement about past ecological damage, however, does not create agreement about what Arizona was like before widespread commercial grazing. Early explorers describe lush grasslands and healthy riparian areas (Sheridan *Arizona* 129). Since then, however, not only has the density of grassland plant species decreased, but species composition also has changed qualitatively. For example, since the 1930s, imported African grasses, intentionally seeded to restore damaged lands, have significantly altered the species composition of even those areas that remain dominated by grasses (Cox 523; McClaran and Anable 92–93). What this means, practically, is that incomplete historical records cannot be decisively filled in by reference to current habitats, even those that are currently ungrazed. As many of my informants bemoan, the scientific baseline—the standard for measuring the success of restoration work—is lost. Without the baseline, interlocutors have difficulty creating agreement over what the land used to look like, let alone establishing what ecological processes created that landscape, let alone determining how to reverse processes of change should they wish to.

Several of my informants explained to me the significance—and challenge—of determining the historic model. As we spoke in her agency's conference room, a member of a county agricultural extension service told me about weaknesses in arguments concerning the effects of cows on particular riverbanks: "You've got a lot of steep slopes. You've got endangered fish in the river. And they're saying, 'Look: you put cattle on there, you're accelerating the soil erosion. It's going into the river. It's going to hurt the fish.' But there's no data to tell you that. There's *no data* that says that."

Continuing on, the agent explained how some scientists have concluded, in the absence of direct evidence, that cattle cause erosion: "It's just these broad-scale computer models that are saying: 'If it's this kind of soil and this kind of slope then you have accelerated soil erosion.'" Developing her critique, the agent told me, "There's no baseline between what's natural erosion and when you get to the point that it becomes accelerated erosion.

We just had a meeting last week where . . . one of the watershed professors at the U[niversity] of A[rizona] says we don't know what that threshold is when all of a sudden you start getting massive erosion." The missing link, as the agent explained, is an accounting of erosion in areas that have not been affected by cattle either in the past or in the present.

In the absence of a clear baseline, debaters can easily deconstruct model-based arguments. The answer to the second stasis question—What is it?[6] (is the erosion a cattle impact)—cannot be agreed upon. The problem is circular. The evidence that would persuade many that cattle cause erosion is a baseline established in the long-term absence of cows. Without such a baseline, there is no fully persuasive reason to remove cows.

It is possible, and best practice, to construct probable accounts of baselines.[7] However, in popular forums, baselines are always easy to dispute, as I learned in a ranch tour following one of my interviews. My informant, the primary rancher at the Rocking Horse Ranch, (not its real name), is a friend of someone in my partner's family, someone I had met once several years before the interview. To cut down on driving time as we left for a vacation in the direction of the ranch, Phil, my partner, joined me for my first visit to this informant. I decided that the preexisting acquaintance, slight though it was, justified a change in my typical practice of visiting informants independently. Nonetheless, I worried a bit about the dynamic. For much longer than I have known him, Phil has been a dues-paying member of the Southwest Center for Biological Diversity, an organization that (among other environmental projects) promotes the abolition of western public lands grazing as a means to its primary goal of preserving species diversity. Phil clearly disapproved of the rancher's enterprise, but promised to leave me to my interview in peace. He sat reading, but also listening, on a couch near where the rancher and I spoke, then joined us at the recorded interview's end when the cattle rancher's partner also came in from tending her horses.[8]

At this point, the two ranchers volunteered to take Phil and me on a tour of Rocking Horse, and I switched off my audio recorder. Phil drove, and I sat in the back with the cattle rancher's partner, leaving Phil and the rancher to discuss—and at times hotly dispute—their differences. At one point they turned to baselines. The rancher pointed out that his land had been overgrazed for the last hundred years and that it is doing poorly in consequence. However, he added, the land had always been grazed, even before cows, and it now needs a degree of grazing to fully recover.

Phil disagreed. He argued that, historically, pronghorn had grazed the land, behaving differently and shaping the grassland differently than cows.

The two could agree on the history of overgrazing and that current grazing levels are lighter, but they disagreed about the specific features of their historical comparison. Overgrazing, yes, was the source of the change from idealized history to criticized present. But what did that imply about a different level of grazing? Would lower levels of grazing have fit into the idealized history without causing disturbance? Can lower levels of grazing fit into current ecological processes and make the future more like the past? In the absence of a functional landscape that matches the ideal, whether or not cows can create or accommodate themselves to the ideal remains an outstanding uncertainty. The rancher's partner interjected that the whole comparison is a "moot point" because "the original ecosystem doesn't exist any more." I agree. Nonetheless, the past remains a regular source for arguments about restoration. In a context in which everyone wants to control landscape changes and an imagined past is preferred to present damage, ecological history serves as a rhetorical resource for arguments about the future.

In the absence of an agreed-upon baseline, many debaters use other forms of historical comparison to make their claims, but this varies in fairly systematic ways by the positions folks take in the debate. When referring to the past to support management decisions, those who value cattle generally use shorter timeframes than those who oppose public lands grazing. I do not mean to suggest that there is no variation across informants or even across different sections of an interview. Nonetheless, my interviews suggest that some typical habits of my informants may be linked to their different perspectives. In the following paragraphs, I illustrate these habits, beginning with informants who believe that cattle are vital to grassland habitat and moving through a range of views until ending with informants who believe cattle destroy desert grasslands.

I take my first two examples from the transcribed speech of ranchers. The cattle rancher from Rocking Horse believes that cattle assist with grassland reconstruction and that, in effect, cows plant grass when appropriately handled. The entire interview makes clear that he is equally concerned with overgrazing and undergrazing, since he believes that grazing animals play one limited and important role in creating balanced ecosystems. In the excerpt below, this rancher projects into the short-term future to explain his management decisions.

"This land has been way overgrazed. That's my biggest ecological challenge. There is really nothing—well, at least 80 percent of what is supposed to be there naturally is now replaced by something that's not supposed to be there, . . . which is all just nature's reaction to being abused. . . . If I reach any given year, at the end of any given year, and I don't have better grass than I did the year before, then I'm way overgrazing. So then I'll sell down again."

This rancher integrates his focus on a one-year cycle of observation with his understanding that cattle help reseed grasslands. He allows that the latter claim depends on appropriate management, and he therefore looks to the short-term responses of plants to give him feedback on his management decisions. At the time of our first interview, this rancher and his partner had recently bought the ranch, which probably contributes to the rancher's desire for immediate feedback. Yet this short-term emphasis is also consistent with other aspects of his management philosophy, a point I will develop more fully in the next chapter.

A second rancher, from the Lazy T-Bar, does not argue that cattle are necessary to grasslands. He nonetheless believes he can graze while improving the health of ranchlands, and he further suggests that cattle might assist in some ecological processes well enough to benefit degraded grasslands. He suggests, for example, that cattle might substitute for fire and help control brush in places where rural towns and vacation homes make it unlikely that the National Forest Service will follow its professed let-it-burn policy. This rancher has a vision of sustainable agriculture that depends, in large part, on finding ways to develop food sources in most locales. In the arid West, he sees grazing as the most obvious form of agriculture. In keeping with his vision, this rancher sells finished beef directly to consumers rather than selling yearlings to feedlots, the more typical practice.

Gesturing from his home down to a wash, green and wet after summer rains, the rancher shared with me one of his success stories. "When we came here," he began, then interrupted himself to point to the trees, "this whole riparian strand through here." He returned to his narrative, telling me the status of that area before he arrived. "There was a little patch of willows just upstream from the bridge and most of the rest was just open sand wash. It was really awful. [It had only] a few relics: old cottonwoods and a few gnarled old willows. And we initiated, for the first five years or so, absolutely just winter grazing, or dormant season grazing only. And then the last few years we've grazed it for a couple weeks during the summer and then sometimes in the winter also. But we've just seen the willows and the cottonwoods explode!"

This anecdote is based in a ten-year timeframe, longer than that of the Rocking Horse rancher's, but still relatively short compared to those I will discuss below. The timeframe does overlap, however, with those of informants whose support for grazing is more blatantly accommodationist. By accommodationist, I mean these informants never suggest cattle benefit grasslands, but they do think grasslands can maintain themselves in the presence of well-managed cattle.

During my interviews, government agents who assist with ranch management in either an advisory or supervisory capacity often articulated this accommodationist position, as I will illustrate with excerpts from interviews with two informants employed by government agencies, who spoke to me as professionals but not specifically as agency representatives. One, a county extension agent, explicitly disputes claims that cattle assist with grass reseeding in any way. However, she wants to help create sustainable cattle ranching in southern Arizona and she believes the ranch community can realize this goal with appropriate will, education, and attention. Because her role is advisory rather than regulatory, she sometimes gets calls from ranchers asking for help when they are threatened by lawsuits. She can only help, she told me, when they collect vegetation data. One of her goals is to teach ranchers to monitor plant biomass by conducting vegetation transects, both for their protection and to give them feedback on their ranching practices. A thorough transect involves clipping all the target plants in a given area, drying the plants, and measuring dry weight.

I asked the county agent, "How many years of data do you need to effectively intervene [in a lawsuit], or months?"

She answered, "We usually like about five years of data to get a good picture, because so many things can affect the data. It can be observer error in plant identification, or something like that. It could be—your weather has a lot to do with how you interpret that data, so for the first, we like to take it three to five years, every year, and that way you can see the normal little humps and things, and then after that we do it every third, about every third year."

Similarly, an informant working for one of the government agencies responsible for granting leases requires several years of data to inform his decisions. He supports ranching, but he also sets limits on the level of grazing permissible in state ranchlands. When making leasing decisions, he looks favorably on ranchers "if they can have documentation showing that,

'Here's ten years of transects,' and it's showing that the trend [of biomass available from desirable plants] is not going down. Even if it's just level at least that's showing a sustainable plant community." In other words, this agent is willing to evaluate sustainability in ten-year chunks, at least within the context of ten-year lease decisions, making a rancher's own practices the standard for evaluation and the start of a lease a practical baseline for measuring the needs of the land. Individual ranchers are thereby made responsible for keeping the land in the condition they found it, regardless of prior assessments of damage, and sustainability is defined in practice as a relatively short-term absence of change.

This practice significantly contradicts the preferences of environmentalists who oppose grazing, environmentalists who do not agree that preventing further change is the true measure of sustainable ecosystems they perceive to be significantly damaged already. Focused on reconstruction, these activists consistently place baselines in the more distant past, often referring to changes dating back to the decades preceding the turn of the nineteenth century.

Near the end of my interviews, after I had developed a specific interest in cow-plant interactions, a staff member from the Buenos Aires National Wildlife Refuge who supports the refuge's no-grazing policy complained to me about the effects of cows on grasslands. I was actively trying to sort through specific differences in attitudes about cow-grass interactions. To gain another perspective, I mentioned, "I hear over and over that cows plant seeds." The staff member rejoined ironically, "Yeah, they plant mesquite seeds."

He based an elaboration in a long-term history: "Cows do eat a lot of mesquite beans. But that's how mesquites came into the valley. When they brought cows into the valley in 1865 these cows came out of Mexico and they came out of Texas. And the ruminants were full of, evidently, mesquite seeds because [early explorers, when writing,] described mesquites only in the foothills. You know, they weren't even out on the grasslands. But cows love mesquite beans, and what a perfect seed-spreader is a cow. They scarify the seed; they spread them. They put them in dung piles; they give them nutrition. They got, you got the moisture there, you got nitrogen; it's the perfect medium for spreading, spreading mesquites. So that's how the mesquites spread through the valley, you know; it wasn't wildlife."

This person's rhetorical habit, like that of others who oppose grazing, is to base claims in an expansive historical perspective. Other informants told me, in frustration, that there used to be a fishing industry along the Gila and Santa Cruz Rivers of southern Arizona. Both rivers used to run perennially, but they are now dry for much of their length and run only with seasonal rain. My informants concluded that cattle grazing, along with overconsumption of water for agriculture and towns, has contributed significantly to the rivers' radical change by trampling plants and eroding banks, by eating grasses that hold together soil.

Notice that, in the above illustrations, those who are most nearly involved in daily operations typically—although not always—refer to short-term ecological changes. Ranchers describe small improvements that they notice or seek to put into place. Those who work most closely with them, government agents, also take a relatively short-term view. However, those with a preservationist or restorationist agenda that excludes cows, the majority of whom are urban environmentalists and more distant from managerial decision-making, tend to take a long-term view of ecosystem change and often reference damage throughout the approximately one hundred and forty years that cattle have extensively grazed southern Arizona. These differences in preferred temporal evidence suggest that, instead of meeting in points of stasis or clear disagreement, debaters might be speaking past each other.

This point is even more strongly suggested by differences in preferred geographic evidence. Once again, the generalized pattern is that those who most strongly advocate for grazing tend to select the most local forms of evidence, whereas those who most strongly oppose grazing tend to select the most broad-based forms of evidence. These different rhetorical habits suggest that the neat lines of argument, laid out as a focused stasis earlier in the chapter, may mask more broad-based differences that operate on a wholly separate plane.

Before I proceed to my next set of examples, I wish to note that there is no clear scientific reason for consistently choosing one type of geographic evidence over the other. Both local and more generalized ecosystem approaches make recognized contributions to scientific knowledge. A range scientist I interviewed spoke from the small scale. When I asked him how best to manage a ranch, he told me that his answer depended on a number of factors.

Reading from what he called the "short list" posted by his office phone, he told me the kinds of things he needed to know: management objectives, geographic location, precipitation amounts and distribution, vegetation types, archaeological sites, topography, current ecological conditions, kinds of animals involved, stocking rate, season of use, timing and length of rest, the history of all those things, range improvements—how the ranch is watered and how it is fenced, utilization patterns, riparian area considerations such as the presence of endangered species or cultural resources, the economics of the ranch, legal aspects, and water quality information.

"If you give me all that stuff," he concluded, "then I can help you determine best management practices."

Most of this scientist's requirements can only be answered in reference to a specific location. Several of the topics assume information based on areas smaller than a ranch; for example, wanting to know how long an area is rested implies that cattle are grazing elsewhere.

In defense of the larger scale of evidence, however, the very concept *ecosystem* points to the usefulness of thinking about land not as isolated sections but instead as a complex set of networks, relationships, and connections. There is practical disagreement over how large an area to consider when analyzing the ecological effects of an action, but the range scientist's microlevel is generally recognized as reciprocally implicated in a much larger system of ecological interactions. A more macrolevel approach informs, for example, the *Draft Comprehensive Conservation Plan and Environmental Assessment* of the Buenos Aires National Wildlife Refuge. According to the draft plan, the U.S. Fish and Wildlife Service decided in 1994 to approach management decisions using an "ecosystem approach." Based on this approach, it identified only fifty-two "watershed-based units" in its care. The unit in which the Buenos Aires participates, referred to as the Gila/Salt/Verde River Ecosystem, is an "approximately 49 million-acre ecosystem [that] encompasses most of Arizona" and a small part of western New Mexico (10–11). The draft argues that management decisions for the refuge need to be contextualized by this larger area, even though the Fish and Wildlife Service must focus its decision-making only on the land it directly controls. This example suggests that, when networks of ecological connections rather than specificity and variation are the emphasis, macrolevel arguments come to the forefront.

During interviews, most of my informants made geographic claims more often than temporal claims, providing me with many more examples to select from to illustrate my understanding of differences. As a result, my remaining selections are more closely connected to issues of cow-grass interactions than the previous time-oriented examples. As in the baseline discussion, I arrange examples beginning with those who think cattle are vital to grasslands, ranchers who argue from the smaller scale. As my examples move along a continuum toward antigrazing perspectives, my informants' referents also tend toward larger geographic areas.

My first example, once again, is from my interview with the cattle rancher from Rocking Horse. One of this rancher's major managerial concerns, in addition to fine-tuning his stocking rate, is figuring out the best way to rotate his cattle through his several paddocks. During the interview, he typically spoke about the management needed for a single field rather than for the ranch as a whole. For example, while explaining to me the role of cattle in breaking up the ground to help grass reestablish, he noted that he included a severely overgrazed field within his yearly rotation plans as a way to improve grass cover in that field, as he believed the field would further degrade without short periods of grazing. This decision contradicts his narrow self-interest, as it requires purchasing supplemental feed; yet it fits within his overall plan to create grassland health in the long term.

The rancher told me of this plan during my second interview at the Rocking Horse, an interview that also included the retired rancher who had previously owned the land. This retired rancher shared the current owner's belief that cattle help reseed land. Speaking about a different area on the ranch, the older man described a section of land, visible from a well-used road, that he had left ungrazed because he feared public censure. However, he argued, "I had kept it looking good so long that it was starting to damage the resource. . . . And so the regional guy, the head of the Forest Service for this district out of Albuquerque was here visiting. . . . And I say, 'This needs to be eat off right to the ground.' And he says, . . . 'Go eat it off. Right to the ground. Just go ahead and do whatever you want to do to it as long as you think it will really improve the resource.'"

The rancher continued, telling me that the land became much healthier after he had grazed it heavily. I asked, "What does eating it off to the ground accomplish?" He explained, "[it] gets rid of a lot of decadent growth that the animals won't eat. Gets—helps to get the hoof action in the ground, stirs things up, new seeds. Water then penetrates the ground a lot better. If the grass is allowed to get old and everything it gets sawed down; water can't get into the ground like it should."

Both these ranchers link their claims about cows' restorative effects to evidence derived from lands smaller than a single ranch. In contrast, two government agents, who do not share the Rocking Horse ranchers' belief that cattle actually improve ecosystem health, refer management decisions to larger areas, whole ranches. While responding to questions about how she thought ranching might become sustainable, one agent referred to a rancher who makes his decisions based on fields within the ranch, but her own decisions are more closely connected to the appearance of the ranch as a whole: "There's a place . . . that . . . had been overstocked: too many cattle; it had no rotation at all; they were just kind of put in three pastures and left a lot. We got a new manager. . . . He let it rest for two years. But in the meantime we were doing other things and we went from three huge pastures to nine—eight or nine—smaller pastures. . . . He just started moving the cattle based on where he knew it had rained or not rained, what the plants looked like. We had, when we rode that first time [immediately after the management change], we saw very, very few [of] what we call riparian species trees, maybe one or something. We had no idea of any potential. And within five years we had new little baby trees coming up in these wash bottoms; we had the deer grass coming up really well, and we . . . gave him an increase in livestock numbers because it showed he could take it."

Similarly, an employee of another government agency explained to me that the agency once needed to pressure a permittee to get him to graze cattle. When I asked him if he were concerned that the land might be damaged if there were no cows on it, he answered, "No. It's just that the grass gets so thick it bends. Starts dying. And then, grass is meant to be grazed. Lots of people argue with me, but if you graze it just right, it won't hurt it. It's that level that we argue about."

Both of the above examples are based on ranch-size arguments. The first describes the establishment, in the presence of cattle, of species previously unknown to a ranch. The second is more generalized but arises, once again, in the context of a discussion about a single ranch. The ecological reasons given for management decisions do not depend on the presence of cows, but are instead meant to demonstrate that, with proper management and appropriate levels of grazing intensity, ecological processes can support and even regenerate grasslands in the presence of cattle.

My final examples are from interviews with environmental activists who want ranching to be abolished throughout the Southwest. The scope of their goals matches the scope of their arguments. Both have contributed a combination of either time, money, or expertise to the Southwest Center for Biological Diversity. One informant argued against the value of public lands ranching throughout the American West, also remarking on other examples of destructive ranching, including Navajo ranching in northern Arizona and Mexican ranching in nearby Sonora. His personal and public frustration with ranching was palpable throughout the interview, and he spoke in anger about pervasive species lost as cattle consumed whole ecosystems, eating grasses and trampling the soil that formed the foundation for sound watersheds and vegetation.

In the second case, an environmentalist and I were specifically discussing the argument that the region's grasses have evolved to require grazing. The environmentalist attributed this point to confusion with grass types in other ecosystems. He told me, "Southern Arizona grasslands are typically and almost universally desert grasslands. The native grass species are bunch grasses and annual grasses, neither of which form sod or anything resembling a prairie."

"What does this mean for the effect of cows on the grass?" I asked.

My informant answered, "The areas between the grass clumps are typically overlain with litter, which impedes surface erosion. If this litter and the soil crust are broken up repeatedly by hooves and action, it turns into a very powdery layer that is easily washed away or blown by wind. This also carries away the seeds of the annuals that would have sprouted with the rain, silts up the water courses, increases the scouring action and erosional potential of the floodwaters, and causes a sort of domino effect of degradation."

In making their arguments against grazing, both these environmentalists discuss ecological damage spread over large geographic areas. Like the retired Rocking Horse rancher who discussed the impact of cattle hooves on water absorption into the soil, the second environmentalist focuses on interconnected ecological interactions among cattle, water, soil, and plants. The conclusions the environmentalist draws from looking at these interactions, however, are opposite to those of the rancher. My informants differ in the management plans they support; they also differ in the geographic scale of evidence they use to support their ecological claims.

As in the case of habitual differences in temporal argumentation, there are plausible reasons why debaters might typically select evidence based on different geographic scales. As mentioned previously, many proponents of grazing currently work on specific sections of land, trying to make fine-tuned management decisions in relation to that land. Ranchers make management decisions based on differences within their ranch; external managers, such as government agents, tend to think of contrasts among the many ranches they are responsible for. Therefore, they tend to reference their remarks to specific pastures or ranches, respectively. Activists instead often work out of organization offices, relying heavily on published studies from multiple regions to piece together a more expansive perspective from a number of relevant ecological indications, at times bypassing a more fined-tuned specificity as a result of looking for the grassland, not the grass. These argumentative practices at times shift when debaters tackle other tasks, as when an environmental organization files a lawsuit related to a single ranch and uses more localized evidence as a result, or when ranchers work together to publicize a broader understanding of cattle impacts. It would be an error, consequently, to generalize from practices in a handful of interviews to the broader system of debate.

Nonetheless, patterned preferences for differently scaled forms of evidence, on both geographic and temporal scales, remains common. In fact, one of the environmentalists I interviewed who actively opposes grazing commented that damage measured locally might look quite different than damage measured on a larger scale. Differences in evidence and procedures for gathering evidence throw open the fourth question in stasis theory, thereby deferring resolution of the more decisive earlier questions and illustrating a need for a different approach to argument.

Skew Rhetoric: Making Space (and Time) for New Collaborations

To review, my informants disagree about the effects of cow-grass interactions. Some of my informants believe that cattle fill important, otherwise nearly vacant ecological niches, helping grass to reestablish even as they graze. Others believe that cattle degrade desert grasslands, interrupting ecosystem processes by selectively grazing plants, spreading undesirable seed, generally changing species composition, accelerating erosion, and degrading watersheds. Still others reject both these positions in favor of the belief that good management practices can sustainably accommodate cattle to desert grasslands in spite of real challenges, remaining practical puzzles, and no direct ecological benefits.

I model this apparent three-way point of stasis in figure 3. The point where the three lines metaphorically intersect represents the geographic point where three different armies might meet or, in the rhetorical analogue, the point that three different lines of argument most sharply contradict one another.

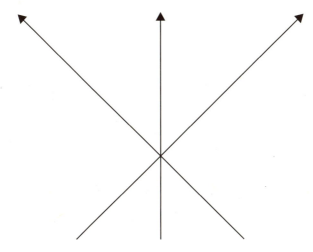

3. An apparent three-way stasis.

This model, however, assumes that there is enough correspondence among the different lines of argument that, while particular points are still under debate, at least the standards for judging them are not in question. In military terms, battle is met, and superior force will take the day. In rhetorical terms, disagreement is clarified, and superior proof will take the day. May the best argument win.

Yet what if the terms of winning, the terms of judgment or logic, are themselves called into question?[9] What happens to hopes for resolution once procedural issues displace the first three stases? Differing preferences for evidence undermine the very basis of agreement in just this way, as the data some find persuasive may not convince another. In figure 4, I model a rhetoric that recognizes that, because the three lines of argument are based on different geographic and temporal evidence, there is no clear point that could resolve them.

In the figure, I represent differences in evidence three-dimensionally to suggest that different ways of pursuing answers are analogous to operating on different geometric planes. In three-dimensional space, which represents not only arguments but also the evidence on which these arguments are based, the three lines no longer meet in ways that allow their resolution. They simply pass by each other. I refer to figure 4 as skew argument, borrowing a term from geometry for lines that are not parallel but never intersect, although if someone looked straight on without depth perception, he or she

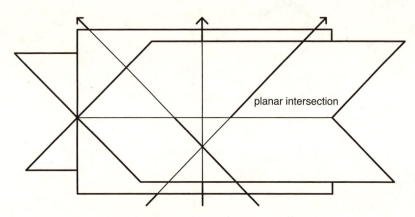

4. *Three skew lines of argument, each lying on a separate plane.*

would see the appearance of an intersection, as in figure 3. Similarly, two (or more) claims that are in disagreement may never meet in a testable fashion because they are based on different ways of mapping the debate, although a more cursory analysis might suggest they are in direct contradiction.

What do intersect, however, are the different conceptual planes that arguments are based upon, as seen in figure 4. One of my informants provided me with an example of what can happen when debaters engage material evidence as well as the claims based on that evidence. My source has limits, as I draw this example from an interview with a single rancher. I lack detailed information on alternate perceptions that might include more skepticism about the project's success. Nonetheless, the case suggests what might happen when those who hold opposing positions create their knowledge collaboratively, instead of just countering one another.

Upon purchasing the Lazy T-Bar, a ranch primarily composed of government leases, a rancher and his spouse advertised their desire to hold public meetings for anyone who had an interest in the public land. At the first meeting, the rancher recalls, a man attended "who had been a principal signer on a number of lawsuits filed against the Forest Service, . . . who was one of . . . the main people in the Forest Guardians," an organization opposed to public lands grazing.

The rancher reported that this activist came to the meeting and introduced himself by saying, "'I'm committed to abolishing grazing on public lands.'" In effect, the man announced he had come to put the hosting rancher out of business. Several meetings later, however, the activist and rancher had become friends, capable of working together collaboratively on shared conservation goals. What had happened?

According to the rancher, one contributing factor was an agreement to share responsibility for ecological monitoring. Each meeting now takes place in a different ranch habitat, providing members with the opportunity to point directly to examples of their hopes and concerns. At times, differences in perception persist, but, according to the rancher, discussion in the presence of evidence can, more often than not, produce agreement.

In a humorous illustration of the challenges of creating agreement, the rancher recounted one frustrating monitoring project in which the group's members were trying to determine the amount of decaying plant matter and the rate of its reincorporation into the soil. This process required categorizing decaying vegetation as "litter one" and "litter two": "Litter one is on the surface; litter two is, incorporated, that's, you know, decaying organic matter incorporated into the surface. So," the rancher continued, "you'd have something that's halfway in and halfway out, and argue about it."

When a debate broke out over which category was more appropriate to a particular location, a person in favor of litter two, said the rancher, "finally 'all right!'" As he retold this participant's frustration, the rancher bent down and, locating a twig at my feet, dug it into the ground. "'Now what is it?'" he at once asked his past audiences and me.

I laughed. Smiling, the rancher recontextualized this disagreement: "But ultimately the upshot is that everybody's seeing the same general thing, and most of their conclusions were not so much about what they were seeing but where they were coming from, and the position or set of values that they felt they had to defend, and, so, then, we would get into a discussion about that and it really came down to, you know, in a nutshell, every person had strong, strong feelings about the land, about the health of the land and their expectations from it, and there was a lot of common ground."

The rancher's story remains as a reminder that evidence does not speak for itself. In the rancher's analysis, discussing evidence makes it easier to understand where other group members are coming from. This basic respect and understanding enabled participants to stop using ecology as a justification for simply contradicting one another and to instead build a dialogue about desires for the land, a dialogue that eventually led to innovative ideas on how to manage the ecosystem to pursue new goals generated out of the discussion.

In contrast to stasis theory, skew argumentation requires that debaters acknowledge that their differences might be based on more than self-interest and that conflicts have other causes than a clash between truth and fiction, reality and self-interested fantasy. Skew argumentation requires that debaters work through the spaces created by their differences, spaces that are as broad and open as the space between the intersecting planes in Figure 3b. The first step is to acknowledge that space exists, instead of trying to flatten disputes into single points of conflict. The next is to recognize that processes for engaging one another cannot be taken for granted but need to be developed out of a full exploration of differences. This approach leaves room for a more creative type of invention, one that is less systematic than stasis theory but more likely to lead to the generation of new ideas. In the process, the forensic bias of stasis theory is replaced by a consensus-oriented deliberative bias, one that assumes that the standard approach to resolving conflicts is the time-consuming process of understanding one another, building respect and shared knowledge, and playing around with problems and solutions in a search for responses that might be mutually satisfying.

[4]

SOCIOECOLOGY AND THE FUTURE OF THE LAND

The Buenos Aires National Wildlife Refuge lies in south-central Arizona, sharing a border with Sonora, Mexico, stretching up through the Altar Valley to the west of the Baboquivari wilderness and the Tohono O'odham Indian Reservation. These 116,095 acres were purchased using congressional appropriations to "provide habitat for threatened and endangered plant and wildlife species, with emphasis on the endangered masked bobwhite quail" (USFWS 7, 5, 1). One late summer day, a couple of years before Wayne Shifflett's leopard frog transplantations (see chapter 2), I drove south from Tucson along Highway 286 to visit the refuge and its visitors' center. The highway crosses the Mexican border in the small town of Sasabe, but shortly before it arrives there, it passes Buenos Aires to the east. No road sign announces the refuge at its northern border, but I noticed a constellation of landscape features that nonetheless signaled the refuge's presence. The refuge generally hosts a lower density of mesquite trees in comparison to the regions I had been driving through and to the ranched area directly to my west. In the absence of a canopy, the refuge's grass is particularly noticeable. At one point, I passed a recent burn, with the trunks of leafless mesquites supporting blackened branches, many with their thinner ends broken off. What little grass remained was short and singed.

At the Buenos Aires visitors' center, about ten miles north of Sasabe and fifteen miles west of the only slightly more inhabited Arivaca, a volunteer shared news of the wildlife refuge. She was most pleased at the recent sighting of the endangered bobwhite quail, which brought the area's known population count to more than forty. She also shared that there were a couple of herds of "antelope" on the refuge at the moment, then drew attention to her error with the craft of an experienced educator, correcting it to "pronghorn" in pleasant and performed self-deprecation. Before I left, the volunteer had loaded me with newsletters and with the United States Fish and Wildlife Service's December 2000 *Draft Comprehensive Plan and Environmental Assessment* for the Buenos Aires. The majority of these publications discuss the refuge's prescribed burn plans. The burns are intended to reverse the incursion of woody plants and to create more grassland habitat for bobwhites and other species.

One goal of the burn program left me particularly puzzled. The refuge hopes to replace introduced grasses, such as the South African Lehmann lovegrass, with native grasses, reversing changes in species composition that have been ongoing since the introduction of new grasses in the first half of the twentieth century. The refuge's first manager, Wayne Shifflett, believes that the burn program will assist with this project. Yet this belief is not widely shared, and many of my informants scoff openly at the plan. This troubled me for two reasons. Most immediately, I love this land. Like others who do, I find it important to know unquestionably the effects of burns on grass species composition. This is the type of knowledge that ecological science is designed to produce and the type of knowledge that enables secure management decisions. At this point, however, no authority has produced a consensus on this issue that holds throughout the public arena.

Disagreement over how and whether to rid the land of Lehmann troubled me for a second reason—a reason that might at first seem at odds with my quest for ecological knowledge. While the rational modern environmentalist in me wishes for a certain response to what I perceive to be an ecological problem, the rhetorical analyst in me wishes to remain sitting on a fence for as long as possible, and to examine the interconnected social, rhetorical, and ecological elements of the problem rather than reduce them to simple ecology. This internal conflict has manifested itself in other aspects of my research. For example, on the first official day of my research I foolishly turned down an offer to be introduced to a rancher wary of environmentalists, in large part because I did not know how to reconcile my environmentalist worldview with my intention to represent the integrity of my informants. I have since come to see my decision as a cause for both regret and amusement, since my research has introduced me to the complexities of debate and humbled me into the recognition that I have no clear answers to use as a ground to dismiss others. Even as the complexity of issues interrupts my knee-jerk impulses, however, I still recognize that I have internalized those voices from our culture that hold tenaciously onto the hope that science will provide single right answers and that ecological knowledge will be freed from the contingencies and aporia that are the bread and butter of rhetoric. Behind this tenacity is a fear that tracing the ways that science is rhetorical amounts to claiming that science is subjective and divorced from reference in the real world. This distance from the world would make humans helpless within it; distance is the conceptual opposite to the socioecology that binds together all of us who live here.

What I have had to learn is that sitting on a fence need not lead to distance and helplessness. Instead, by granting validity to multiple beliefs and inventions, symmetrical analysis demonstrates that possibilities are not as limited as they might at first seem. Attending to the rhetoricity involved in creating these different possibilities simply highlights the (partial) role of human agency in creating and choosing among different possible socio-ecological futures. Fence-sitting, therefore, can create new openings for agency, rather than foreclosing grounds for decision-making, as I at times fear.

In this chapter, I explore some of those possibilities by tracing the socioecological relationships connected in my informants' rhetoric. Along the way, I discuss some fundamental work in science studies that has opened the door to new epistemologies. A full review of relevant contributions is beyond my scope and specialists may find the review I do provide initially redundant with well-established scholarship. For nonspecialist readers, however, this discussion will introduce basic resources for responding to science-based claims and tracing their referents into both social and ecological aspects of reality; and for all readers, I promise a rhetorically-inflected reading of science studies. The outcome of a rhetorical approach to scientific knowledge is a fuller accounting for difference, one that uses knowledge claims as starting points for understanding alternative values and ways of acting in the world. This accounting works to understand the forms of validity that substantiate multiple perspectives, cultivating grounds for respect that are essential to the creative invention of skew argument.

Validating Difference

It becomes more challenging for debaters to accept multiplicity when science is presumed to produce certainty and a clear route to action, as seen in the previous chapter. Nonetheless, and in spite of publicity surrounding some debates internal to the scientific community, one of the more common cultural beliefs about science is that scientists can act as spokespersons for nature and, consequently, as arbiters of social action (Latour Politics). To address this belief, which problematically reifies knowledge and thereby undercuts human agency, humanistic and sociological scholars have been working to develop ways to refigure science as valuable knowledge without according to it the invulnerability of reified and single right answers. These alternatives examine how both humans and nonhumans are necessary to validate knowledge produced within science. Increasingly, scholars interested in agency also are attending to the constitutive role of language in shaping knowledge and action.

With his 1962 publication of *The Structure of Scientific Revolutions*, historian Thomas Kuhn challenged the idea that science is a direct means for knowing an objective nature. Similar charges had been made earlier, such as by Ludwik Fleck in his 1935 *Genesis and Development of a Scientific Fact*, but a whole host of historical contingencies helped to bring Kuhn more publicity than earlier work in the same vein, including post-war disillusionment with the institutions that built the atomic bomb and, within the academy, the spread of skeptical and reflexive approaches to knowledge production, especially approaches associated with the so-called rhetorical turn and postmodernism. In combination with the work of Robert Merton (collected in *The Sociology of Science*), Kuhn's approach to science helped to open a new, interdisciplinary field of science studies that examines how social relations, subjectivity, and language are all implicated in the construction of scientific knowledge.

Kuhn's famous argument is that scientific work is conducted through the guidance of epistemic structures he calls paradigms, a word that more or less means "puzzles." A paradigm helps scientists to select what research questions are worth pursuing and what evidence is significant. It then guides the interpretation of evidence. Under normal conditions, Kuhn argues, a dominant paradigm is so taken for granted that it need not be articulated. However, as evidence accumulates that cannot be interpreted within a dominant paradigm's strictures, a crisis develops that creates a scientific environment more conducive to the production of new scientific theories. If a theory is proposed and accepted that can account for a wide set of the available evidence while still providing additional puzzles for researchers to address, it is likely that a group of scientists will begin operating under that new paradigm. As examples of paradigm shifts, Kuhn offers the Copernican revolution and the substitution of Einsteinian relativity for Newtonian dynamics.

A new paradigm cannot fully invalidate the old one, Kuhn claims, as neither solves everything. For a new paradigm to dominate to the point that it need no longer be articulated usually requires the death of adherents of the old paradigm. In other cases, two different fields of inquiry may develop out of a previously unified community. Kuhn argues that the coexistence of multiple paradigms indicates there is more than one plausible way to interpret evidence. Further, the loss of a paradigm always will entail some loss of scientific knowledge, even if much old knowledge is incorporated within the new paradigm and much new knowledge is gained from pursuing its puzzles. Kuhn's theory suggests that interpretation, which is traditionally attributed to the humanities, is also typical of scientific knowledge production.

Paradigms influence more than interpretation. They also can help create divergent knowledge by governing systematic differences in research agendas. An activist opposed to grazing might look to research that asks questions such as: How many species will die in the next half-century if cows are not banned from the Southwest? To what extent have major rivers silted up over the last century? But a rancher might want answers to questions such as: In an average rainfall year, which of two pastures, given differences in soil and vegetation, should be grazed, earlier in the season? These different agendas are based on different assumptions. The first questions assume damage, and researchers looking specifically for harm are much more likely to find it. The second questions assume that one of the two fields should be grazed first and so the answer, however scientifically arrived at, will include cows. These background assumptions illustrate how researchers are likely to embed assumptions and expectations within their studies and then reproduce those assumptions in the process of research.

To state the matter radically: the process of doing science cannot entirely separate out researchers' expectations from their results, which, I should clarify, does not mean that expectations can control or predict results. While researchers may at times be surprised by results, only rarely will researchers' basic paradigms shift, because they have confronted aspects of the world revealed to them through their own carefully constructed research. Kuhn argues that paradigms are tenacious because, in addition to guiding interpretation and research agendas, they also guide vision. This claim is roughly equivalent to saying that scientific theory selectively blinds scientific observation. Kuhn makes this point literally by discussing the eventual discovery of X-rays. Kuhn argues that prior to 1895, X-rays could not have been predicted by prevailing theories. Therefore, scientists never noticed the X-rays they regularly produced, either because they literally overlooked them or because they disregarded them as meaningless experimental noise (58–59). At times, vision is constrained by belief and expectations. More generally, what knowing subjects create as knowledge is shaped by the expectations they bring to their research.

While Kuhn's aim is to explain how paradigms govern experimental science, I wish to extend his term as a useful way to think about how interpretation shapes less controlled forms of ecology-based argument as well, probably to an even greater extent. As I spent time with those who cared about the land of southern Arizona, I heard these differences in vision and interpretation on several occasions. For example, the Buenos Aires National Wildlife Refuge has been a focal point for contention since its creation, as discussed in chapter 2 and, more briefly, in the introduction to this chapter. Different parties to that contention have different expectations of the refuge burn program's impact on grass species composition, and these expectations guide vision. A pro-management refuge worker I interviewed is quite pleased to see a marked return of native grasses. This worker recognizes that the refuge is still a long way from eradicating Lehmann lovegrass, but still sees the balance shifting in favor of natives. A second government agent, who oversees ranching operations elsewhere in the state, disagreed with the refuge worker's assessment. He informed me that while he was on a refuge tour, his guide bragged about all the natives, but the visitor identified only a few natives along the road and otherwise nothing but Lehmann for as far as he could see.

Both of these speakers have similar scientific values in terms of evidence. They have both conducted the vegetation transects described in chapter 3, and both value this method as an appropriate way to understand grassland ecology, although the claims I report are supported not by systematic research but by professionally-trained judgment. In this less formal setting, even more than in Kuhn's controlled research settings, my informants are inclined to see what they expect to see. Behind their different observations are different assumptions about the effectiveness of fire in restoring grassland, with the second, critical, informant claiming that "Lehmann's responds well to fire" whereas the first, pro-management, informant claimed fire could make species composition more like it had been in the past.

Later in my research I again traveled south from my Tucson home base to ranchlands near the border of Mexico, including Rocking Horse and other area ranches. Here I spoke with an environmental activist opposed to grazing, a Forest Service agent, an agriculture extension agent, Rocking Horse Ranch's retired rancher, and the couple who bought the ranch from him, all of whom were familiar with aspects of Rocking Horse and land near it. The environmentalist and retired rancher had particularly divergent interpretations of the land, its problems, and appropriate management. As we viewed roads together, the environmentalist pointed out to me a particularly bare and water-scarred pasture as evidence of harm done by cattle. He noted the general lack of plant cover and drainage problems and then ascribed the problem to overgrazing, with the complaint that the land desperately needed rest. When I later interviewed the retired rancher, I asked him to help me "read" the same pasture. To frame my question, I noted the location, but did not mention that I understood the land to be damaged. However, to the rancher also, the land was in such poor shape that its damage was readily visible, and instead of describing the land he instead explicated causes. Unlike the environmental activist, however, his explanation pointed[1] to slightly different features of the land, different processes for its degradation, and a significantly different prescription for its recovery.

"What's caused that are the development roads," the rancher tells me. "The water does not get to run on the land—it runs down the ditches to the draw."

"OK," I say, simply to indicate that I'm listening. The younger rancher noisily places a beer on the wooden table in front of the older man, causing the latter to turn to his host: "Thank you, señor. You might be all right after all."

I laugh, and the speaker turns back to me. "No, but that's what's caused most of that. And some of that country, it's not been, it's not animal impact that's caused the problem it's just . . . the way it goes, you know. That black brush has gotten in there and stopped a lot of stuff from growing and it needs to be eradicated. And other things. The way to eradicate that and develop seed growth, or plant growth, is—"

At this point, the speaker interrupts his comments to me. "I haven't talked to you about this either," he tells the younger man. "In those real dry areas where the ground is capped and there's nothing growing there? Throw a block of salt out there."

The younger rancher: "Oh, yeah."

The retired rancher continues. "One block. And let your cattle fight over that block of salt: dig up the ground, with their hooves. And then move it to the next spot. That's how you can get your ground broke up real quick without any mechanical means. It's really better. But these are the kind of things that need to be done. You know. So."

Turning back to once again primarily address me, the rancher concludes: "That's all I can say about that. The water is not allowed to get on the ground like it should because of the roads and the ditches and things like that. It's caused big draws."

The conversation left me wondering about the disparity between the views of this rancher and those of the environmentalist I spoke with earlier. In these contrasting descriptions, the rancher and the antigrazing activist are discussing the same landscape and noting similar aspects, but highlighting slightly different components: the antigrazing activist looks to the absence of plants, while the rancher looks to the presence of undesirable plants. More significantly, the two attribute significantly different causes to the shape of the land. The views diverge yet further when they move from explaining damage to prescribing preferred management plans: rest for one, cattle concentration and agitation for the other. A difference in vision leads to a rift in explanation and a gulf in application. Both see the land validating their views.

According to Kuhn, paradigmatic differences are produced and maintained by education. Kuhn implicates the reproductive tendencies of textbooks, which create normalized and simplified accounts that obscure the complexity and ambiguity of scientific practice. Many scientists do later develop an experiential knowledge of the messiness of practice and learn to integrate science's usefulness with clarity about its partiality and its limits. Yet, for the many who do not become scientific practitioners, textbooks remain primary representations of science. Even scientists, Kuhn argues, remain formatively shaped by the paradigms presented in their introductory learning.

I find reason to extend Kuhn's claims about textbooks to other reproductive learning processes. There is an old adage that the only way into ranching is through inheritance or marriage; in other words, economic barriers to entry help ensure that there are close social ties between new ranchers and older ones who assist with their education and enculturation. There are exceptions that challenge the adage's claim, as in the case of the retired rancher and his successor quoted in the previous paragraphs. Yet, as the conversation showed, the retired rancher felt a responsibility to train the new rancher, and separate interviews confirmed that, in spite of some differences in philosophy, the younger man is greatly interested in learning from the older and has largely adopted the same basic grass management principles. In response to this type of enculturation, which I routinely saw evidence of in my interviews with ranchers, a rancher is likely to arrive at management puzzles that are typical of the ranching community. How do I ranch sustainably? How can I take better care of my resource? What is the best time of year to graze grass so as not to interfere with its growth patterns? It is much less likely that a rancher in the midst of day-to-day practice, without external prodding, will ask if ranching in southern Arizona is ecologically viable.

This is not to say that all ranchers come up with the same answers to the same questions. In fact, there is currently substantial motivation for innovation in ranching in southern Arizona. One of the more agreed-upon responses in my interviews is that the worst ranching practices, particularly from an ecological perspective, will drive ranchers out of business. Activists, ranchers, and government agents agree that there is no more room, either politically or ecologically, for the most flagrant abuse of the land. My informants claim that the worst ranchers, at least in the next generation, will be forced out by lawsuits or the economic crisis resulting from not having a strong resource, or else they will sell out in search of fiscally greener pastures. With this negative spur to action, combined with the increasing number of role models for how to respond better to ecological problems, a number of ranchers are recognizing that their community's traditional beliefs are failing them, and they are changing long-term practices and experimenting in order to come up with ranching that better fits ecological needs. There is plenty of room to experiment, adapt, and create new knowledge about how ranching can play a positive ecological role in the region. What makes ranchers' creative applications of knowledge cohere within a single paradigm is not acritical acceptance of past practices, but rather the incorporation of new answers into the old problem of how to ranch well.

The educational route of antigrazing activists may be less homogenous, but there are still patterns that influence the paradigms activists bring to their ecological understanding. Many organizations that protest public lands grazing have leaders or staff trained in wildlife biology, especially those that emphasize the importance of managing public lands in ways compatible with species protection, such as the Southwest Center for Biological Diversity, whose cofounder Peter Galvin is an experienced wildlife researcher. In addition to formal study, environmentalists frequently train each other. Those who do not work full-time within environmental organizations attend meetings and lectures or share newsletters and Internet sources with other activists. More involved members may attend work parties (for example, to eradicate introduced plants seen as invaders in important habitats), or they may participate in demonstrations (such as public protests against Forest Service visitor fees). Frequently, environmentalists further share social links, hiking together for example, and discussing the land together as they do. These formal and informal routes for education help create a shared understanding of ecological relations and a shared approach to land use questions. Where do cattle directly harm endangered species? What indirect damage is done by grazing? To what degree does cattle's erosive impact measurably alter crucial habitats downstream from where they graze? What other ecological processes are changed upon the introduction or intensification of grazing? In these questions, cattle, an introduced species, are assumed to alter ecosystems that would better be preserved as is; what remains to be specified is the kind and extent of damage.

Applying Kuhn's educational focus to grazing issues illustrates that the way debaters understand grassland ecology is significantly shaped by tradition, cultural heritage, and social networks. All else being equal, these social networks will reinforce the association of certain ecological arguments with certain groups. Implicit in this claim is another, one that argues for the importance of getting out of preformed groups and speaking to each other across differences. If ideas are communicated through social networks, then a reorganization of those networks might very well lead to shifts in both knowledge and management actions.

Kuhn primarily addresses social aspects of knowledge production. He treats scientific objects as constants, regardless of the ability of scientists to access them within a particular paradigm, and regardless of the meanings and interpretations scientists assign to these objects. Others, building in the space that Kuhn has helped to create, have taken science studies in new directions. Rather than focus exclusively on the subjectivity of science, as does Kuhn, many of these scholars are working to build an epistemic that integrates human and nonhuman responsibilities for knowledge production. This valuable work includes Anne Fausto-Sterling's *Sexing the Body* as an example of particularly deep engagement with specialist science and

Steven Epstein's *Impure Science* as a good illustration of the politics of science, including scientific reference, written from a social movement perspective. Here, I will concentrate on a close reading of Latour's *Pandora's Hope* for its development of what I find to be a particularly compelling science epistemic, one that I then extend to consider the role of science-based claims in discussions of grasslands management. By using Latour to more particularly account for the role of nonhumans in the construction of knowledge, I mean to add a little resistance to my uses of Gieryn's work in the previous chapter and Kuhn's within this one, which might erroneously suggest that any claim has equal potential to be persuasive within an argument. The claim that cows frolicking on tundra will turn it into a rolling grassland is idiosyncratic and ridiculous, for example: ridiculous because the referents of the claim do not support its sense. The role of reference in scientific argument adds resistance to claims that scientific argument is simply socially produced. It is not; it is socioecologically produced.

Latour builds his approach to scientific reference by analyzing his participation in field work in a Brazilian rain forest. He argues that language is linked to its referents through a chain of translations. In his example, a nonhuman thing (such as soil) becomes meaningful, inscribed into language, by first turning into a hybrid thing/sign (such as soil in a pedocomparator that acts as a conceptual table) that at once contains the referent and its sense. This chain of translations allows Latour to argue that language is actually constituted by, and constitutive of, the relationships between subjective knowers and the things that they know.

This theory of reference is not the theory of fact Latour ultimately seeks. Latour claims that social agreement is required for a fact to become stable. Both humans and nonhumans need to be mobilized to participate in that agreement. A fact is constructed from the use of scientific or technical instruments that create material associations (such as the association of a cellular organism with the chemicals that fix it and the microscope slide it is mounted on). These instruments provide scientists with access to material associations. Latour calls this first link the "mobilization of the world." Facts additionally require the mobilization of a community of scientists socialized into the relevant skills and criteria to make each scientist a credible judge capable of persuading others through the experimental process. A fact is further constructed and stabilized through the mobilization of allies, such as funding sources, and the mobilization of public representations of science. Finally, a fact is constructed by linking all these mobilizations together in stable associations that Latour metaphorically calls knots (100). If enough relevant "actants" are mobilized into an association that remains stable over time, they create a fact. That fact is a knot at the center of the links. In other words, facts are the relationships between the actants involved in their constitution. The more links that are involved in tying the knot, the harder it is to undo the fact.

An article from the *Journal of Range Management* can help illustrate Latour's claims: The abstract—or rather, "highlight"[1]—of this 1971 article, "Lehmann Lovegrass on the Santa Rita Experimental Range, 1937–1968," summarizes its argument:

> Thirty years' experience shows that Lehmann lovegrass readily estab-
> lishes itself from seed under adverse conditions, reseeds itself quickly
> after fire or other disturbance, can withstand heavy continuous yearlong
> grazing, and can invade established stands of velvet mesquite. However,
> it is less palatable than native perennial grasses during the summer
> growing season, and has almost completely replaced the native peren-
> nial grasses on and adjacent to seeded areas within its preferred range.
> (Cable 17)

For the sake of focus, I will discuss only aspects of the article that are used to make the claim that this particular variety of grass "can withstand heavy continuous yearlong grazing."

In order to argue about the extent of Lehmann lovegrass in a way that is persuasive to his audience of science-trained readers, Cable presents vegetation transect data showing changes in Lehmann's presence over time. He notes, for example, that in transects between 0.1 to 3.0 miles from lovegrass plantings, only four transects had Lehmann lovegrass in 1955, "compared to 14 transects in 1962 and 65 transects in 1968" (18). So far, the technical procedure for data gathering, the scientists who have gathered this data, Cable, who interprets it, and the grass itself are responsible for claims that Lehmann lovegrass can spread on its own.

However, cows also must be a part of this persuasive collaboration if Lehmann lovegrass behavior is to be linked to grazing. Cows are recruited into the collective of knowledge-makers in association with an experiment in which scientists use an aerial spray to reduce the density of mesquite trees. In this pasture, especially but not exclusively in the sprayed area, Lehmann lovegrass spreads rapidly after reseeding, so that within thirteen years Lehmann lovegrass is producing 978 lb/acre on the sprayed areas and

600 lb/acre on the unsprayed areas. This difference is explained by association with another collaborator in the creation of this fact: native grasses. Lehmann lovegrass, an introduced grass from Africa, has outcompeted the native perennial grasses, especially in the area disturbed by spraying. Here is where the cows come in. Cable points out that during the ten years prior to the experiment, "yearlong stocking in this pasture averaged 2.3 head." Afterward, "stocking averaged 6.3 head" (20). Cable explains that the increase in stocking is attributable primarily to mesquite control (mesquite are a limiting factor on grass production), but also to the increased carrying capacity that results from the spread of Lehmann lovegrass. In other words, since management is assumed not to send cows to graze where they have no feed, the increased presence of cows is a historical indicator of the increased presence of grass. Cows have become proof of grass production.

Historical contingencies intervene to help make further associations, or links, as Latour would say, between cows and Lehmann lovegrass. Light rains during the 1965 monsoon season mean that "58 cattle from a 4,900-acre pasture, where annual grasses [especially dependent on summer rains] normally produce most of the forage," are moved into the sprayed pasture discussed in the previous paragraph (21). The cattle graze the Lehmann lovegrass intensively, to a "relatively uniform stubble height of about 2 inches. . . . No harmful effects of the heavy use were apparent in the lovegrass growth the following summer" (21). It is only because of a management decision made under the duress of a drought that Cable has available the necessary association needed to conclude that cows can graze Lehmann extensively without destroying the crop. By this time, Cable's list of associations includes vegetation transects, aerial spray, mesquite, Lehmann lovegrass, native perennial grasses, annual grasses, annual climactic variation, and cows. This leads Cable to conclude, among other things, that Lehmann lovegrass "is the only perennial grass that has demonstrated the ability to establish itself . . . on heavily grazed areas" (21). The persuasive task complete, Cable's article enters the range science literature and is regularly cited over the course of decades, even as range science attitudes toward the controversial Lehmann lovegrass decline, overall, from hesitant favor to ambivalence or hesitant disfavor toward management plans that promote the grass.[2]

By examining the mobilization of both the nonhuman and human world in the constitution of a fact, Latour's approach to knowledge provides a fuller accounting for the essential role of reference within science while nonetheless underscoring social contributions to its constitution. Latour's approach also accounts for the persuasive appeal of science, for his theory makes it clear that stable facts do not allow the separation of language from its referents. Instead, Latour simply expands those referents to include the entire mobilization necessary for fact production. In the process, he makes it clear that both humans and nonhumans are necessary to validate claims about the nonhuman world.

In a move useful to studies of future-oriented deliberation, Latour also argues that facts have "historicity," a term he borrows from the philosophy of history to mean not just that time passes but that, in passing, it transforms the world (*Pandora's* 306). To refine his point, Latour distinguishes between two types of history: linear and sedimented. Linear time refers simply to the passing of years, whereas sedimented refers to the way human understanding of a single year changes as time passes. So, in linear time, in 1864 spontaneous generation existed, and airborne germs did not. In sedimented time, after Pasteur's persuasive 1865 experiments, airborne germs always existed, even in our reconfigured understanding of 1864, a process Latour calls retrofitting (172–73, 170). Working in linear time, Latour argues that historicity shows the reworking of relationships between humans and nonhumans, with spontaneous generation referring to one set of relationships that were then undone and refigured as Pasteur persuaded others to accept a new set of relationships indicated by the concept of airborne germs.

This distinction does away with the dichotomy between epistemology and ontology, as Latour asserts (*Pandora's* 145–46). The relationships that constitute rhetoric's epistemic function are ontologically real. For my purposes, Latour's insights are most valuable when extended forward to examine the constitution of knowledge in the future, especially in a field where science and management are inextricably linked, as Cable's article demonstrates. That is, existing relationships, held together in rhetoric, help shape the facts created in the future. If some persons believe that cows are able to participate in the restoration of a grassland, their understanding will lead them to graze cattle. In contrast, those who believe grazing seriously degrades the ecosystem remove cattle whenever they find adequate means. In the latter case, the claim that cows restore grassland becomes, of necessity, historically untrue. Relationships between cows and grass would be severed, and facts based on that relationship would disappear. No cows means no cows planting grass.

To further illustrate the role of management action in fact construction, recall the fenceline photographs mentioned in the previous chapter. Surf the Web or open books that either criticize grazing or discuss its management: fenceline photographs abound as arguments for and against particular management plans. A typical photograph will show two pastures, demarcated by a fence, with noticeably different vegetation in either pasture. Perhaps one side is bare dirt, the other lush vegetation. Perhaps one side is laden with wildflowers while the other has relatively few. Perhaps one side is burdened by a mesquite forest or snakeweed incursions, while the other sports thick grasses. Below this photograph, a caption will identify a management action that makes one side preferable to the other.

Many such photographs appear in *Waste of the West*, a scholarly, author-published, book-length polemic that has become a cult classic among environmentalists opposed to grazing. One typical caption reads: "Luxuriant riparian vegetation turns to trampled, barren mud at fence. The cattle responsible for the contrast lie in the shade of a large oak at right" (L. Jacobs 102). A similar-looking photograph taking an opposing view, in Allan Savory's *Holistic Resource Management*, is captioned: "Severe overrest resulting from rotational grazing has killed large areas of grass in the right-hand paddock. These plants are grey, oxidizing, and dying and are thus ungrazed. Plants on the left are green, growing, and grazed" (262).

Invariably, fenceline photographs show that ecological processes respond to human intervention. The different human choices on either side of the fence create different landscapes. Truth really does depend on which side of the fence one is on. Different beliefs might have different means of validation, but they all are constituted in a network of relationships that are helping to uphold them.

Debate over the ecological impacts of cattle will not proceed far without its scientific methods, its experiential and local knowledge, its standards for comparisons, and its classification of different types of grass, soil, and climate. These all are crucial to knowledge about ecological interactions. However, so is human agency, and especially the control of ecological interactions created by managerial and experimental manipulation of key factors in those interactions, such as the presence or absence of cows, the time of year that a specific area is grazed and for how long, or the use of different strategies to shape vegetation—strategies such as reseeding (but which seeds?) or species removal (such as by chaining or spraying mesquites). Managerial decisions are influenced by available ways of knowing, but they in turn influence what type of knowledge is generated. This general point might especially apply to grasslands ecology, a science that typically does not proceed via twenty-four hour petri dish incubations or similarly controlled laboratory experiments.[3] In contrast, most range science experiments tie up parcels of land for several years before they produce peer-reviewed knowledge. Wildlife ecology, which is frequently more heavily based in field work and observation than in experimental manipulation, also can take many years to arrive at something a community agrees is a fact. Sociologists often point out that one cannot experimentally manipulate a whole society just to generate knowledge. Ecologists are up against a similarly complex problem. A part of this complexity is that social decisions integrally shape ecological relationships at any given time and location, to the extent that the two cannot be disentangled. It is more thorough, consequently, to think in terms of socioecology, a concept that does not separate the knower from the known but instead recognizes that they are mobilized into relationships with one another that are simultaneously epistemological and ontological.

The Socioecology of Cows, Grass, and Management

The county extension office where I sat waiting for an early interview, my first with a trained scientist, greets visitors with a clutter of posters, papers, and a large industry book on how to diagnose plant problems and then treat them with proprietary products. A few moments after I arrived, the extension agent emerged from her office, smiling warmly. She led me to an open conference room where, for the next hour, she shared with me her wide range of professional, practical experience working with a large number of area ranchers and other members of the public. This was only my third formal meeting with a person or group as part of my research, but simply by asking questions about the sustainability of ranching and best management practices and by listening to others interact, I had already started to puzzle over contradictory claims that I was beginning to delineate along the lines of 1) cattle assist with grass reseeding; 2) cattle and desert grasslands are fully incompatible; and 3) cattle are not ecologically beneficial, but they can be managed to do no harm. The agent held this latter position, but she was familiar with the others and accustomed to working with persons holding a wide range of views. Her familiarity was key to helping me identify a major source of the claim that cattle can help grasslands.

In response to a question about changes in management, the agent told me that she thought many ranchers were learning to pay more attention to grass cover and rotate their cattle more often. This comment made me recall other claims that had confused me. "I've heard from several people," I said, "that running cattle can actually increase the soil, increase the grass cover, and it's not a mechanism that I understand. And I was wondering, do you believe that?"

Laughing broadly and pleasantly, the agent told me the claim comes from a management system known as Holistic Resource Management, which she also believes is the source of ranchers' greater and beneficial attention to grass and to rotation. She believes that Allan Savory, the developer and primary promoter of Holistic Resource Management, has also caused damage, in large part because, she thinks, the Savory System, as it is known, misleads ranchers into thinking they can run too many cattle. This tip-off toward Savory provided my first guide into rangelands literature to look for sources of competing claims, claims that differ enough for rhetorical scholar Anthony Chiavello to call Savory a producer of "anarchy" in range science. The extension agent's comments also gave me one strong indication that differing views about cow-plant interactions were linked to views about a number of other ecological processes and management actions. Later, I would additionally come to suspect that these different beliefs about best management practices were linked very closely to different desired outcomes, and that truth and values were inextricably linked.

Even though all those I interviewed sought healthy grasslands, they evaluated that health by different criteria, including differences in opinion about the value of Lehmann lovegrass. After visiting Buenos Aires, I began searching academic journals, especially the *Journal of Range Management* (widely read by my informants), in an attempt to learn more abut the interrelations of cows, Lehmann lovegrass, native grasses, and fire.

As I read, guided by my desire to remain sitting on a fence for as long as possible, I discovered a set of definitions that captured the three different ecosystem outcomes I was beginning to imagine. Rebecca Richards, Jeanne Chambers, and Christopher Ross, the writers offering these definitions, borrow them from a National Academy of Science publication on mine revegetation and apply them to both fire and mining sites. Following their lead, I further extend the terms to also cover range revegetation. Richards, Chambers, and Ross write:

[R]ehabilitate refers to producing an alternative ecosystem that is consistent with existing land uses but that has a different structure and function from the original system, such as pastures and croplands; restore
refers to the manipulation of natural processes of ecological succession
to create self-organizing native ecosystems as they exist before land
disturbance; and reclaim refers to creating ecosystems that are self-
organizing and exhibit a high degree of similarity to the original or
undisturbed ecosystem but may include introduced species that respond
like the organisms they replace. (626, emphasis in the original)

Each of these terms—rehabilitate, restore, and reclaim—indicates a way to
respond to land that is out of equilibrium due to a disturbance radical
enough to destroy vegetation, expose topsoil, create erosion, and injure
watersheds. Arizona's agreed-upon history of overgrazing, exacerbated by
turn of the century drought and El Niños, regrettably fits this bill. Below, I
suggest that each of these terms refer to different possible socioecological
futures for Arizona. By performing this symmetrical analysis, I hope to shift
the ground of debate. To borrow a term from Donna Haraway, I hope to dif-
fract an argument about truth and singular approaches to ecosystem health
so that, as the argument passes through the lens of my analysis, I can
instead turn it into an argument about multiple hopes, desires, and futures,
an argument about control over the land and about the way that scientific
knowledge can differ alongside differences in the future.[4]

Collectively, I will refer to these futures as grassland (re)construction, a
term that indicates that each of the revegetation plans invents a future different than the present, with the ambivalent "(re)" pointing to the frequent
use of constructed understandings of the past to validate desired futures.
Popularly, most people use the term restoration, if any at all, to refer to their
efforts to create a healthier, more sustainable grassland ecosystem. Restoration is a highly valued term; one of the functions of Richards, Chambers,
and Ross's definitions is to also give a degree of legitimacy to the alternative
plans suggested by the terms rehabilitation and reclamation. According to its
technical definition, restoration refers exclusively to attempts to create an
ecosystem identical to that prior to significant disruption—in this case,
prior to the devastation associated with the rapid postbellum expansion of
grazing followed by rampant overgrazing and weather patterns that exacerbated damage. Whether or not cows could have fit easily into that past
ecosystem with better management is a point of debate. For a restoration

project to seek that past ecosystem in full, however, requires prohibiting grazing, for starters.

The Buenos Aires is the largest open grassland in Arizona that is no longer ranched, although occasionally stray cows (primarily from Mexico, I am told) make their way onto the refuge. The Fish and Wildlife Service's December 2000 Draft Comprehensive Plan and Environmental Assessment notes that the area "was a flourishing cattle ranch" from the mid-1860s. It adds that by the end of the nineteenth century bobwhite quail—the refuge's raison d'être—had disappeared from the United States because they "could not survive in areas drastically altered by intense grazing and drought" (7). However, quail remained in Sonora, Mexico, to the south, and the Fish and Wildlife Service determined that bobwhite quail could be reintroduced to Arizona by habitat restoration measures (7). The plan supports this purpose. Its executive summary lists eight goals, four of which are directly related to restoration and management for wildlife habitat, while the remaining four focus on recreation, education, community partnership, and cultural resources (i).

The decision to remove cows from Buenos Aires is one of the more charged (positively or negatively, depending on viewpoint) management decisions made on the refuge; yet, on a practical level, it is likely one of the easier management goals, requiring only the maintenance of fences. Other management goals present ongoing challenges. The nature of those challenges are in part evident in Richards, Chambers and Ross' definition of restoration. The present tense use of "exist" in the definition is at odds with terms such as "manipulation" and "ecological processes." The latter terms suggest the dynamism of grassland ecosystems; the former, "exist," suggests a static timelessness that erases historical processes of change.

One area that this tension manifests is in the extensive roots of the challenge to remove the introduced Lehmann lovegrass, which has proven more intractable than cattle. After its original introduction in 1932 and subsequent testing to select a robust strain, the Soil Conservation Service began a program of Lehmann seed production and distribution to rehabilitate disturbed land along roadways and on rangelands throughout Arizona, New Mexico, and Texas (Cox and Ruyle 25; Cox et al. 53–54). Within a few years, Lehmann had begun to colonize areas that had not been seeded (Cox and Ruyle 25). Subsequent field studies, including Cable's, suggest that Lehmann has a competitive advantage over native grasses, so that many associate Lehmann with monocultures and the reduction of grassland biodiversity. One substantive component of this competitive advantage is that it has a high recruitment rate for new seedlings, with plants establishing relatively easily (Cox 523). This makes it particularly difficult to eradicate Lehmann, as new plants are likely to take the place of old ones that have died off.

Nonetheless, Buenos Aires Refuge staff are committed to eradicating the introduced lovegrass, and they have some hope that the refuge's prescribed fires will help in the restoration of native grasses. The *Draft Comprehensive Conservation Plan* notes that, since 1988, a prescribed burn policy has led to burning about 14,000 refuge acres per year in a rotating pattern intended to promote biodiversity. While one key motivation for the burns is to curtail woody plant (i.e., mesquite) encroachment, another is the much finer sorting out of native from introduced grasses (Fish and Wildlife Service 64). In addition to burns, the refuge intends to use other "remedial measures that enhance the native grassland restoration process," including the planting and seeding of native grasses and the "limited use of herbicides" (97). The plan's use of the word "remedial" implies that refuge management hopes that these types of interventions will be temporary and that, eventually, the fire cycle will be able to sustain native grass populations and bobwhite quail habitat on its own.

The effectiveness of this approach has not yet been established to the satisfaction of everyone concerned. In an informal assessment of the effectiveness of the burns, the refuge's plan notes:

> Refuge personnel believe the prescribed burning program has been successful as re-established native perennial bunchgrasses are apparent on burn units. Masked bobwhite quail appear to be using burned habitats with increased frequency. A long-term monitoring/research project is necessary to quantify fire-induced changes to plant communities. (64)

By invoking two standards of evidence—what personnel have seen and a monitoring program—this assessment points to some of the uncertainties and potential conflicts that so frequently appear in ecological debate. As I discussed previously, standards of evidence vary. The evidence necessary to convince refuge staff to continue with a prescribed burn program is not the same as the evidence necessary to convince external audiences of the wisdom of their choice. To address this disjunction in acceptable evidence, the refuge's draft plan indicates a need to conduct more grassland habitat surveys and to hire research organizations such as universities to "monitor permanent vegetation transects to evaluate the role of fires on vegetation" (96). This dovetails with its objective of improving baseline habitat and wildlife data, which it then intends to maintain by developing a GIS database. Among other things, this database will help keep track of the fire management system and its impacts (95).

All these objectives and strategies point to a desire for more knowledge to help guide action to meet already determined goals. Yet this desired knowledge does not depend only on the observation of grasses and fires. It also requires that the refuge's managers successfully persuade others that it should have funding to acquire more personnel. The refuge will only be able to use the cooperation (or noncooperation) of native plants to decisively claim the benefits (or drawbacks) of a frequent fire cycle if it is able to hire new, appropriately trained staff.

The refuge's restoration challenges are heightened by its physical location amidst lands whose managers have other goals. It is not surprising, then, that refuge staff wish to work cooperatively with neighbors, such as private landowners in Mexico (96). Implicitly, the *Draft Comprehensive Conservation Plan and Environmental Assessment* argues that restoration cannot be easily contained within the boundaries of the refuge, advocating an ecosystem approach to management requiring education and collaboration with other agencies and private landowners (9–11). The refuge may have clear-cut borders in terms of managerial control, but it does not in terms of plant and animal movement. Strategies to prevent invasive plant introduction include such cautions as washing equipment brought onto the refuge, spot surveying all heavy traffic areas during the summer growing season for introduced plants, developing provisions to address the potential introduction of plants in such products as mulch or gravel, and ensuring that horses, which the refuge allows recreationally and for hunting if users bring their own feed and water, be fed either alfalfa or pellets (101–02, 83). All these references point to networks of movement that do not respect the refuge's boundaries. They also suggest that it may not be enough for neighbors to respect the refuge's goals, or *vice versa*, as species movement inhibits the establishment of "separate but equal" management areas. So much for fences.

This ecological interconnectedness is not the only cause of political battles for management control, but it certainly raises the stakes and helps support the attitudes of those who wish others to adopt their own preferred management approach. Many battles over management take place externally, between refuge managers and others in the broader political arena.

The battles also are internalized, however, as managers need to set priorities and balance goals. In the case of the refuge, the Fish and Wildlife Service aims at a full restoration of past habitats and ecological processes. Yet actual practice suggests that some aspects of restoration—as technically defined by Richards—are much more important than others. For example, the current presence of humans (most of it recreational, with an estimated 35,000 visitors per year between 1993–1997) is orders of magnitude higher than in the past that the refuge hopes to ecologically recreate (75). While some believe recreation is fully compatible with habitat restoration, others argue that recreation is not an "ecologically benign" use of the land (Sheridan "Cows" 146). That the refuge staff itself agrees with this contention is suggested by its decision to restrict access to a particularly sensitive part of the refuge's avian habitat, Brown Canyon (78). Managed recreation, then, is seen as compatible with restoration goals, but managed ranching is not, leading anthropologist Nathan Sayre to argue critically that the refuge symbolizes nature for ideological reasons alone (230).

The refuge's opposition to cattle ranching flies in the face of the ecological beliefs of those who believe that cattle actually help to maintain grassland ecosystems, such as the ranchers from Rocking Horse. Following Richards and her coauthors, I associate the goals of these ranchers with rehabilitation, which "refers to producing an alternative ecosystem that is consistent with existing land uses but that has a different structure and function from the original system, such as pastures and croplands" (626). This approach to ecosystem (re)construction allows more flexibility than does restoration, which has a historically prescribed end. A rehabilitation approach would, for example, allow different component species than a historic ecosystem and a different set of ecological processes for their maintenance, with the possible inclusion of human managerial decisions as more than a remedial part of that ecology even in the ideal end, not just the practical meanwhile.

Notably, agriculture serves as Richards et al.'s primary example of this type of ecosystem. Although ecosystems are associated with "nature" in opposition to humans, the extension of the term ecosystem to include agriculture effectively incorporates humans, their symbol use and politics, and their management actions into the ecological processes that shape the land.[5] Ranching fits within this understanding of ecosystem in a way that is not possible within a restorationist perspective. The current ranching couple at Rocking Horse and the retired rancher from whom they purchased their ranch are committed to maintaining a sustainable grass-based, ranched ecosystem that is best described as rehabilitative.

These ranchers argued that there is an identity between their interests and those of the land. The retired rancher explained the basics of sustainable ranching as the primary current rancher interjected his agreement: "Rotation. Look at your grass. I tell you what I do. I look at my grass instead of my cows. Right? If I take care of my grass, my resource, the resource will take care of my cows. That is my first concern—the resource." Later, the current primary rancher told me that, until the land has a chance to more fully recover from prior overgrazing, he has decided to voluntarily graze only about half of the cattle allowed by his leases. He told me: "The only way this thing can operate and actually rejuvenate the land or even carry on for a long period of time as a ranch is to not make any money." This decision reflects a greater concern for the land and its long-term carrying capacity than for short-term financial solvency, a decision enabled by his partner providing the couple with another source of income, but one that nonetheless challenges the couple financially. For all these ranchers, ranching means creating an ecosystem that can be sustained over time.

As discussed earlier in this chapter, these ranchers also believe that at times the action of cattle hooves cutting up the soil is necessary to reestablish grass cover. This idea is consistently promoted by Allan Savory as part of Holistic Resource Management. Savory promotes an alternative approach to ranch management that differs significantly from more traditional approaches. As a result, many of Savory's claims are quite controversial (Chiavello 301). To begin, Savory distinguishes between what he calls "brittle" and "nonbrittle" environments, with the former referring to more arid regions such as Zimbabwe,[6] his homeland, where he originally developed his system, as well as to much of northern Mexico, Texas, New Mexico, Utah, and Arizona.[7] Savory devotes most of his attention to these brittle environments. His primary argument is that healthy grasslands alternately require rest and disturbance. While Savory notes, cautiously, that fire might be an appropriate disturbance at times (125), he particularly promotes what he calls "herd effect" as a means for managing grasslands.

Herd effect refers to having cattle cut up ground with their hooves, as they might in the presence of predators. Savory writes: "Normally, grazing or walking animals place their hooves carefully, avoiding coarse plants and barely breaking the soil surface, but still compacting the soil to a degree. When herd effect occurs, the same animals break down coarse plants, raise dust, chip soil surfaces, and open the soil to aeration" (178). Savory believes the best way to create herd effect while ranching is to excite cattle temporarily by offering, for short periods only, dietary supplements such as hay, molasses, or—in the suggestion picked up by the retired rancher—salt. Savory also defines herd effect as "the hoof action of excited animals on plants and soil," and the ranchers at Rocking Horse, especially the retired rancher, have picked up the use of the words "hoof action" in their routine speech (Bingham and Savory 61).

This is Savory's most controversial claim, as he himself seems to recognize through his attempts to forestall objections. In his analysis of a range of Savory's publications, Chiavello notes that, by 1988, Savory's arguments take on a more propagandistic tone, suggesting that Savory "has lost the point of his rational attack" (313). Nowhere is this so pronounced as when Savory introduces herd effect. Savory argues, for example, that the belief that livestock damage plants is "*deeply held throughout the world*," and he calls it a "tragic irony" that "some of our most serious academics have rejected the one idea that has more promise of solving the riddle of desertification than any other" (Savory 176, emphasis in the original). Savory's critique of academics preserves a space for his ideas against routine dismissal.

Yet Savory has not been wholly disregarded by the academy; instead, many of his ideas have been tested through traditional academic experimentation and found wanting. Two studies conducted on the Anvil Ranch southwest of Tucson compared how seeds respond to five different treatments, including light and heavy trampling by cattle, two mechanical means of disturbing the soil and, as a control, leaving the soil undisturbed (except, inadvertently, by a rainstorm). The first study, "Effects of Seedbed Preparation and Cattle Trampling on Burial of Grass Seeds," does report significant differences in seed burial by treatment, supporting the claim that cattle do help plant seed, especially when they are heavily trampling the ground as a consequence of being excited (Winkel, Roundy and Blough). However, for cows to plant seed is not the same as for them to help establish seedlings. Further, the connected study suggests that, in the wettest years, there is no need for seedbed preparation through any of the treatments and, in the driest years, treatments cannot significantly counteract the negative impact of water shortage (Winkel and Roundy 180).

The most interesting results come from a year with moderate rainfall. In this year, Winkel and Roundy find a trend for South African grasses, including Cochise lovegrass and Lehmann lovegrass, to do best in the most disturbed beds (heavily trampled, imprinted, root plowed, or ripped), with this trend being statistically significant in the case of Lehmann lovegrass. Amongst native grasses, sideoats grama and blue panic grass also fared better in the most disturbed beds. Nonetheless, the lovegrasses had "much higher" emergence than did the native grasses, to the extent that the authors need separate graphs with different scales to plot emergence (178). Given this difference in scale, Winkel and Roundy conclude that in wet years the lovegrasses could establish themselves without assistance, whereas sideoats grama had an "acceptable" establishment rate only in the root plowed or ripped plots, and only in the moderately wet year (180, 179). This held true even though, as Winkel, Roundy, and Blough report, heavy trampling and other significant disturbance buries a portion of small love-grass seeds too deeply for seedlings to emerge, even though the native annuals can handle greater planting depths than the smaller-seeded perennial.

What these and other studies suggest is that, under certain, very limited conditions, the hoof action of cattle can help establish grass seedlings. Yet this hoof action will disrupt the existing composition of vegetation and preferentially assist those grasses that most easily re-establish, namely Lehmann. Those ranchers who use heavy impacts of cattle as part of their grassland (re)construction can expect significant vegetation changes to accompany their managed ranch ecosystem.

In accord with this, both the retired rancher of Rocking Horse and the primary current rancher approved of Lehmann, although the current rancher qualified his judgment by saying to me privately that he "thought" he liked it, too, reserving certainty for more experience. The older rancher shared his views of the grass while discussing some of the recovery he had seen on the ranch during his tenure. He had told me that the ranch included some bottom country, and "part of it was grazed every summer during the growing season for forty years. And it still wasn't that bad. But it was not in good shape." To address this problem, he explained, "We cross-fenced it, [which allows for greater control over rotation and rest] and in two years, which people say it takes longer, in two years it was back to being very lush."

"When it recovers," I then asked, "is it the same species that come back?"

The rancher replied, "Generally. Generally is. We have had an invasion, which I like, of Lehmann lovegrass. It's not as nutritious as the native grasses. It produces a lot more forage, takes less rain, greens up earlier in the spring, stays green longer in the fall and saves the runoff, the erosion, and things like that. I think that's why the county's planted it along the highways. That's what they've found. I think it's a great grass. Half the ranchers in the country disagree with me."

During this discussion, the current rancher interjected that Lehmann also stays in the ground longer. The context of this conversation was the rancher telling me about some of the management practices that he thought made the ranch more sustainable. These practices include additional fencing, more regular rotation, and paying attention to the growing season. All these practices are associated with Savory's system, even though they are not used exclusively by system adherents.

There is a suggestive correlation between these ranchers' clear borrowing from Savory's management system, first developed in the south of Africa, and their acceptance of a controversial south African grass. I can only speculate whether the fit between these is more than coincidental. The Rocking Horse ranchers, however, are clearly trying to (re)construct a grassland ecosystem in a location that has suffered historically from extended overgrazing in their own estimation (especially according to the younger rancher). Some of the land these ranchers graze has been so damaged by bulldozing in preparation for later-abandoned development plans that erosion has become a primary ecological problem. The consensus is that Lehmann will establish in areas that are so damaged that natives cannot survive there, which is why, historically, the lovegrass has been widely used to create a grass cover. Even now, the Highway Division of the Arizona Department of Transportation regularly reseeds roadsides with Lehmann, and the Natural Resources Conservation Service of the United States Department of Agriculture lists the lovegrass as a conservation plant, meaning that it has "known characteristics and proven soil and water conservation uses when used in their areas of adaptation" (Davis, Englert, and Kujawski 21). Attempts to conserve soil, create grass cover, and sustain ranch uses while accepting significant changes in species composition fit Richards, Chambers, and Ross's definition of a rehabilitative future.

There are those who support cattle ranching who would like to see the ecosystem otherwise develop a species composition more similar to past grasslands, and these persons take a different approach to management. I had the opportunity to visit two ranches that fit this type of reclamation goal: the Lazy T-Bar and, even more clearly, Rancho Sonoroso, located in different counties. The manager of Rancho Sonoroso, who self-identifies as a conservation rancher, unequivocally calls Lehmann lovegrass a "prob-

lem." Like the ranchers from Rocking Horse, those who manage these reclamation ranches consider fencing and rotation to be important aspects of
creating a sustainable operation, and the Lazy T-Bar rancher also recommended Savory's work to me, citing its influence on "all of us [ranchers]."
Yet these ranchers did not use terms like "hoof action" that are attributable
to Savory, and their language actually showed similarities to those of both
conservation- and preservation-oriented environmentalists, especially when
speaking about ecological processes.

These ranchers repeatedly demonstrated that they care about goals
shared with restorationists. On a tour of Rancho Sonoroso, the primary
rancher's retired father, who had been scanning the roadside with the
expectation of seeing a favored plant, called out to his son to stop the truck
and back up. We halted by a green, leafy bush. Red tubular flowers still
clung to stems in spite of having dried in the summer heat, and the state
land agent present identified it as bush penstemon, which everyone agreed
was a rare, preferred forage plant. The retired rancher challenged me to say
if I knew how to keep a rare, preferred forage plant around in an area that
had been grazed for a hundred years. When I admitted I did not, the retired
rancher, pleased, announced that you didn't graze it in the growing season:
that's how!

Like the Rancho Sonoroso managers, the primary rancher of the Lazy
T-Bar also pointed to particular species as an indication of his success.
From his house, we could see a wooded creek area, which the rancher
pointed to, explaining: "When we came here, this whole riparian strand
through here, . . . there was a little patch of willows just upstream from the
bridge and most of the rest was just open sand wash (I mean, it was really
awful) and a few relics, old cottonwoods, and a few gnarled old willows.
And we initiated for the first five years or so absolutely just winter grazing,
or dormant season grazing only. And then the last few years we've grazed it
for a couple weeks during the summer and then sometimes in the winter
also. But we've just seen the willows and the cottonwoods explode!"

The rancher additionally attributed this success to first (re)constructing
a healthy riparian area on private land, then using the evidence generated
from this combined managerial-ecological process to convince the Forest
Service to allow him to take measures that would deter drivers of quads and
motor bikes from using the public portions of the creek. As with the managers from the first ranch, this one understood the value of a healthy water
source for his cattle, but the way he spoke about the riparian area stressed

the value of other species—cottonwood and willows—and valued healthy habitat for their sake as well. It is likely that those ranchers I have identified as rehabilitationists also value these species, but the reclamation ranchers were unique among my rancher informants for bringing up species diversity by their own preference.

In addition to valuing biodiversity, the reclamation ranchers also sought to establish ecosystem types more continuous with the preranching ecological history of the region. For example, the Lazy T-Bar included a woodlands. The rancher wished to (re)construct what he called a savanna, a more open grassland with only a few dispersed trees. He had collaboratively developed an elaborate plan for doing this in a way he believed would also be economically sustainable. Yet, he also supported the use of other means to (re)construct these historic ecosystems, including the return of a closer-to-historic fire cycle. He spoke animatedly of his disappointment when the Forest Service did not effectively follow through on a prescribed burn plan and suppressed a natural fire elsewhere on the land he grazed. Similarly, Rancho Sonoroso's primary rancher showed great interest in the effects of fire on his mesquite grasslands, claiming that frequent fire maintains low levels of mesquite but that once the cycle is interrupted more extreme measures, including more intense fires, are necessary to rid areas of established mesquite.

While these ranchers share many typical conservationist and preservationist concerns, they are critical of some claims made by persons in these groups, considering them extremist. Unlike the environmentalists I interviewed who opposed grazing, and who agreed that they preferred to have some private lands developed rather than to have grazing on the much more extensive public lands, these ranchers condemned the development of previously rural areas. The retired father from Rancho Sonoroso cited subdivisions as a primary problem for sustainable ranching, while his son included subdivisions within a larger problem of water overuse, arguing that the water consumption in developments was on an entirely different scale than ranching, although he quietly added that environmentalist criticism is primarily directed at watershed destruction. Similarly, the rancher from Lazy T-Bar criticized environmentalists for supporting a federal decision (now overturned) to limit grazing in one region of the state for the purpose of protecting a threatened species. This rancher claimed that Forest Service biologists, after being challenged, admitted that they knew little about the animal's needs or even whether the animal on the ranch was the same species as the one listed as threatened. The rancher understood this case as but one example of a general, overweening environmentalism.

In both these examples, the ranchers distance themselves from what they understand to be knee-jerk antagonism toward ranching. As the first rancher related, "It's very easy to sit back and look at something and say that it's wrong and it's bad and therefore it shouldn't exist. And that's a prejudice thing too. It can be. It can get there. . . . You know, a lot of people hate cattle." To these ranchers, a pure restoration goal unreasonably ignores what they consider to be the realistic possibility of integrating cattle ranching with many of the same ecosystem goals as are held by restorationists.

Still, in spite of these criticisms, the ranchers are willing to work with environmentalists. The son from Rancho Sonoroso even acknowledged the value of antigrazing activists: "Because what it does, it creates the production community, ranchers, that are saying: 'Oh, I didn't know I was doing something wrong.' Because then you start to do a little better job of managing, start to look at other aspects, deer habitat, water pollution in the stream. Whatever. Whatever you're looking at, you start to do a little better job, because you become aware. And if you weren't aware—if those people out there on the front lines of environmentalism weren't doing that—then it [the production community] wouldn't react. Thing is, they're [front-line environmentalists] needed."

This ranchers' assessment matches that of social movement sociologists who argue that a "positive radical flank effect" occurs when a particularly progressive or radical group pushes for changes that, while not enacted in themselves, make other groups appear more mainstream (Haines 32). This assessment is also echoed by an informant from a moderate environmental organization who notes that the most radical environmental organizations make ranchers more willing to collaborate with his.

The key distinction between reclamationists and restorationists, however, is not their judgments of environmental organizations but their understanding of cattle impacts. In spite of having goals similar to restorationists, reclamationists are distinctive for believing that cattle might fill a valuable ecological niche as a replacement, which, according to Richards, Chambers, and Ross's definition, is a central justification for accommodating new species within ecological processes.

This is especially true in the case of the Lazy T-Bar rancher, who, identifying himself as an "applied ecologist," told me, "I try to figure out, how does this work, how can we mimic this system . . . and derive an agricultural product, and how can we use these animals to bring the system back into function." The word "mimic" points imperfectly to the historic past idealized by the restorationist, but the reclamationist goal is modified by hope for local, sustainable agriculture. In another context, the rancher developed his vision, saying that the "interface between agriculture and ecological restoration is like hand and glove." His hope is not to need to choose between restoration and agriculture or to make tradeoffs between the two, but to create a reclamation area that integrates both.

In accord with this desire, the rancher from Lazy T-Bar held that cattle can help replicate some of the effects of fire. Fire's role in the western ecosystem has changed over years of fire suppression, which has led in recent years to less frequent, more intense, and broader areas of fire. While Smokey Bear policies bear a lot of responsibility for fire suppression, there is also broad consensus that livestock are responsible for earlier suppression because they ate the understory that carried frequent, low intensity fires (Bahre; Grissino-Mayer and Swetnam 168). On its face, the hope that cattle will now serve as an approximate substitution for fire contradicts this consensus over historic effects. Supporters of this belief argue that for grazing to work in this capacity requires specialized management; it requires that "you do it right," as the county extension agent I interviewed asserted. The agent, however, argued that cattle are, at best, a partial substitution; cows (beneficially, she claimed) do not take an entire plant in the way fire does, but they also (detrimentally) do not recycle in the same way ash does (a point the agent explicitly made in contradiction to some claims that cattle excrement is a significant recycling process). However, since government entities are generally unwilling to let fires burn, especially near homes or other development, many believe that cattle now serve as one of the better brush clearing alternatives.

Many also argue that cattle substitute for decimated populations of grazing animals such as pronghorn, although this point is in turn contradicted by those who point to differences in behavior. Not incidentally, differences in grazing habits also help account for why the extension of the Savory System to arid environments of the United States West has been so fraught with contention. As the extension agent critically relayed, Savory's claims about hoof effect are based on observations of African game such as zebra and wildebeests, ignoring how more sedentary cows typically have lower birthing rates if they are moved frequently. She additionally discounted the substitution value of cattle by arguing that grasses of southern Arizona are different than those of, say, the Great Plains, which evolved together with buffalo and reproduce by tiller, unlike those of Arizona, which typically reproduce by seed.

The challenge of managing substitutions in ways that fit cattle into ecological processes illustrate that reclamationist goals are not yet worked out in practice, just as the tenacity of Lehmann lovegrass raises questions for restorationist goals, and uncertainties about the applicability of the Savory System raise questions for rehabilitationists. Each of the three goals is joined to different research problems, different knowledge claims, different management plans and—as a consequence—different socioecological relations. Recognizing these differences and the uncertainties attendant on each is a good step toward creating space for the creativity of skew argument.

Socioecological Rhetoric as a Rhetoric for the Future

What my analysis suggests is that the debate over whether or not "cows plant grass" can be fruitfully reconfigured as a debate over different possible futures, rather than over reified scientific truths about the present. The National Academy of Science's mining site designations of rehabilitation, restoration, and reclamation, which I have chosen to apply to southern Arizona's grasslands, are merely a convenient way of considering the ecosystems that might result from basing management actions on one set of truth-claims rather than the other. In this designation, those who value cows as an effective management tool for grassland (re)construction and who also value the grass cover provided by introduced African grasses such as Lehmann, a colonizer of disturbed soils, are following a route to rehabilitation. That is, by stressing the importance of cattle grazing they are advocating what they consider to be a viable habitat that accommodates the human activity of ranching while nonetheless seeking a renewable grass resource. Those who oppose cattle grazing on southern Arizona's public grasslands, and who promote grassland fires and native plant revegetation, are instead trying to (re)construct a full restoration of a past habitat known primarily through the accounts of early European explorers. Finally, those who follow a last set of claims that do not consider cows essential to habitat (re)construction but think that they can nonetheless be integrated with ecosystem goals, perhaps as a partial substitute for fire or wild grazing animals, are more in line with a route to reclamation and an attempt to (re)construct a habitat similar to a disappeared past, but one that accommodates a degree of change, substitution, and human activity for agricultural purposes.

Each of these scientific-managerial positions is more complex than its representation within my analysis, and each contains variation with it. Additionally, the categories of rehabilitation, reclamation, and restoration are, within this context, my own applications, creating artificial boundaries that do not fully contain the arguments debaters make. However, what my reconfiguration points to is that the debate over grazing southern Arizona's grasslands, which primarily occurs as contradictory statements over what is true scientifically, depends heavily on a static conception of the environment that is in fact changing dynamically. Certainly, most of those involved in this debate recognize change, but their evaluation of whether those changes are positive or negative frequently suggest a linear continuum where changes lead toward the disappearance of a taken-for-granted valued habitat. Instead, multiple possible futures are at stake, as all those in the debate are attempting, differently, to alter the habitat to create a future that is different than what the ecosystem is today. Which future habitat is most valuable cannot be taken for granted, but will only be decided within a power-laden political arena. Consequently, any scientific truth-claim about what helps or hinders ecosystem health can only be verified and enacted within a particular set of managerial actions, aimed at a particular set of goals. These goals, then, together with the desires motivating them and the human activities oriented toward them, are deeply implicated in the debate. Arguments about socioecology, even when conducted primarily through ecology-based claims, will not be resolved solely through an appeal to a version of science that does not address these other divisions.

[5]

FROM IDENTITY POLITICS TO DIALOGIC IDENTITIES

Throughout this book, I have argued that the claims speakers make help to constitute knowledge and, through human agency, to turn understanding into action, to give substance to reality. This argument is not a particularly new one: it is fairly typical within the contemporary human sciences to reject what James Carey and others have critically characterized as a "transmission" model of communication (language is at best transparent and at worst encumbered by extraneous noise) and to instead accord language a more constitutive role. As people make meaning of the world, whether in stories of self and histories (chapter 1), in mapping and naming landscapes (chapter 2), or in science-based claims about ecological processes (chapters 3 and 4), they select features of experience and draw them into relationships with speakers or writers and audiences.

These relationships are consequential. The process of constructing them in language forms understanding, shapes decisions, guides action, and participates in the construction of the world. Science helps to decide the best actions for maintaining healthy relationships within society and nature. Naming provides concepts that formulate goals. Mapping guides plans for enacting those goals. Histories give us our moral lessons for the future. The stories we tell about ourselves shape our identities, what we believe, and how we act. A rhetorical perspective on language emphasizes this active component of meaning, showing how understanding points to the future, not just the present or the past. By also pointing out the contingency of claims, rhetorical analysis underscores that there are multiple possible futures that cannot be clearly adjudicated outside of deliberation.

This hope in deliberation answers the commonly held belief—rooted in a transmission model of communication—that some views are right and others are wrong, which flattens rhetoric into a process of convincing others of a preformed set of ideas (or failing to convince others, or compromising, as the case may be). Once contingency is recognized as an inherent aspect of all truth-claims, deliberation instead becomes a way to dialogically invent (that is, simultaneously discover and create) an informed plan of action.

Yet contingency does not imply a lack of constraint or responsibility. The concept of socioecology acknowledges that any action will impact others within a relational system. Through the symmetrical rhetorical analysis of the previous chapters, I have sought to show how attention to a reality that admits contingency might further mutual respect and create space for those who differ to speak together about how to relate to one another and to their world. This dialogue need not imply agreement, but it does imply willing-ness to grant validity to others' perspectives and openness to evaluate one's own position and to possibly transform it from another's point of view. James Zappen, in his reading of Bakhtin, advances this understanding of dialogue. Zappen explains that "[d]ialogized heteroglossia," a Bakhtinian concept referring to the interaction of diverse discourses, "is the interani-mation of languages that occurs as each language is *viewed from the perspective of the other*" (11, emphasis added). This perspective does not erase differ-ence, but it does imply transformation.

Rhetorical analysis can create space for dialogue, and it also performs some dialogizing transformation itself, but in this final chapter, I wish to focus explicitly on actual dialogues, between myself and my informants or reported by informants. Within these dialogues, I focus my analysis on explicit identifications, making a full circle back to my first chapter, but with a twist. Rather than set narrative identities apart as a way to fence off sections of a field, I will rely on my informants to put identities in relation-ship to one another and reconfigure them in dialogue. I begin by examining stereotypes that constrain thought but end with an examination of how informants dialogically invent new identifications that imply the transfor-mation of consciousness and learning from one another.

The Reification of Conflict

Those who wish to engage in dialogue must address grazing issues, and address one another, in a context saturated by conflict. This conflict per-sists, in part, because of the ready availability of negative stereotypes. These reified representations of identities do not welcome potential interlocu-tors, and those who wish to speak do so in the knowledge that their words will likely be prejudged. More insidiously, even the best-intentioned speakers frequently internalize aspects of stereotypes, and they must struggle against their own consciousness to responsively engage others. This struggle indicates the reification of conflict, the ossified association of people with stock arguments. Those who struggle against stereotypes prepare for more open dialogue.

The need to struggle presumes the dominance of negative stereotypes, which have indeed become ubiquitous enough to form a shared cultural knowledge, a part of the discursive context in any conversation about grazing politics. These stereotypes are readily invoked with quick labels: the granola-eating activist, the trustafarian, the cowboy, or the dude. It's easy to look at quick markers of identity, such as occupation or even dress, and overlay these stereotypes on particular people. At a Steering Committee meeting of the Sonoran Desert Conservation Plan, I watched during the public comment period as the angry yelling and document waving of a rancher was followed by the more approving and hesitant queries of an environmentalist who kept glancing down at prepared comments. "Cowboy hats and Birkenstocks speak past each other," I wrote in my notes, selecting actual yet stereotypical aspects of dress to metonymically represent my observations.

One particularly common stereotype of ranchers recurred throughout my interviews, illustrating how reified identities can become a shorthand to commonplace arguments. I mean commonplace, in this context, in the Aristotelian sense of *topoi*, as a metaphoric place for discovering widely-shared, topically-related arguments. For example, I began one interview with my standard opening question, asking my informant to explain how he became involved in grazing debates. The second part of his answer invoked a stereotype, though his purpose was to refute its accuracy.

"I got to know the ranchers in the region because most of the valley is undeveloped, particularly like my neighbors . . . who ranch around the subdivision where I live, and live in that subdivision. And as I begin to get to know these people the stereotypes that (at least certain) environmentalists present of ranchers in Arizona began to ring less and less and true, and—"

I interrupted. "How would you characterize that stereotype?"

My informant paused a moment to choose his words, then answered, "that grazing is uniformly ecologically destructive, that these people are kind of welfare ranchers, that—." He interrupted himself, then continued, "You know, that they're sort of ripping off the land for their own benefit."

My informant was correct. I did know this stereotyped image of the "welfare rancher," as did others with whom I interacted. Two of my informants invoked the stereotype to advance their critiques, and two others (beyond the one just quoted) alluded defensively to the negative identity. This type of widely shared, negative stereotype is a common development in social movement rhetoric, as sociologists Scott Hunt, Robert Benford, and David Snow perceptively argue. The development of antagonist identities, they claim, works rhetorically to identify a clear target that can help to mobilize members of the general public to oppose public lands ranching. The image of the welfare rancher gives a face to problems perceived by activists, casting the new drama of the West.

This antagonist identity has taken the particular form of "welfare rancher," however, not only because of its generic value as a concrete target but also because of its aptness for pointing to a set of interconnected problems. Activists also mobilize participants by creating interpretive frames that give relief to problems in ways that audiences can easily recognize, as Snow and Benford argue in "Ideology, Frame Resonance, and Participant Mobilization." When environmentalists critique welfare ranchers, they do so to point to integrated economic and ecological concerns, arguments my informant glosses as "ripping off the land." Typical expansions on this idea include arguments that, because ecosystems cannot themselves sustain significant grazing, ranching requires government subsidy in the form of drought assistance, grazing leases priced below market value, and financial support for the construction of stock tanks, fences, and other public lands improvements (as these are legally called, despite activists' derision).

The widespread appeal of the arguments cohering around the stereotyped identity of the welfare rancher is attested to by their tenacity as well as by their present ubiquity. Important concepts behind the phrase became popularized in the mid-twentieth century, largely through Bernard DeVoto, a government critic and polemicist who wrote a number of scathing articles opposing public lands policy and practice during his tenure as *Harper's* Easy Chair editor. His oft-quoted argument in the 1947 essay "The West against Itself" is one of the early national press sources to iterate key arguments against public lands grazing, and certainly one of the most vociferous (Merrill 192–93). For example, he writes: "Cattlemen do not own the public range now: it belongs to you and me, and since the fees they pay for using public land are much smaller than those they pay for using private land, those fees are in effect one of a number of subsidies we pay them" (50).

Throughout his essays, DeVoto conceptually links subsidy, grazing fees, and public lands.

Other writers would later summarize these arguments in the phrase "welfare ranching." Edward Abbey's influential 1986 article, "Even the Bad Guys Wear White Hats," also published in *Harper's*, may be one of the first mainstream invocations of the stereotype, introduced by Abbey as "welfare parasites" (Abbey 52). The stereotype now announces a widely reviewed, 2002 book edited by George Wuerthner and Mollie Matteson, *Welfare Ranching: The Subsidized Destruction of the American West*.

More locally, the phrase is used liberally by Tucson's own Lynn Jacobs, who, throughout the 1990s, acted as major spokesperson for environmentalists opposed to grazing. Jacobs devotes a chapter of *Waste of the West* to the subject. He argues, for example:

> The environmental consequences . . . more than justify ending public lands ranching. But, adding insult to injury, we the people are forced to subsidize this plunder. . . . [S]tockmen have stuck us with the bill—without our consent or even our knowledge. . . .
>
> They perpetuate a land abuse system—often called *welfare ranching*—that eats up billions of tax and private dollars. In fact, in terms of net production public lands ranching is among the most heavily subsidized businesses in America. . . . Most stockmen themselves admit that most public lands ranching operations would collapse without this artificial support structure. What does this say for an industry whose members boast of self-sufficiency and resourcefulness? (368, emphasis in the original)

Jacobs's tone and argument, like DeVoto's, illustrates the indignation and frustration felt by those who perceive public lands grazing as a clear wrong. In addition to its evident critique of industry economics, Jacobs's assumption of "we the people" versus "they the stockmen" helps to create a rift important to the construction of antagonist identities. Through arguments such as this, the welfare rancher has become a reified, even sloganized, identity that works to keep audiences from identifying with ranchers.

Those who support grazing must somehow confront the arguments that cohere within the welfare ranching identity. Their position is made more difficult because of the typical association of ranchers with right-wing politics. In this context, the term welfare rancher inverts the Republican whipping boy of welfare recipients, turning a stigmatized identity of the right-wing's own making back upon itself. In response to this stereotype, one of my informants attempted to unravel stigmatizing discourse by challenging the economic assumptions that generally inform denunciations of any type of subsidy; another, in a more typical move, simply tried to deny the local relevance of the stigma by arguing that ranching's contribution to rural economies more than compensates for any government inputs. Claims about ranching's value to rural communities, however, are as hotly contested as the ecological ones discussed in chapters 3 and 4.

Ranching supporters are not assisted out of their defensive position by associated negative stereotypes that add so many additional blows. Even the mythical cowboy, in this context, is maligned. A staff member in a government agency, who personally supports ranching when he believes it is well managed, nonetheless gently criticized some of the effects of cultural mystique. "Some ranchers, you know," he told me, "they just don't want to get into [ecological] monitoring. They just want to be a cowboy. And I don't blame them, either, because I would like to be out there most of the time, but it's not possible to do that."

Another informant, a retired rancher, similarly associated the cowboy image with nostalgia for an unsupportable way of life. His critique of cowboy culture suggests that some ranchers believe that activists opposed to grazing are at least partially correct in their stereotyping, a claim made explicit by yet another informant. "I've talked to many cattle growers," a county extension agent told me, "who have said, you know, if our neighbors aren't doing what they need to do to take care of the land, then they shouldn't be here.

"Of course," she continued, "everybody doesn't share that, but some of them realize for them to stay in business they can't afford to have their neighbors doing a bad job because too many people are watching them now. Some of them, the smaller outfits, are going to have to diversify on their income basis, and some people are doing it."

These comments point to the economic consequences of drawing attention to ecological problems. The term "welfare ranching" incisively exploits the nexus of economics and ecology by pointing to western ranchers' reliance on public lands. The term argues, as do DeVoto, Abbey, and Jacobs, that ranchers degrade land in a form of plunder. As one rancher exclaimed, "How do you argue with the degradation of the resource if you can prove it, and no money coming in for the use of it?" But, he added, the economics of ranching are now improving due to development pressures and the public desire to conserve land.

As a consequence of stereotypes, however, those ranchers who wish to create dialogue must first work to destabilize reified meanings about ranchers that negatively identify them to others. These types of disassociating arguments often operate through clearly diachronous or synchronous arguments; that is, by either claiming that negative ranching is a thing of the past or else by claiming that while some ranchers still engage in harmful activities, others do not. The Lazy T-Bar's rancher provides an example of a diachronous argument, one embedded in a discussion of changing ranch practices. I quote at length to illustrate the context.

"You know," the rancher told me, beginning with a characterization of past practices, "if you're allowed to have four hundred cows here, then you put out four hundred cows and scatter them over the whole ranch, and then there will be minimal impact in any one place because there's only a few here and a few there and a few there." He continued his historical narrative by pointing to a change in ranch practices: "And then, the idea that, 'oh, there's degrees of palatability of forage plants and that they'll eat all of this species and not touch this one until there's nothing else available,' didn't dawn on people until the late fifties, early sixties, and, in fact, it was considered innovative. They developed a three-pasture rotation system at the Santa Rita—Santa Rita Experimental Range south of Tucson—and that was considered very, you know, progressive. If you have three pastures and you rest one of them, you know, once, in a three-year time period.

"I mean, that's like! . . ." exclaimed the rancher to point to how archaic it seems to call progressive a minimalist three-pasture response to cattle's forage preferences. Bringing his narrative up to the present, the rancher continued, "So, we've come a long way since then."

He then added, "There's a few old-timers that have survived all the economic crunches that don't rotate cattle, and we have a saying in the cattle business that the industry will change one funeral at a time because those old-timers aren't going to change.

"But their kids are changing. Their kids have changed and their grandkids. And there's a group of people my generation that, as a rule, are college educated. They are—they're very committed to a healthy landscape and a sustainable agriculture and very interested in learning new . . . things. So that's maybe the leading edge. And the trailing edge is being sucked along or forced along by a combination of tighter governmental controls, public pressure, and economics. . . . The real feedback loop is if you do a better job and you get paid for it, you're inclined to do a better job. And so, where you can make a little more money if you do a better job of managing your livestock and managing your ranch, or, you know, the other choice at the other end of the extreme; if you're going to lose your ranch if you don't change your ways because the economics just won't support that tacky way of running it, that's sort of rolling up the tail end of the carpet, you know."

I acknowledged my understanding, and the rancher then synthesized the significance of his diachronous argument to current debates. "People will say . . . 'give me an example . . . of a ranch that's being mismanaged,' and it's harder and harder to find an example like that because they're being weeded out."

In effect, this diachronous argument works rhetorically to neutralize critiques by locating them in the past. Most environmentalists who actively oppose ranching are unlikely to agree. Synchronous arguments, in contrast, respond more complexly to criticism, as they require that ranchers participate in current critiques of ranching while simultaneously validating those critiques, indicating that ranching is diverse and that some ranchers are changing practice. This strategy helps to neutralize the personal impacts of stereotypes by limiting their scope. Further, by illustrating more than superficial effects of dialogue in their own speech, interlocutors suggest they have considered others' views and, by extension, they are worthy partners in dialogue. I will discuss these synchronous arguments in the next section of this chapter, moving along a continuum to increasingly dialogic exchanges.

While ranchers must struggle against reified meanings that paint them as swaggering cowboys who lack social and ecological responsibility, environmentalists also must confront stereotypes. They are by turns depicted as power-hungry fanatics, out-of-touch with the land, with work, with people, and driven by a petty aesthetic opposition to cowpies. Once again, the ubiquity of these stereotypes makes them too easy to invoke, as is evident in the following exchange, in which a rancher dismisses environmentalists who oppose grazing. My own leading question pits ranchers against environmentalists and illustrates how oppositions have structured my own consciousness and understanding in spite of my efforts.

The retired rancher at Rocking Horse was telling me how he had helped to mediate conflicts between the Forest Service and other ranchers. I wanted to know more concretely why conflicts arose in the first place, but my query was reductionist: "When the conflicts come up, is it often environmentalists calling the agencies, or what's the source?"

The retired rancher found it easy to follow my lead. "Ah!" he responded. "They're always doing something. What's one of them?"

The rancher answered his own question: "Earth First!ers. A big problem. Cutting fences, shooting up signs. But they were such a radical group. They weren't really interested in environment at all. That wasn't their issue.

"The real environmental people, I mean, you can understand what they're talking about. Maybe we have to change a bit. We got to meet some-place in the middle."

I queried, "What was the Earth First!er issue, do you think, if it wasn't environment?"

"Getting the ranchers off the land," my informant answered. "That's what it was. . . . And it didn't work. And because we have shown, and are showing, the benefit of ranchers grazing the resource, what the benefit has been to the resource."

In this excerpt, the rancher argues that a primary distinguishing charac-teristic of "real environmental people" is the ability to understand and have a conversation. This type of identity work,[1] which splits real from, implic-itly, fake environmentalism, allows the rancher to disassociate the socially valued label "environmentalist" from critiques of ranching, serving to claim environmentalism for his own purposes. Perhaps surprisingly from the perspective of Wise Use co-optation of environmental rhetoric, how-ever, the rancher does not claim he himself is an environmentalist, but instead characterizes environmentalists as others he can dialogue with. The rancher at first characterizes this dialogue as compromise ("We got to meet someplace in the middle"), but he then develops this point to suggest that compromise is more than a truce or a bargain; it requires true change from all participants. In the process, however, he cuts out one self-identified environmentalist voice, that of Earth First!

Another common stereotype of environmentalists paints them as white, elite, and out of touch with their dependency on the environment and the challenges of earning a living.[2] The Lazy T-Bar rancher elabo-rated on this stereotype at some length, claiming that "it's sort of true." As he finishes his remarks, however, he recognizes that his own rhetori-cal strategies match those he decries, and he adds an element of reflexiv-ity to his comments.

We were sitting on a lawn directly outside of his ranch house, close enough to string an extension cord from a bedroom window to my laptop. At more than two hours of formal interview, sandwiched between more informal conversation and a tour of the ranch house, the interview was one of my longer ones, a gift from the rancher's articulate mind and welcoming behavior. We were discussing best practices in ranching, and I asked, "Do you put much stock in the environmental concerns of people who want to shut ranching down? Are there any of those that you consider valid?"

"Oh yeah," the rancher immediately replied. "They're all valid. They have, they're all based on, some degree of truth. But unfortunately, there, there are other things that enter in." After several digressions, the rancher explained, "Getting back to your question about the environmental movement, per se. As a general rule (this is sort of a nasty generalization, but it's sort of true) the environmental movement to a certain extent is a movement of the privileged in that it's generally white people, college educated, good jobs, oftentimes with a recreational interest in getting out in the back country and an expectation that it ought to be pristine and therefore unused. . . . There isn't a ground-swell of Mexican-Americans for environmental whatever, or . . . black Americans. . . .

"It's, as a rule, people who are a little further removed from dirt under their fingernails and labor [who] can enjoy the luxury of an expectation that the land ought not to be used for something. If you go to northern New Mexico . . . and the Hispanic people there have been working that land and using that land for four hundred years. . . . I'm not going to defend their methods, but there has to be some element of sustainability there . . . that suggests that if you have a close linking with a working landscape . . . you can revere and love the land and still work with it."

In the above selection, the rancher develops an elaborate class- and race-based stereotype: the environmentalists are "educated" with "good jobs" and able to "enjoy the luxury" of not using land. He associates this stereotype with unreality: the expectation that the land is "pristine and therefore unused" is ironically joined to a "recreational interest in getting out in the back country." Ranchers are seen as workers and more real. They have "dirt under their fingernails," understand "labor," and, as a result, have a "close linking" with the land. The land itself is given the characteristics of labor, a "working landscape." In the same way that the term "welfare ranchers" drives a wedge in a coherent right-wing platform, this opposition of environmentalism and labor questions a coherent progressive platform, reproducing a common political dynamic.

After further discussing traditional Hispanic ranching in northern New Mexico, the rancher continued, "If you're sitting in an office in Tucson in front of a word processor, it's easy to say ranching is bad, because first of all ranching is just this little box. . . . There isn't a sense of what that means. Or grazing is bad because grazing is destroying plants and creating erosion and there's profit involved. . . . In the absence of knowledge, misinformation can flourish and it's unchallenged. And if there isn't some venue for dialogue, or better yet, some way of experiencing what these two cultures can experience, then it's easy to demonize the other. And see, I've just done it!"

At this point, the rancher starts, in a very small way, to work on destabilizing the stereotypes he has just invoked. He continues to associate environmentalists with distance from the land, but in so doing, he begins a switch from critiquing people to critiquing a way of thought. In particular he denies a "little box" way of thinking that keeps environmentalists from developing more genuine knowledge. He suggests that through dialogue and experience, the situation might change. Then, he self-consciously recognizes his own contribution to stereotyping. This recognition suggests the speaker struggles between his ready access to commonplace negative characteristics attributed to environmentalists and his commitment, amply demonstrated elsewhere, to creating dialogue with others.

Like ranchers confronted by the ubiquity of the welfare rancher image, environmentalists respond to negative stereotypes in an attempt to more favorably portray their identities. An activist who works for the Southwest Center for Biological Diversity, an organization well known for its opposition to the effects of public lands ranching, rejected being identified as an antigrazing activist, clarifying that neither he nor his organization opposes ranching. Instead, he supports the protection of threatened and endangered species and opposes ranching for its negative impacts on biodiversity. This reframes his identity positively, through association with his goals.

Similarly, an informant who works for a moderate environmental organization claimed that the organization has addressed negative perceptions by attempts to create dialogue. In an excerpt from a late September 2001 interview that, in many ways, parallels the diachronous argument about ranching made by Lazy T-Bar's rancher, this informant told me that at one point he felt his organization had little credibility in rural communities.

I asked why, and the informant responded, taking personal responsibility for problems and changes. "I think the no credibility in the beginning is a reflection of the fact that we really weren't committed to community-based conservation. And I can attest to that as someone who wasn't. It wasn't that I made an overt decision. It's just that we didn't think, really think, about conservation that way. We didn't think about going into the community and engaging the community. I think we were pretty presumptuous about what we thought was good, and presuming that of course it was good for the community because we couldn't perceive any downsides; then of course it's got to be good. And so we kind of viewed our activities as either neutral or beneficial, so it was like, just go and do them. It wasn't like you had to worry that much about what people thought. I think also instances where we did know that we had issues, I think we just had a more cavalier attitude like, screw it, you know, some people aren't going to like it, but that's just the way it is. No one's ever going to be happy.

"And I think sort of in the late eighties, early nineties, [my organization] made—the [organization] overall made a huge shift into recognizing that conservation in the long run can only be successful if you engage people at the local level. It's the kind of rhetoric that's out there everywhere today."

"Right," I assented.

My informant continued. "But we've pretty much bought into that. I think, you know, we haven't questioned it. It's been pretty much rock solid, and it continues to be. And I was just at a board meeting this weekend, and one of our board members talked about it in light of the New York City tragedies. . . . Maybe this is a time to . . . engage at a greater level in community-based conservation and put all our resources in that direction. So that helped a lot. It's a matter of just sitting down with people and truly listening and taking the time to talk through these things and acknowledging their points of view have merit and trying to work out a solution that meets their needs as well as yours, and I think we've done that in a lot of different places. And it's resonated enough times that now we have bought a little bit of standing. So it's worked out well."

Like the Lazy T-Bar rancher in his argument that bad ranching is going out of business, this informant claims that change over time has addressed earlier critiques. A primary difference, however, is that the speaker here personally implicates himself in that learning process. Yet, both informants' speech challenges the reification of identities, pointing to possibilities for learning and change.

Speakers making these types of diachronous arguments provide a first challenge to stereotypes. Yet the words of my first informant suggest an even better approach to changing minds. According to that informant, as he gets to know the ranchers who live around him, the stereotype "rings less and less true." Direct contact, he implies, moves people from representation to relationship. While represented identities can easily become reified into stereotypes, relational identities support the possibility of developing new, more open-ended meanings about one another. In the following sections, I discuss further the desire for dialogue and, as I draw to this chapter's close, I look at how dialogism in my informants' speech leads to the invention of new identifications that have not yet been assigned positions in a conflict.

Desire for Dialogue

It can be a long path from stereotype to dialogue to "dialogism," the term Bakhtin uses to describe the active transformation of one's own words in response to another's. I will discuss dialogism later; here I focus on the simple desire to speak to one another. Diachronous responses to stereotypes might be seen as a first expression of dialogue because they acknowledge some truth in stereotypes while attempting to change views. This suggests some engagement with representations received from others. However, diachronous arguments tend to leave preexisting community identities intact: old ranching practices are replaced by new practices, old forms of conservation by new forms. These temporal changes often suggest new grounds for collaboration, but ranchers and environmentalists remain distinct groups whose primary allegiance is to those they are identified with. Synchronous arguments are a further step along this continuum. They create a more complex picture of current practices, suggesting that fuller engagement is necessary for adequate understanding, challenging the one-dimensional picture created by stereotypes. Just as informants switch between stereotypes and diachronous arguments, they switch between diachronous and synchronous arguments. My own claims about the effects of these arguments refer to rhetorical practices, therefore, not to informants.

My first example of a synchronous argument is excerpted from my first interview with the primary rancher at Rocking Horse Ranch. When I asked him my typical question about best management practices, this rancher used his neighbors to exemplify how different attitudes shape management practices. Pointing to a map showing his ranch boundaries, he told me: "Then you go over here and your neighbor—the road runs along the other neighbor, which is Mr. Anderson's [a pseudonym]. I can say his name 'cause I'm going to brag about his land. He's got grass out there that just looks like hair on a cat. You know, it's just beautiful. Just beautiful grass.

"And I made mention as I was driving with the old rancher from here. I said, 'Look at the beautiful grass over there; isn't that nice?' In the rain, you know, a rainy afternoon. And he says, 'Yeah'; he says, 'Devon, he wastes his grass.'

"Well, how the hell the hell do you waste your grass? You know, and I thought about that. And I thought, you know, if I had a hundred dollars and I gave him ten, would he think that I'm wasting ninety?"

"Right," I concur.

"It doesn't make sense," the rancher continued. "It ain't your grass. You're getting given that grass." This comment referred to a gift from God or nature, not a gift of public land. "How the hell can the rest of it be wasted, when it wasn't yours in the first place? It's not a blade of grass's mission in life to grow up and be eaten by a cow. Its mission in life is to reproduce and make another blade. So that's, that's why this is overgrazed."

In this example, the rancher compares attitudes of two neighbors. In his reflective follow-up, "I thought about that," he identifies with a perspective that dictates less grazing. This example gives credence to claims that some ranchers overgraze, but here the rancher takes ownership of those arguments. The rancher names people, but his purpose is to compare management practices, which deflects attention from identities to actions.

These types of synchronous discussions are, in effect, attempts to show more discerning judgments than those indicated by broad-based stereotypes. At times, they can serve as the basis for collaboration across different groups. For example, in a synchronous argument, an informant from a moderate conservationist organization distinguished among ranchers in ways that critiqued some but upheld others as worthy of collaboration. I asked how the organization is involved with ranchers.

My informant told me, "We certainly dealt with the ranching community up in the legislature. In fact, it was mostly our experience in the legislature which prompted us to take the initiative and try to put something together [a dialogue], because we just saw ourselves butting heads on public policy initiatives that, from our perspective, there didn't seem to be a reason why we should be opposed. If anything, we should be supportive of each other, and we weren't at all. So, at that point, we thought, well, we got to figure out something here and try to establish a dialogue, and that led to the [establishment of a working group/think tank]."

After explaining how conflict led to this desire for dialogue, my informant continued, "Unfortunately, I don't think it was—I think it was very, very modestly successful on that latter point [policy initiatives], and I can only speculate as to why. The fact is there's only a handful of people that represent the agricultural community—the ranching community—in the legislative environment. They've been doing it a long time. . . . They're well connected in terms of the relationships they have, and I'm not sure that they accurately reflect the breadth of ranching interests in Arizona. They sort of have one sort of particular viewpoint that certainly reflects some ranching interests, but there's a lot of other people out there now that are basically as disenfranchised politically as we are."

I asked, "What sort of concerns do you see as being disenfranchised?"

My informant answered, "I think that their interests may not completely lie with maintaining ranching as a sustainable economic activity on the land. I think there's a lot of other agendas going on. Which are understandable." He explained that some ranchers might care more about "being in a position to maximize" the development value of their land, identifying more with economic interests than with ranching itself. Developing the idea, he continued, "You know, ranching just happens to be, maybe, part of your family's past, or just a nice way to make a living in the interim. Again, I'm kind of speculating because I don't have the kind of relationships with these folks that allow me to really understand what motivates them. But I think [ranchers] who we've developed more of a . . . bona fide relationship, they [similarly] view the political element of the ranching community as, by and large, a real estate community."

While this speaker expresses understanding for economic interests, my informant also distinguishes between ranchers whose primary concern is financial and those who give priority to ranching as an activity with value in itself. The latter, the speaker suggests, are amenable to conservation goals, making it possible for the development of dialogue and "bona fide" relationships. These types of distinctions enable more complex actions than those suggested by identity politics drawn along stereotypical lines. Rhetorically recognizing the complexities of identity is a precursor to developing new approaches to socioecological problems.

The desire for dialogue indicates a desire to know others and, perhaps even more poignantly, a desire to be understood on the basis of shared conversations. This latter wish is particularly clear in an excerpt drawn from the finale of my interview with the current ranchers of Rocking Horse. The primary rancher's partner had just noted her frustration with the way she is treated in town when she introduces herself as a rancher, telling me that, like those who criticize her, she also cares about the environment. She is tired of others automatically assuming she is harming the land before they even talk to her.

"What I noticed is that, if you're a rancher today, you're worse than a car salesman, a used car salesman, or a lawyer, or some of those other things that don't have a good reputation," she told me. She explained this is "because the environmentalists hate us, because we're supposedly destroying all the range and all the wildlife habitat, and the animal rights people hate us because people eat the cows, you know, to slaughter eventually, and, then, the public doesn't like us because we keep them out of certain areas where they like to go whipping around with their ATVs, or—"

"—And throw beer cans," her partner chimed it.

"So," she continued in a moment, "it was kind of weird for me because I've always considered myself an animal lover and I've always considered myself an environmentalist. So what we would like to do is to be good stewards of the land here, and the same thing with the cattle."

Later, echoing his partner's words, the primary rancher replied to my standard, open-ended closing question by calling for an increase in dialogue. At the same time, like his partner, he asserted an environmentalist identity, challenging stereotypical views of ranchers.

I asked, "What one thing would you like the general public to know?"

He responded, "Well, my blanket statement would be to talk to ranchers. . . . If we're environmentalists, as we say we are, we want to share that with people, you know? So come and talk to us about doing it and we'll help you do it."

Here, the call for dialogue represents a desire more than a reported practice. Additionally, its primary emphasis is on ranchers as speakers, though it gives them a secondary role as listeners. That is, the ranchers wish to share their environmentalism and help others. Yet the invitation, "come and talk to us about doing it," adds a degree of bidirectionality to the wish, as it suggests a willingness to accommodate the goals of others. In the context of the larger interview, the rancher may very well have been thinking about helping others use ranchlands for their own purposes, as in the case of a horse club that the couple found scouting state lands in preparation for a trail ride without obtaining legally-required permits. The ranchers helped the group through the permit process, but they remained frustrated at discovering the club's plans by accident, rather than through the club or the state. During their discussion of this incident, as in their closing comments, the ranchers repeatedly stressed their willingness to talk to others about how the ranch is used. In the process, they challenged common perceptions of ranchers, arguing that those who listen to ranchers will revise their stereotypes.

The expressed desire for dialogue was common, though not universal, throughout my interviews. Those who reported actually creating dialogues that defied standard lines of identification were more rare, though my snowball selection of informants favored public figures in a way that emphasized dialogic practices. Regardless, those who expressed desire for dialogue believed that face-to-face conversation could shift people away from antagonisms. The county extension agent I interviewed is typical. As a routine interview question, I asked her whom she interacts with most frequently while doing her work.

She answered, "The Bureau of Land Management has a statewide advisory council that's made up of recreation interests, not just grazing, so we did a workshop for them this spring to bring them up to date. And then, with these field people, they not only just do the monitoring, but they have the rancher with them and so it's a one-on-one education of how to monitor. So getting that data and getting the data used is probably the top priority."

"How do the recreationalists get involved in the monitoring?" I asked. Referring to an earlier part of the interview when the agent had told me about running a well-attended workshop on ranchlands, I appended: "Like when you did the workshop for them?"

Answering the first question, the agent responded, "They don't—very often."

Answering the second, she added, "The one workshop that we did, where I mentioned that we had them there, was to make them aware that this [monitoring] is going on in the field and understand a little bit about what range monitoring is. The hope is if there's people in the Sierra Club or some of these other conservation organizations that are concerned about rangelands, it would be nice if they did come out with you . . . and do the monitoring because that way when you gather the data together you're more likely to see the same thing on the ground. . . . We don't [always] agree on what we see. But if you're out there together then you can at least talk it out, and even if you don't come to agreement, you understand where the other person's coming from. . . ."

The agent continued, pointing out some of the benefits of talking together: "I see a real shift where ten years ago the enemy was the Sierra Club and the Audubon Society and the Nature Conservancy. And they're not the enemy anymore from the rancher's perspective. There's still, well, there's still some feelings, but . . . they're not opposed to having them coming out on the ranch anymore as one of these coordinated efforts." Dialogue, she suggests, has created the conditions necessary for further dialogue.

Dialogism: Transformation and Invention

Those among my informants who express a desire for dialogue and who, at times, successfully create a place for dialogue indicate a hope that debate over grazing can move from conflict to a cooperative approach to the inter-connected cultural and social, economic and ecological problems—to the socioecological problems—that have generated conflict in the first place. These efforts, however, as the county extension agent's monitoring example suggests, often are constrained by limits to time and resources. On-going dialogue takes commitment. Where dialogue occurs, it often is unevenly structured, with those whose livelihood (and physical location) is tied to the land (such as ranchers and extension agents) having more oppor-tunity for long-term involvement than those whose primary economic and social commitments are elsewhere (as is routinely the case for most mem-bers of such organizations as the Sierra Club and Audubon Society).

These barriers prompt a closer look at dialogue, what it offers, and how it functions. If dialogue is defined merely as a face-to-face meeting among individuals, then individual limits on participation become major con-straints, and the exchange of ideas occasioned by such meetings may seem too little benefit to justify the costs of commitment. Yet dialogue can do more than facilitate individual exchanges. It also can offer a transformation of consciousness and the invention (as opposed to the exchange) of new ideas, as suggested by the Lazy T-Bar advisory team that brought together a ranching couple, a Forest Guardian member, and other members of the general public for ecological monitoring (see the end of chapter 3). These potential rewards are the promise of dialogue: that participants may do more than compromise or even cooperate; that they may encounter possi-bilities they could not imagine outside of dialogue; that they may receive more from dialogue than they put into it.

There is little to assure the actual realization of these idealized possibili-ties. The transformative potential of dialogue depends, in large part, on the ability of participants to shift identifications, to move out of the reified roles offered to them by representations of conflict in widely-available cultural stories. Dialogue may facilitate processes of reidentification, but its success is as indeterminate as persuasion always is. In the remainder of this chapter (this section and the next), I explore forms of rhetoric that enable new identifications, focusing in this section on explaining rhetorical principles developed, primarily, from Kenneth Burke's approach to identification and Bakhtin's approach to dialogue and its theoretical sibling, dialogism. Here, I use my experience to illustrate these general principles. Yet, I give the emphasis in the final section to the words of three informants. Their comments richly illustrate that dialogism can contribute to transformed identifications and that these new identifications can offer more cooperative approaches to the politics of grazing southern Arizona's public lands.

My experience at one ranch, the Lazy T-Bar, exemplifies in miniature a process of reidentification that I engaged in, more substantively, throughout my entire research project. As is often the case in qualitative study, perhaps especially with semistructured interviewing, the particularities of timing, setting, and even mood influenced the nature of my interview (Fontana and Frey 661). Aspects of an interview can be controlled. As always, I led with my stock page of questions for a semistructured interview. Other aspects are more accidental, but sometimes equally or even more significant. In this case, I had scheduled an interview at the Lazy T-Bar for a Monday just following a vacation with Phil. By the time we were returning home on Sunday, I balked at the thought of getting in a car the next day and driving several hours to my informant's ranch. I had all my interview equipment with me, so I called the Lazy T-Bar, received an invitation to come a day earlier than planned, and Phil and I changed course. Although I only recorded the exchange between the rancher and me, Phil's presence and the presence of the rancher's family during parts of our meeting still shaped the interview. Even the vehicle we were driving, different than what I would have driven on Monday, made a difference.

We arrived as the rancher's family was sitting down to lunch outdoors. The rancher and his wife (who, on weekdays, works in a skilled profession in the nearest town) immediately gave Phil and me the water they had poured for themselves. We had eaten just before arriving, and turned down an offer to share lunch. As they ate, we spoke conversationally. I learned that I partially shared an educational history with the rancher's wife. Both the rancher and his wife had spent a fair amount of time where Phil and I had recently been on vacation. They liked to kayak; I had run rivers in driftboats all my life prior to moving to the desert, and we shared our vacation pictures of Phil navigating rapids in his first rubber ducky trip. Our chatter focused on inconsequential commonalities. When I expressed my discomfort at arriving in a vehicle with a Southwest Center for Biological Diversity bumper sticker on its rear window, a point that had caused me a degree of anxiety, the rancher and his wife shrugged disinterestedly. No matter.

Yet, the Southwest Center and the truck (as Phil calls his Toyota Land Cruiser) came up again later, as a linked pair. At one point in the interview, the rancher named the Southwest Center for Biological Diversity as a group whose claims have valuably shifted perceptions and prompted better ranch management, but whose alleged refusal to engage in dialogue troubles him. Within a couple of minutes, without prompting, he transitioned to a critique of the direction taken by the environmental movement.

"I think that I have common ground with most environmentalists I know," began the rancher, "but I think those that want to shut grazing down . . . , an analogy might be that you have a kid who reaches up and puts their finger on a hot burner and burns their finger and there's clearly some damage that's been done and harm and pain and so these extreme environmental groups say, 'That's it. We're selling the stove. In fact, we're unplugging the gas. We're not doing this anymore.' Instead of saying, 'OK, we recognize the danger here. We recognize the problem. We need to devise some methods to make this safe, or to make it workable.'"

The rancher, using an example I would later recognize as sharing a structure with an example from Bingham and Savory's *Holistic Range Management*, asked me to think through the different effects of 365 cows grazing an acre for one day as compared to one cow grazing an acre for 365 days. He explained the example's significance to his critique, in the same breath characterizing environmentalists opposed to grazing in an exceptionally derogatory way: "To me, grazing isn't any one thing, it's infinite variations on a theme. . . . My biggest criticism with the folks like [particular leaders of] the Southwest Center [for Biological Diversity] is that their level of intolerance . . . , I would equate it with the same kind of thing that we might have expected from, from Governor Faubas in Arkansas in the sixties or George Wallace. . . . It's a very intolerant view of what amounts to a human necessity. I mean, my cows aren't attacking a civilization; they're emblematic of the need for humans to feed themselves. And today in America, 2 percent of the population are actually engaged in agriculture. . . . Where I depart company from those folks is that, number one, they won't engage me in a person-to-person discussion about these issues."

At this point, I asked the rancher if he had indeed tried to talk to these people, and he indicated he had. After a further question, he clarified that they would speak to him "if you catch them at a booth or something," but that they did not participate in the ongoing dialogues about management that he wanted. After a short example about logging, structured like the 365 cow example and making the point that sustainable agriculture is possible, the rancher added, "We've screwed up, because the environmental debate ironically to me is about logging and mining and grazing and electrical generation, but it doesn't seem to be about population control, doesn't seem to be, you know, anybody talking a whole lot about—"

"Consumption," I stated, as the rancher searched for a word. In my engagement with the conversation, I unintentionally disregarded a rule of interviewing, and significantly collaborated in the rancher's idea.

The rancher indicated agreement, and I continued. "I haven't heard that for ages."

"Yeah," said the rancher, then developed the line of argument. "If you happen to be a Datsun B210 driver, then you can bitch about gas-guzzling SO—SUVs." In a performed under-his-breath comment, the rancher clarified the meaning of his original acronym: "SOBs!"

I laughed, as did Phil, who had been listening.

"But, you know, and yeah! Personal lifestyles, and we have this media, fantastic way of educating the masses. And what's the overarching message that comes from the television? You know? It's: 'Buy! Buy this stuff. Be trendy. Be cool. You got to have the new stuff. You got to keep getting something different all the time.'

". . . Where's the screaming and crying about that?"

"Right," I said.

The rancher then linked his critique of consumption back to the agricultural theme structuring his comments, using the discussion of broader environmental issues as a context for his lifestyle choices. "I feel like if we can't devise sustainable agricultural methods we may as well go ahead and have a good time because it's going to be a short, you know, short time to no future. . . . We're sitting here today with this population line going this way," he said, tracing his hand across the air in an upwards diagonal like a graph line, "and the arable land line going this way." The hand plunged.

". . . We're working with an extremely marginal environment, and it's extremely productive for a marginal environment. Once you cross a threshold in terms of, you know, the productivity of the earth. And we're surfing on fossil fuels right now, big-time; you know, nitrogen fertilizer is a petroleum by-product. And that's the basis for this, you know, the first so-called green revolution that put all the third world countries back on the map as producers, and it isn't going to last. I mean, I don't think it's going to last."

Throughout this exchange, the rancher situated grazing within global issues of production, consumption, and population. He argued, here and elsewhere, that developing sustainable agriculture is among the most important challenges facing civilization. While he never claimed that he or other ranchers had achieved a sustainable system, he consistently suggested that sustainable agriculture is a goal his activities legitimately participate in enacting. Intentionally or not, the rancher's use of "sustainable agriculture" inverted the common stereotype of the "welfare rancher," linking ecological and economic practice in a positive rather than a denigrating way.

Though both the rancher's passion and my framing interest for the interview maintained sustainable agriculture as the focal point for this discussion, another context for the exchange, whether intended at the time or not, was calling me to reflexivity about my own position in a system of consumption and production. After the recorded interview, Phil joined in our discussion. While his environmentalist critique of ranching was evident, he approved of the rancher's desire for a let-it-burn and proactive burn fire policy, and the two shared an aversion to chaining as a means of controlling woody incursions. They began discussing at length means to reverse riparian damage through forms of erosion control, considering both the practical and political measures necessary to install gabions or stop-check dams that could slow the rush of Arizona's monsoons and contribute to watershed restoration. Their conversation focused both on ranch arroyos and the river washes running through Tucson and other urban areas.

As we said our thank-yous and goodbyes, the rancher jokingly asked us if our Land Cruiser is one of those gas-guzzling SUVs. "SOBs," we returned, in unison, and Phil added that he uses the Toyota primarily to drive to "Sprawl-Marts" and buy cheap plastic consumer goods that will break in a couple of years. Our host laughed and waved us off, telling us he needed to practice throwing Depends out of windows.

These light-hearted exchanges were exaggerated as well as friendly, and the hyperbole had the effect of helping me keep some emotional distance from the critique of my consumptive practices. Yet, as the rancher's use of the conditional tense to say that "If you happen to be a Datsun B210 driver, then you can bitch about gas-guzzling SO—SUVs" indicates, his point was not so much that our choice is wrong as that it is too easy to use relative difference as a moral high ground to avoid questioning one's own practices. I left more personally conscious of what I already knew, that no one holds the franchise on damaging the earth and that socioecological reform will not come from targeting ranching in isolation. While the broader public may call ranchers to attend to the impacts of grazing on ecosystems, ranchers, as agricultural producers and part of that public, have something to teach our consumption-oriented society as well. None of us will develop better means of participating in socioecological relationships if we close down the conversations that enable us to learn from one another. The rancher's ability to call me to self-reflexivity is as responsible for my change as is his land ethic.[3]

More significantly, my changing perceptions are the cause of a research process that, relying heavily on interviews, has placed me in continuous dialogue with those who I had previously known primarily through the representations of others. My learning through research is joined to a process of change that is basic to rhetoric. Throughout this book, I have discussed language's role in shaping perception and understanding and, consequently, their impact on relationships and action. Yet rhetoric also is oriented to persuasion, or, more broadly construed, to change. According to Kenneth Burke, rhetoric's basic process for creating change is by shifting identifications. Rhetoric, he writes, is "*the use of language as a symbolic means of inducing cooperation*" (A Rhetoric 43, emphasis in the original). Yet the need to induce cooperation implies a conflict to address, so "The Rhetoric . . . considers the way in which individuals are at odds with one another, or become identified with groups more or less at odds with one another" (Burke A Rhetoric 22, emphasis in the original). Rhetoric, therefore, though primarily oriented toward identification, implies both identification and division in a tense relationship with one another: "[P]ut identification and division ambiguously together, so that you cannot know for certain just where one ends and the other begins, and you have the characteristic invitation to rhetoric" (Burke A Rhetoric 25). The challenge facing those who wish to foster dialogue is to induce them to identify in a shared project, but this may require dividing them from contrary goals.

These processes of division and identification are both apparent in the above example. The rancher's characterizations of environmental activists participate in ubiquitous negative stereotyping and create a division between "common ground with most environmentalists" and those whom the rancher cannot talk to, a division remarked on in earlier examples as well. Given our earlier attention to our branded vehicle, the choice to combine criticism of the Southwest Center with a critique of fuel consumption led me to consider whether I am at all implicated in a "screwed up" environmental debate and overconsumption, suggesting the possibility that the criticism is personally addressed to me and not just a critique of an absent other. Yet the rancher destabilizes these divisions to subordinate them to identification, indicating that even the Datsun B210 driver is identified as part of a consumptive system, and we all participate in "the need for humans to feed themselves." With everyone irredeemably identified in the problem of consumption, the remaining challenge is to cooperatively develop appropriate production systems. The rancher does not claim to have done this, but he does argue that we should identify with the way he is framing the problem, asking us to participate in a dialogue about best production practices, such as watershed restoration.

Conversations such as this one contribute to change in my self, a change in my own way of thinking and being with others that I attribute directly to my research. I came to the study strongly identified as an environmentalist and personally sympathetic to arguments for a wholesale end to public lands grazing. I kept a distance between sympathy and agreement, but I had less sympathy for, and less understanding of, ranchers and their supporters.

My understanding changed quickly as I spoke to others. In part, their stories reminded me of aspects of my own experience I had not attended to. I began recalling and constructing narratives based on my childhood visits to my uncle's ranch, such as the one opening this book, and I developed new sympathies for ranchers' self-representations. I began puzzling through how having parents who hunt has shaped my environmental ethic, especially as I found myself responding negatively to representations of hunters and internally distinguishing my parents' ethic from practices I heard my informants deriding. I also started wondering if the number of farmers and millworkers in my family had unconsciously shaped research interests I had previously tied exclusively to my desire to find a site of rhetorical conflict where I could develop my scholarly interests in the rhetoric of science and the rhetoric of social movements.

Soon I connected my disciplinary investments to other forms of social concern. Even more than the renarrating of my self in response to my informants, new learning is basic to the way I ultimately came to identify my research questions. Learning what the rhetoric of the range has to teach my discipline, and vice versa, requires building relationships between the questions raised by disciplinary communities and those raised by informants. My interest in science-based argument, for example, became a more specific interest in attitudes toward Lehmann lovegrass and claims about cowgrass interactions after several informants discussed these as important to their management decisions. Out of my informants' own concerns, I developed curiosity and investment in programs aimed at restoring native grasses. This informed my literature searches, explicitly shaped questions in my later interviews, and became a primary focus for analysis. (My apologies and thanks to the unquoted hydrologists who gave time to inform my understanding of watersheds.) As I drove from site to site, puzzling about the contradictions between informants' claims, I began thinking of myself as a vehicle for putting claims and counter-claims into conversation with one another, and I understood the generosity of my informants as one way of enacting dialogue.

There remains a tension, however, between my role as a field researcher and my role as a writer, a tension between the participatory role I figure as a vehicle and the representative role I take as I select and analyze my data. Another way to describe this tension is one between rhetoric and rhetorical analysis. The distinction is not perfect, as rhetorical analysis is itself a type of persuasion. That is, I hope that readers find enough grounds for identifying with my claims (e.g., that narratives have epistemic and political impact, that metaphors literally matter, that contradictory ecology-based claims participate differently in visions of future socioecologies) that readers will responsively engage with those claims. Yet this mode of argument is different in orientation than the arguments made by my informants. While rhetorical analysis is oriented toward understanding arguments and their impacts, the rhetoric of my informants is oriented toward explaining and justifying perceptions and, in public forums, toward motivating certain actions toward people and the land.

One approach to the tension between participatory and representative forms of debate has been developed by anthropologists associated with critical ethnography, who frequently call on researchers to recognize that those we write about are also part of our audience (Papa and Lassiter; Plummer; Richards; Stacey). One approach that has informed my research since its proposal is developed by George Marcus in his often-cited article "Ethnography in/of the World System: The Emergence of Multi-Sited

Ethnography." Marcus's approach to qualitative research (specifically to ethnography, though his argument has wider relevance) is premised on the idea that researchers construct the connections they represent, and that these representations are, in fact, their argument. Objects of study, Marcus argues, are defined through "different modes or techniques" that "might be understood as practices of construction through (preplanned or opportunistic) movement, and of tracing within different settings of a complex cultural phenomenon given an initial, baseline conceptual identity that turns out to be contingent and malleable as one traces it" (106). My movements during research shape my understanding (and representation) of grazing conflict, which is, after all, a rather placeless construct despite my attempts to locate it in southern Arizona. Indeed, one of my informants lives in central Arizona, and my textual sources are even more diverse. Even without these messy borders, my argument would be identified with movement, so that a primary source of my claims that dialogue can lead to cooperation, invention, and the transformation of consciousness is that diverse informants have engaged me in dialogue, changing my mind in the process.

Admittedly, some of Marcus's emphases differ from mine. I would claim this as a study of "cultural logics," an approach that has clear affinities to rhetorical analysis of socioecological relations. Like Marcus, I see my study focused on a "cultural formation, produced in several locales," instead of on "a particular set of subjects" (99). My informants' contributions are essential to this project, but they in no way capture my informants' subjectivity, nor can I claim they represent the organizations they work in or the social roles they perform. Still, they indicate, in their very particularity, forms that argument often takes. I recognize that I have given little attention to political economies, which Marcus values alongside cultural logics, and which forms a basis for his focus on systems. Yet, his words apply to my understanding of this research, which "constructs aspects of the system itself through the associations and connections it suggests among sites" (96). In sum, my representation is an active response back to an audience that potentially includes my informants, and my representation is an argument made from my mobile perspective, not from theirs. With each claim I quote or otherwise respond to, I recontextualize the words of others, drawing new connections. Significantly, however, I could never have made this argument without my informants' shaping influence on my perceptions.

Marcus's argument reminds analysts what readers, perhaps especially readers from my field site, already know: an academic study is not the last word on any subject. This claim resonates with a key point made by Mikhail Bakhtin, whose contributions have significantly shaped much social and humanistic thought on dialogue. All language, Bakhtin notes, is a response to another. And all words, once spoken, call for an active response on the part of the listener. While a listener may respond silently, or after a delay, receiving words nonetheless requires active interpretation.

Bakhtin's starting point for understanding language is dialogue. All language use is situated, Bakhtin claims, and all language carries aspects of its context with it. Even our first words, he points out, are learned in contexts created by others:

> [Early] influences are invested in the word (or in other signs), and these words are the words of other people, above all [with respect to infants] words from the mother. Then these "others' words" are processed dialogically into "one's own/others' words" with the help of different "others' words" (heard previously) and then in one's own words, so to speak (dropping the quotation marks), which are already creative in nature. ("Toward" 163)

As a result of this starting point, Bakhtin claims that all language and understanding is, basically, dialogic. The epistemic properties of language imply, therefore, that knowledge is always an interaction and an invention of relationships.

Bakhtin, however, does not limit his interest in dialogue to this descriptive theory of primary dialogism. He also takes a normative interest in what he calls a secondary dialogism, which, unlike primary dialogism, cannot be taken for granted. This secondary dialogism refers to the degree to which speakers use language in ways that invite continued dialogue, interpretation, and response. Bakhtin argues that it is possible for language to become more monologic, stripped of its interactive origins, in ways that control its interpretation. He refers to this as the reification of knowledge, a point that resonates for me (with respect to the natural sciences) with Latour's understanding of how facts are stabilized, and with my discussion, in chapter 3, of how authoritative invocations of science can shut down dialogue. With respect to my own work, the impulse I feel to make my words more authoritative than they are, to suggest, for example, that my interviews are somehow representative of particular organizations or even an entire system of debate, is an impulse toward monologism, an attempt to protect myself from active responses that are likely to include disagreement as well as qualified assent. I work to resist these forms of authority in the hope that responses to my words might include invention, the development of new ways of thinking that do not conform to mine, ways of thinking that, nonetheless, would have been impossible without my own response to the words of my informants.

I am equally interested in how the words of my informants invite dialogue by moving, by degree, away from the monologic pole of language use toward the dialogic pole. Bakhtin refers to these poles, alternatively, as reification and personification. In terms of identity politics, these poles are the differences between flattening stereotypes that call for the annihilation of the other (through the abolishment of welfare ranching or the marginalization of activist concerns) and open-ended identifications that allow for cooperation and, more significantly, for learning, a process of becoming resulting from negotiating identities in relationship with others.[4]

Dialogic Relationships and Reimagined Identities

The pull of monologism is evident in my first excerpt, an exchange with the rancher from the Lazy T-Bar. Ultimately, however, the rancher chooses to explicitly distance himself from stereotyping others. At the same time, he crafts a new identity that serves as an opportunity for shifting forms of identification. The rancher had just complained to me about a challenging management situation. He wanted to lay a fence on public lands in the hope of increasing his control over what land is rested, which is generally recognized as a necessary component of revegetation efforts. Fences can have other impacts, however, and an environmental organization demanded that a full environmental assessment be conducted. In consequence, at the time of our interview, the fence had not yet been approved. I summarized the story as I understood it.

"So," I said, "let me make sure I understand the situation right. . . . Some environmentalist groups have got the Forest Service agency to require these environmental assessments . . . , and because of that you can't do something that you think is going to be ecologically more beneficial."

The rancher affirmed my summary but then backed away from what might be perceived as my negative inflection of his language about environmentalists. He elaborated, "I think that's true. I don't want to paint the ecological groups with, you know, a bad brush. But . . . they have wanted, or have been, I think, very successful in forcing the Forest Service to follow the law. . . . Anyway, the net result for us is that we are essentially dealing with a landlord who won't let us paint the bathroom or fix the leaky faucet. And yet we're sort of required to do that but not allowed to do it. It's a very frustrating situation to be in. . . .

"One of the real significant changes that we made [when we purchased the ranch] was to invite the community to help us manage the ranch.

"And underneath my rancher clothes, I think, inside I'm really kind of an applied ecologist. . . . I try to figure out, how does this work, how can we mimic the system . . . and derive an agricultural product, and how can we use these animals to bring the system back into function. And I think West-wide, most ecologists would tell you that we have an explosion of woody vegetation due to all the following reasons: historic overgrazing, fire suppression, possible changes in climactic cycle. But we have watersheds and hydrologic systems that are out of function and it's causing a lot of problems. It's not going to get better with creeping subdivisions."

In this excerpt, the rancher makes a quick transition from his frustrations, which have themselves been framed with a desire to not "paint the ecological groups with, you know, a bad brush," to a discussion of ecological issues. His discussion of these issues is in no way distinguishable from an environmentalist articulation of similar concerns, with the notable exception that the rancher contextualizes these issues by pointing to development pressures, which some environmentalists consider a red herring for ruling out political solutions that simultaneously limit development and grazing. This statement of concerns leads the rancher to recharacterize his own identity as that of an "applied ecologist," suggesting that his rancher identity is as superficial as his clothing.

The rancher's assumption of a superficial connection is reinforced elsewhere in our interview, when I asked him how he became involved in ranching. Rather than give the traditional answer of family connections, the rancher instead began with principles, claiming that he thought sustainable agriculture should be the basis of culture. In arid Arizona, he continued, ranching was a more appropriate form of agriculture than alternatives. This narrative, like his identification as an "applied ecologist," suggests that problems of arid production have more meaning to him than an identity rooted in tradition.

Notably, the rancher chooses to make his transition from discussing his frustrations with others to discussing ecological problems by means of what might at first seem a non sequitur, his indication that he and his wife asked the community to help with ranch management. It is this invitation, and the resulting dialogue, that serves as the impetus for the rancher renaming himself an "applied ecologist."

The dialogue formed out of this invitation has become an exemplar, to me, of how dialogue can lead to invention. As discussed in the final section of chapter 3, the shared ecological monitoring processes the group ultimately engaged in formed a basis for new approaches to ranch management. A key aspect of this success, however, as related to me by the rancher, was getting to a point where people could share monitoring in the first place. At the first community meeting, the rancher asked everyone to introduce themselves as individuals, setting as a ground rule the expectation that participants speak only for themselves. So, to borrow the rancher's primary example, a participant who had a leadership role in the Forest Guardians and came to the meeting with hostility toward ranching could speak about the basis of his hostility, but could not speak as a representative of the Forest Guardians. This eliminated the type of conflict dynamic typical of representative politics, where individuals' responsibility to represent absent others locks them into prefabricated positions. Otherwise, the participatory forum thereby created did not limit the subject of dialogue. Like the Forest Guardian who moved from avowedly wanting to put the rancher out of business to forming a friendship over shared goals, the rancher lost his identification with ranching "clothes," throwing off a preformed community identity and crafting a new one.

In my second excerpt, the father and son from Rancher Sonoroso invoke and respond to others' arguments. They do not accept others' arguments in the form they are presented, but neither do they dismiss those arguments nor form counter-arguments whose purpose is to simply reinforce a previously-formed position. Instead, their comments suggest that they have internalized aspects of common critiques of ranchers, taking on those critiques as their own words. Yet they struggle against the tendency to apply the critique universally, disassociating themselves from it with a synchronous argument.

While discussing competing interests in the land, the father criticized the behavior of some recreationists, such as ATV (all-terrain vehicle) users: "They're not really concerned about environmental needs, whether they should drive up a sand wash or a hill that causes erosion. To them it's just a challenge, and that's to me—"

The son interrupted to shift the direction of the conversation from environmental problems caused by others to environmental problems charged to ranchers: "—One of those things that, philosophically, is in a very hazy area is the environmentalists, activists in the far end like the Southwest Center, they'll say, 'why are you leasing land for a dollar fifty a month per cow [when the government is not making money and the] land is not being taken care of?'" Answering these represented criticisms, the rancher claimed: "Well, that's not entirely true. I mean, there's some people trying to ranch reasonably, and there's some people that are not. That's a hazy area, because how do you argue with the degradation of the resource if you can prove it, and no money coming in for the use of it?"

Though the rancher may have intended this as a rhetorical question, I asked it seriously. "How do you answer that?"

The father replied, "The cattlemen say, 'well, we're taking good care of the land.' That's not necessarily true. It certainly hasn't been true in the past. They're standing on shaky ground. And, so, that's where the conflict comes, from the far left, and the far right. And then the cattlemen start arguing—'but it's a way of life!'"

The retired rancher continued, "You better marry a rich goddamn woman if you want to be a cowboy!"

"Yeah," chimed in his son. "The 'way of life' really doesn't hold water. I mean, it does hold something."

"If you're rich, or you're not in debt, or you're not in a drought—"

"But, you know," the son interrupted, as the father turned to brush some saddles. "Let's say if you were, if you were making buggy whips. Right? They don't, they don't have buggies any more and everything goes to cars. Do we, as a society, continue to support that buggy-whip guy? No! . . . By his own bootstraps, he figures: 'Oh, instead of making buggy whips, I'll make a spark plug or I'll make a—'"

"Or go into something else. Or go into the furniture business!" the father interjected.

"That's—that's—exactly. So you know, the kind of way of life that won't hold water, if it's not economically viable. . . . We have a scenario now that's changed, and some economics are being put back into it."

These comments presume a three-way exchange. Outsiders critique cattlemen, and cattlemen defend themselves as stewards of the land or on cultural grounds. Yet the ranchers in this conversation add another voice, one that discounts the defenses of cattlemen and calls instead for ranchers to watch their ecological impacts while developing an economic base for their business—or to get out of the business. This third voice internalizes the criticisms of activists but refuses to accept activists' conclusions.

In an excerpt following closely after this exchange, the primary rancher develops his response to environmentalists, using an analogy to southern racism, an interpretation he shares with the Lazy T-Bar rancher, and then adds layers of other negative identifications, including the suggestion that activists are like overreacting children and equal to neo-Nazis, a term often used to malign radical environmental groups such as Earth First! (DeLuca 6). Yet the rancher stops short of following through with his initially quite negative characterization of activists and, in a move unpredictable by any formal rules of coherence, instead talks about the positive impacts of the group while imputing abusive behaviors to some ranchers and ignorance to ranchers as a whole. Like the above exchange, the lack of coherence in this discussion leaves open the rancher's own struggle with the meaning of environmentalism as he internalizes aspects of it in his thought and his action.

To stay out of the welcome summer rain, we were speaking in a tack room, and the rancher's retired father had distracted himself for a moment with a bridle. This allowed the son to speak with fewer interruptions than during most of the interview.

"A lot of people hate cattle and want to get the cattle off the range. I make an analogy. It's just the same as people in the South in the forties and fifties. They did not want to be on the bus with the black person. They did not want to eat in the café with the black person. They had a prejudice. It wasn't based on any reality; it was a true prejudice. There are true prejudices out there. They may be educationally created through reading literature and stuff about how terrible the cows are and all that kind of stuff, but it's really the same thing. It's no different than neo-Nazism. You know what I mean? There are people out there who abuse the land. There are people out there that run red lights. There are people out there that abuse their children. But that doesn't mean everybody who has a child abuses the child. That doesn't mean everyone who runs a cow doesn't have a long-term sustainability.

"And I think you have to have that pendulum of those movements that are out there, that front line out there that are saying: 'OK, all cattle are bad, got to get them off.' Because what it does, it creates the production community, ranchers, that are saying: 'Oh, I didn't know I was doing something wrong.' Because then you start to do a little better job of managing, start to look at other aspects, deer habitat, you know, water pollution in the stream. Whatever. Whatever you're looking at you start to do a little better job because you become aware and if you weren't aware, if those people out there on the front lines of environmentalism weren't [making you aware], then it [the production community] wouldn't react. Thing is, they [front-line environmentalists] are needed."

As the rancher moves out of his analogy between environmentalists and racists, he argues that these environmentalists have a role in changing consciousness. Notably, he makes this claim by representing a conversation in which a rancher (such as himself) acknowledges having something to learn from the claims of environmentalists, which he then follows up, returning to his own voice, by pointing to specific aspects of the environment that require attention. After giving this example of why dialogue is needed, the rancher then claims that the dialogue partners—front-line environmentalists—are also needed. He suggests that, by themselves, ranchers will not learn everything they need to; their own growth requires the voice of another.

These ranchers' comments suggest a possibility for dialogism that does not require face-to-face dialogue. When I asked the rancher to represent different positions, he put them into conversation with each other, showing radical environmentalists and conservative cattlemen in disagreement. Yet, as he speaks for himself, he develops an active response that shows mixed identifications with these diverse others.

My final excerpt illustrates even more clearly the construction of a new identity. In this example, a Buenos Aires Wildlife Refuge worker represents the outcome of a conversation with a rancher. The speaker supports the refuge's controversial no-cow policy, telling me explicitly that "cows are no help," a belief placing refuge practices inherently at odds with ranch management. In spite of the persistence of this disagreement, the refuge worker identifies with the rancher in other respects, as the two together develop a new identity that indicates a different emphasis in management and a shift in the way both perceive their relationship to the land as well as to each other. This new identity provides a way for those who disagree to speak to each other and share, dialogically, in a process of socioecological change.

The refuge worker, referring to his interlocutor, explained to me the agreement. "Mr. Exel (a rancher; not his real name) and I agree that ranchers should look at the ranching condition, as they're grassland farmers, they're not cattlemen. . . . They should look at themselves: 'We're grassland farmers.' I look at myself as a grassland farmer. Mr. Exel looks at himself as a grassland farmer."

The refuge worker continued. "So many of them think of themselves as, 'No, we're a rancher.' No. You're not a rancher. You're a grassland farmer.

"You take care of the grasses; you only use cows as a tool. That's not the end. The end is the grass. And they never get this concept. The most important thing you have is the grassland. It's not wildlife. It's not cows. It's the grassland. And once you get the grassland reestablished then these other things are, basically, they're maximized because they'll take advantage of the good grassland conditions."

In this reported conversation, the introduction of a new identity—a grassland farmer—is represented as an agreement, making it impossible to differentiate the influence of the rancher and the wildlife refuge worker in the identity's construction. The place of the new identity's invention, by implication, is the dialogue itself.

You're a grassland farmer.

In their introduction to *Ecospeak*, Jimmie Killingsworth and Jacqueline Palmer argue that rhetorical analysis can reflectively mediate public arguments "by identifying various discourses," including environmental discourses, "before they are galvanized by dichotomous political rhetoric... At the very least, such analysis can reveal possible identifications and real conflicts passed over by an ever-too-glib retreat into ecospeak," that is, typified, rehearsed, and rehashed oppositions (10). Killingsworth and Palmer suggest critical tools serve a normative purpose: to induce more thoughtful, and ideally more cooperative, approaches to problems. I identify with this approach. One personal consequence of my rhetorical analysis is my increasing commitment to the view that solutions to socioecological problems are found in the dialogic interaction of multiple viewpoints.

In this epilogue, I wish to briefly consider this claim from a more critical standpoint, primarily by further contextualizing it within my particular field site and then by briefly situating it within a theoretical context. With regard to my field research, the questions that ultimately came to be of most interest to me, those concerning the role of dialogue and deliberation in the environmental politics of southern Arizona, were not the same as those I began with, which were oriented toward understanding how my informants attribute meaning to "sustainable grazing" and seek to persuade others of their understandings in a conflict-laden situation. As my questions shifted during analysis, the dynamics of face-to-face forums came to be of more interest to me, without an opportunity to return to the field for further data. Within my transcripts, I found information on three participatory forums: the Sonoran Desert Conservation Plan (SDCP), the Lazy T-Bar's ranch management group, and a third group. In the Lazy T-Bar's case, my data is not triangulated, though I have used some print sources to inform the account I base mostly on the primary rancher's testimony. This late interest in dialogism, and the resulting limitations on my data, must be accounted for.

One approach to the limits of a single study is to juxtapose my understanding with the conclusions of other field research. Though the data on my three cases is limited, the perceived promise of the collaborations discussed in this book are in line with a growing body of similar research that examines the role of participatory forums in addressing environmental conflict. In response to deep-seated conflicts that are often framed as stakeholder politics, it is becoming increasingly common to develop participatory decision-making processes that involve long-term deliberation, trust building, and consensus building. Scholarly studies of such face-to-face forums typically celebrate their pragmatic accomplishments for policy and management, particularly when they sustain long-term engagement and find real ways for all participants to contribute. Edward Weber finds that grassroots ecosystem management, a collaborative form of decision-making, can "resolve environmental conflicts" while also increasing accountability (226). Tarla Rai Peterson explains that a grassroots group is able to develop solutions equally acceptable to farmers and environmentalists because members commit to building trust by deferring to each other's expertise (148–57). The multiple cases of community-based initiatives reported in *Finding Common Ground* lead Ronald Brunner to claim that the book can "assist policy makers in improving natural resources policy and governance from a common-interest standpoint" (7). It would be easy to expand this promising list with studies by Zita Ingham, Craig Waddell, Gregg Walker and Steven Daniels, and others. Reports from crossover presses also are frequently glowing, as in many of the contributions to *Making Sense of Intractable Environmental Conflicts* (Lewicki, Gray, and Elliott). *Nature-Friendly Communities* uses Pima County as a showcase community because of its Sonoran Desert Conservation Plan (Duerkesen and Snyder).

Although I find these studies generally sound, they, like my own, nonetheless have two main limitations that keep me from wanting to wholeheartedly endorse participatory forums as the single best solution to environmental issues. First, many of these studies tend to focus on the views of participants. In fact, researchers sometimes act as participants themselves, such as Craig Waddell in his mediatory role in Great Lakes Basin water quality discussions. The investment of participants is often carried over into research, at the expense of perspectives of non-participants. Edward Weber smartly notes in his discussion of the Applegate Partnership that the most "hard-core contemporary environmentalists" are less likely to be satisfied with collaborative governance initiatives because "existing land-use practices, extractive or otherwise, are treated as legitimate although in need of serious improvement" (222). In my research, I encountered an environmental activist who declined an invitation to participate in one deliberative forum because its basic premise is that environmentalists and ranchers can find common ground. An analysis that fails to account for non-participation is necessarily limited.

A related challenge is that many qualitative researchers, myself included, respond to ethical issues around representation by choosing to portray their informants positively. This can subtly color findings. Peterson, for example, in her discussion of the Agriculture Wildlife Coexistence Committee, notes self-reflexively: "I've had considerable difficulty extracting myself from the fuzzy cocoon formed by the AWCC members, and perhaps [my] description reflects that mood too completely" (156). With less cause than Peterson, whose data is more extensive, I have allowed myself to be persuaded by the charisma of those who believe in their dialogue. The emotions of interper-·sonal interaction saturate my analysis. This again contributes to overrepresenting the insider's perspective on participatory forums.

Rather than rely exclusively on studies of participatory forums, therefore, I prefer to examine how different positions taken in grazing debates are responses to one another. This approach situates claims about dialogism by recognizing how conflict can support its development. Karen Merrill's history of grazing debates illustrates that dichotomous pro- and antigrazing positions developed within larger struggles between conservationism, spearheaded by Gifford Pinchot, and what came to be known as preservationism, led by John Muir, from the first half of the nineteenth century. Within ranching communities, defensively conservative arguments are in many ways a reaction to adamant critiques of ranching within the preservationist camp of environmentalists. The power of the antigrazing position has grown over the past three decades, and the increased need to reckon with these environmentalists has spurred the development of a middle position. Social movement scholars, such as Herbert Haines, frequently refer to this type of development as a positive radical flank effect and, in a similar argument, rhetorical scholar Marilyn Cooper notes the "synergistic" relationship between radical groups such as Earth First! and moderate groups such as the Nature Conservancy ("Environmental"). Cooper continues: "the success of the environmental movement will in large part depend on different groups employing different strategies and playing different roles in the debate" (238). I explore similar dynamics in "Activist Rhetorics and the Struggle for Meaning."

One helpful way to more fully theorize rhetorical interactions is to look at responses to Habermas's formulation of the public sphere. One of the primary values of Habermas's concept is that it provides a way to examine how private people create, through dialogue, a sphere of public opinion that can exert some sort of pressure on governing authorities (The Structural 27). Acknowledging that there has never been full and open access to this sphere for all classes, Habermas has nevertheless held up the public sphere as an ideal for political communication. In "Discourse Ethics: Notes on a Program of Philosophical Justification," Habermas makes clear he does not believe the public sphere should operate through an *a priori* rationalism, as he is often charged with thinking. Instead, he argues that the only valid universalizing principle is a version of the Kantian imperative, namely, that "All affected can accept the consequences and the side effects [that a norm's] *general* observance can be anticipated to have for the satisfaction of *everyone's* interests" (65, emphasis in the original). When particularized to participatory forums, this leads Habermas to state a basic principle for the ethics of discourse: "Only those norms can claim to be valid that meet (or could meet) with the approval of all affected in their capacity *as participants in practical discourse*" (66, emphasis in the original).

On their face, at least, the deliberative forums I have discussed approximately accommodate Habermas's ethical principle. While not all the forums assume consensus will form out of dialogue, they all work to that end, evaluating the formation of agreement as success. In the process, they create new publics, arenas for testing ideas and actions against the perspectives of others. This approximation of the Habermasian model suggests that his critics might be valuable for thinking through the limits of the participatory groups that inform my study. I wish to primarily focus on Nancy Fraser's approach in "Rethinking the Public Sphere: A Contribution to the Critique of Actually Existing Democracy."

One of Fraser's key claims is that, if a society is multicultural, even if it is ideally egalitarian, it requires multiple public spheres to accommodate multiple forms of expression (125). In my study, the mediation of environmental discourse, agricultural discourse, and ecological discourse assumes the independent construction of these as distinctive discourses with something to contribute. Habermas also recognizes the importance of this point when he argues that conflict and content are prior to participatory discourse ("Discourse" 103). In other words, to celebrate collaboration through difference requires first valuing the formation of those differences. When these differences come into direct conflict, however, dialogue requires the ability to negotiate them. As I discuss in chapter 2, there is an important distinction between differences identified with discourses and differences identified with persons, a la stakeholder politics. Discursive differences can be dialogised, whereas the latter can only be staged in dialogue.

Fraser's more famous argument is that Habermas's ideals do not apply to "actually existing democracy," meaning stratified societies. In hierarchical societies, Fraser argues, the formation of subaltern counterpublics is particularly important. These counterpublics allow alternative public opinions to form outside the scrutiny of dominant groups. Only when these alternative opinions gain articulateness and strength can they valuably challenge hegemonic opinion. As Fraser writes: "subaltern counterpublics have a dual character. On the one hand, they function as spaces of withdrawal and regroupment; on the other hand, they also function as bases and training grounds for agitational activities directed toward wider publics" (528). Fraser's claims, taken together, point to different ideals for communication in stratified and egalitarian societies, requiring analysts to consider structural power. I hypothesize that situated power relations in grazing debates contribute significantly to the success of dialogic forums.

Participants come to these forums affiliated with organizations—agencies, environmental nonprofits, cattle associations, etc.—that are not on an egalitarian footing. Yet they are not simply placed in hierarchical relationships, either, suggesting a political structure that requires some exploration. The multiple routes to power in United States democracy have created some fundamental uncertainties that makes collaboration structurally beneficial at this historic moment. As a result, where conflict once played a largely solitary role in public grazing debates, consensus-oriented groups are now forming and also play a significant role. In part, this is because of the diffusion of new forms for participatory democracy, with President Clinton's 1993 "Forest Conference" or "Spotted Owl Summit" especially helping in this regard, despite many participants' dissatisfaction with its direct policy outcomes. At a grassroots level, the development of participatory forums has become widespread enough in rural areas of the western United States that Edward Weber considers such groups to be a new movement (5).

Another, perhaps even more basic reason for the development of new participatory forums in Arizona is that the balance of power is volatile enough that it is unclear who is winning in environmental conflict. Historically in Arizona, ranchers have held the clear upper hand, with legislative strength continuing even until now (C. Davis "Politics" 74). Yet, environmentalists are increasingly winning in the courts. A landmark case in November 2001, allowing environmentalists to bid against ranchers for grazing leases, serves as an exemplary example of increased environmentalist power. In 2003, the Forest Guardians made the first successful bid against a rancher, allowing them to rest from grazing 162 acres near the Babocomari River (Tobin). The very real possibility, on both sides, of each group winning in one arena only to lose in another creates uncertainties that may lead to cooperation, and the urgency is famously enhanced by rapid housing development in Arizona. Many (though sometimes not the most preservation-oriented environmental groups) interpret this development as a loss for both ranchers and environmentalists.

In short, extrinsic aspects of the rhetorical situation are ripe for the artistic creation of what Lawrence Prelli calls a discursive "interdependence structure," where participants agree that coordinated action is preferable to the status quo, even though outcomes might be suboptimal "from the vantage of individual value perspectives" ("Topical" 246). As Prelli notes, coordinated action allows "some movement toward solutions to problems that otherwise would continue unabated if deliberations remained polarized over value differences" (246). In other words, it has become easier to persuade participants that they need one another to pursue their own goals. The need for cooperation in response to political uncertainty is different from the public bracketing of inequality critiqued by Fraser, and it creates conditions where people are more dependent on one another's contributions.

A model of a reticulate public sphere, advanced by Gerard Hauser, provides an appropriate way to situate participatory forums within a broader public, including groups persistently at odds with each other (*Vernacular*). Briefly put, the reticulate public sphere can serve as an umbrella concept for such ideas as the Habermasian public sphere and Fraser's counterpublics, metaphorically suggesting that opinion formed in one public arena will influence that in another so long as they share the same basic reference world. Hauser's approach, with its focus on rhetoric and discourse, is complementary to the radical flank effect, which focuses on the structural role of social movement organizations. Both emphasize the interactive nature of diverse aspects of the public and serve as a reminder that valuing dialogic forums also means valuing the exigencies leading to those forums, including radical critiques.

I next wish to draw attention to significant differences between the three participatory forums that figure in my book and to suggest how they affect aspects of rhetorical dynamics. The first obvious difference is an immense divergence in the scale of groups. While the Lazy T-Bar's ranch management group is attempting to create a plan that encompasses a single ranch and a proposed spinoff wood product business, and a second deliberative forum has no specific management site and instead hopes to pressure legislators, Pima County is trying to plan for somewhere around four million acres—the six million in the county minus those independently governed by the Tohono O'odham and other Native American nations. It goes without saying that face-to-face dialogue will be more complicated, given the larger number of constituents and the greater stakes in the county's plan.

The stakes are higher in the county's plan for another reason that is not as immediately obvious. Here, I return again to Fraser, who urges scholars to distinguish between strong publics, those with some sort of governing authority, and weak publics, those without such authority, adding that in actuality there is a continuum between strong and weak publics. Stakes are higher in stronger publics.

It is not immediately obvious where to place the forums I discuss on such a continuum. At first glance, the Sonoran Desert Conservation Plan, as a government-authorized planning process, would clearly qualify as a strong public. However, lands within the county are not necessarily controlled by the county, as is immediately evident by excluding lands under the separate governance of the Tohono O'odham Nation from the mapping process. The bulk of the remaining lands are owned by three federal agencies, the Arizona State Land Department, and private citizens and corporations.

The county's direct regulatory control of private land is through zoning and mitigation ordinances and, secondarily, by less frequently used incentives (Duerkesen and Snyder 267–70). Its other methods for gaining control are outright purchase and persuading a federal organization, the Fish and Wildlife Service, to approve its habitat plan. These methods require coalition-building to first persuade voters to allow the county to go into debt in order to purchase private lands and then to avoid lobbying and lawsuits that would stymie attempts to get its habitat plan approved. In the process, the county has faced major setbacks, such as a cooling of state support which, considering the sizeable amount of state land within Pima County that might be developed, is significant to the plan's success. As put by the Pima County administrator in his cover to the recently released final draft of the Habitat Conservation Plan, which awaits public comment before a Fish and Wildlife decision: "the long term success of the regional biological reserve will require the other local jurisdictions to honor the reserve guidelines, as Pima County has through the Conservation Lands System" (Huckleberry "Re: Draft" 2). In other words, the county's lack of control over key public lands will diminish the regulatory power of the Section 10 permit it seeks. However, it appears likely that the Section 10 permit will be granted and, in a move that should have more impact, the county has successfully passed the May 2004 bond measure that funds other portions of the plan, notably land purchases. So, even while the county could never expect to automatically enact its plan, participants were right to assume that the stakes of either non-participation or cooperation would be quite high.

The Lazy T-Bar ranch management group, on the other hand, might appear to be a strong public with respect to its limited purview. However, most ranching practices are bureaucratically regulated. As long as the group recommends practices typical of ranching, it can expect authorization to enact them. It has been more creative, however, especially in its goals to reverse woody plants incursion by developing a wood products industry, and it has not been able to get necessary approval from the federal agency that holds the majority of its leases. Even beyond this, the ranch couple's compliance with the group's suggestions is voluntary, as was their decision to initiate group meetings. From these perspectives, the group serves merely in an advisory capacity, a clear weak public. The final deliberative forum also is a weak public, one that relies on persuading others, such as legislators, to enact its recommendations.

I speculate these differences contribute to each forum's rhetoric. When someone comes to a ranch management group and says to a rancher, "I want to put you out of business," as reportedly happened at the Lazy T-Bar, there's very little risk involved in continuing the discussion. The activist has available the same third-party coercive strategies as always: lawsuits and lobbying. For his part, the rancher has no need to respond directly to the activist. There's no pressure to reach agreement. The group's basis for collaboration is everyone's assertion that they care about the land, not their assumption that they can ultimately work together. Without the a priori assumption of consensus, there's more room to explore differences. Zita Ingham finds something similar in her study of a Montana community whose conflicts, perhaps not incidentally, were mediated by a southern Arizona nongovernmental organization, the Sonoran Institute. By forming an image of a shared future, Ingham found, members of the community are able to maintain deliberation in the absence of agreement. These open-ended discussions are less viable in cases such as the Sonoran Desert Conservation Plan, which explicitly seeks to make decisions with concrete outcomes that participants wish to control. In short, the ranch management group may have been more cooperative than the Sonoran Desert Conservation Plan in large part because of its nonbinding character and its potential distance from decision making. This complicates my praise of the ranch group's approaches to ecology-based deliberation and strategies for decision making.

My last point examines the aesthetic basis for much of my discussion. My discussion of my interviews, in particular, is based on opposing what I consider to be dialogic rhetorics in my informants' speech to reified arguments, such as ecology-based arguments in stasis or the agonistic identity framings characteristic of social movements. I use representations within private interviews to stand for more public forms of discussion, and I analyze types of rhetoric within private comments in ways that suggest their public impact. This approach, despite serving as a political commentary, operates primarily as an aesthetic of politics because it doubly distances what I critique from a primary political context: the first distance is my reliance on my informants' representations of publics; the second distance is my own representation of my informants' words.

Ken Hirschkop's recent critique of Bakhtin's work is useful for thinking through the implications of this approach. In an *Aesthetic for Democracy*, Hirschkop contrasts Habermas's public sphere with Bakhtin's public square along two axes: structural-cultural and historical-idealist. Hirschkop argues that both Bakhtin's strengths are related to his exclusive identification with the cultural/idealist ends of these spectrums. He contends that Bakhtin's attention to culture allows him to see inequality in discourse in ways that other analysts have missed, and to valorize dialogism as an ideal response to such inequality. Similarly, in my own analysis, I am drawn to dialogic discourses because they are accompanied by reflexivity and a willingness to learn.

However, Hirschkop argues, the poverty of Bakhtin's historical analysis prevents him from recognizing the extra-linguistic modernist and Christian values that drive what appears to be entirely a linguistic theory. Further, and most damningly from my perspective, Bakhtin's allegiance to a model of historical becoming that ignores structural conflict leads Hirschkop to argue that Bakhtin's subjects are freed "from the burden of making decisions" (261). In short, Bakhtin valorizes dialogism irrespective of whether it provides a ground for sound decisions. I think my analysis shares Bakhtin's biases. I consider dialogic rhetorical strategies to be an inventive way to respond to politically gridlocked conflict, but for those who want assurance that invention will lead to sound socioecological action, I have only hope to offer. That hope is grounded in the reflexivity of rhetorical analysis, which, as Ken Hirschkop claims of Bakhtin's clown, can help create an "intermediate space in which we see our language whilst inhabiting it" (261).

24 JANUARY 2006

It is almost five years since my first interview for this study. Since then I have married Phil, received my Ph.D., given birth to a daughter, and kept on studying grazing issues. Unexpectedly, I have also moved across the world, to a different hemisphere and a different season. For the last seven months, I have lived in Aotearoa/New Zealand, where I work at Massey University.

It is greener here. During my campus interview, the pasture hills and valleys, alternating with the deep green of dark bush reserves, made me immediately feel at home—home like in Eugene, Oregon, where I grew up, on the wet side of the Cascades. Although Phil swears our daughter, Rain, is named after the desert monsoons, in whose summer season she was born, I confess that eight years in Tucson could not make me feel like a desert person, and when my new colleagues ask how I am responding to the climate change, I point to Rain as proof I wanted to be somewhere like this. Yet today, as I hang in my office a hummingbird ornament sent by Phil's sister, and then browse the Sonoran Desert Conservation Plan's web site for one more fact check, my heart is suddenly in pain, and my eyes water at a photograph of a saguaro. Immediately, my imagination develops the web site's black and white picture. In the cactus's lime-green side are Gila woodpeckers and the brown boots they co-create with the saguaro. Ants cross the desert sand; a creeping pipevine lies low against the floor; a chuparosa holds back on growing leaves so that its handful of inch-long red flowers appear extravagant. Over it all, the smell of creosote, the feel of dry heat. It is a scene I love, one with little movement in it until the sun sets. Socioecologies may develop as processes, but I hope this desert can always be found in the edges of Tucson, for it is unique in the world. There are no hummingbirds in Aotearoa, and something about that makes humans different, too, makes me and my family different here.

We now own a "lifestyle," meaning a home on a bit of land, a common way that Kiwis remind themselves they are a rural people. For several years I did not eat beef, respectfully joining Phil's ten-year boycott, although I quietly and permanently ended that practice for both of us sometime during the dissertation, once many discussions had changed my views and softened Phil's. Upon buying our new home, one of Phil's first acts was to buy heifers. I like to call it ironic, but this is a completely different environment, the sort that the U.S. Homestead Act of 1862 would have worked in. Our pair of Murray Greys has not been able to keep our two acres of grass in check, and we have had a couple of paddocks hayed.

There are problems of socioecological health here, like elsewhere, but they are markedly different than in southern Arizona. Aotearoa's most significant habitat and species issues are distinctive to the island, due to its isolated evolutionary history. Birds that evolved flightless in the absence of predators developed few defenses against the hunting of first immigrants and the ongoing predation of introduced species, infamously rats. Bush is stripped by possums deliberately introduced for their pelts, and one heated public debate swirls around side effects of possum poisoning.

Agriculture, the most representative site of human-nonhuman negotiations, is at issue here as everywhere, though with its own unique stamp. Here, Kiwi farmers are increasingly held responsible for pesticide runoff into waterways. Population, however, has not reached a pressure point except, perhaps, in Auckland and Wellington, and development, consequently, does not serve as a whip to conservation, although throughout Aotearoa Māori have mourned for lost land, lost faith, and a changing way of being-in-place as new immigrants inadequately honored cultures and treaties.

We live in time and develop strategies to cope with the changes its passing brings. Often, it is easiest to ignore change, but sometimes we are reminded of the constant vulnerability of our present, as when an infant grows into a child or a move around the world shifts the ground from under our feet. I wish that we may all feel that vulnerability sharply enough to listen to the voices of others and know what we love. Whether we listen or not, we all, humans and nonhumans, will keep on becoming each other's future.

This study is shaped by the goals of ethnography, but its claims to ethnography are debatable. The term ethnographer once had as its clear referent an anthropologist who studied, in depth, a clearly bounded time and space. As a preface to critique, Renato Rosaldo explains this traditional anthropologic ideal:

> Anthropology favors interpretations that equate analytical "depth" with cultural "elaboration." Many studies focus on visibly bounded arenas where one can observe formal and repetitive events. . . . Most ethnographers prefer to study events that have definite locations in space with marked centers and outer edges. Temporally, they have middles and endings. . . . Their qualities of fixed definition liberate such events from the untidiness of everyday life so that they can be "read" like articles, books, or, as we now say, *texts*. (12, emphasis in the original)

My own study cannot be considered an ethnography in this tidy sense. However, it is inspired from first design to final analysis by the approach to ethnography advocated by critical anthropologist George Marcus. In "Ethnography in/of the World System," Marcus explains the work of the ethnographer as studying "cultural logics," and uses this purpose to identify as ethnographic the work of researchers such as myself who, in the process of studying a system rather than a space, use "multi-sited" methods that range from place to place (and, by extension, time to time) in the process of "following" a particular cultural logic such as, in my case, an argument. My emphasis throughout has been the cultural logics that circulate within public argument and that are evident primarily in language, though I also seek to understand language in contexts of pragmatic action, especially in deliberative and managerial settings.

In search of additional disciplinary description, I have raised questions of ethnographic description in two conference settings. The first was a 2004 seminar, funded by the National Science Foundation, on studying up in multi-sited ethnographies of science. This was attended by junior scholars (such as myself) from disciplines such as communications, sociology, and anthropology, organized by Gene I. Rochlin and Todd R. LaPorte, and hosted by the Institute of Governmental Studies at UC Berkeley. Here, Joan Fujimura defined ethnographies by the questions they raise, namely their open-ended attention to a research field (however defined). She juxtaposed ethnographies with case studies, which instead emphasize hypothesis testing, and suggested that my work, as I had represented it, adhered to an ethnographic approach. I selected my site, a field of argument because of the long-standing conflict over grazing issues and the involvement of both activist organizations and scientists in seeking to change socioecological relations involving grazing, allowing me to pursue my scholarly interest in social movement and popularized scientific rhetorics. Yet these interests did not entail a testable hypothesis of what I might learn, and my emphases and questions evolved in response to what I heard in the field.

I again raised the question of ethnographic definition in a qualitative studies workshop organized by Roxanne Mountford at the 2004 Conference on College Composition and Communication. There, in a discussion group led by Paul Anderson, we approached the question by focusing on ethnographic data collection, thinking more in terms of Geertzian "thick description," which, despite primarily pointing at ethnographic style, also depends on extensive data collection at a single site. With the advent of postmodern ethnographies and multi-sited ethnographies (again following Marcus), it has become increasingly difficult to define the boundaries of a single site. While it is plausible to define a field site in metaphoric rather than geographic terms as I did in "Debating Ecology" (2004), Marcus's attention to asymmetries of power, a defining feature of critical ethnography (see also Cintron's "The Timidities" and Horner), suggests the value of distinguishing between more rhetorical and cultural qualitative studies, such as mine, and those that put more emphasis on material conditions and structure. These latter would be enhanced by data collection more closely focused on particular agencies, or political processes (such as a fuller account of the Sonoran Desert Conservation Plan), or individuals more extensively located in a network of historic, social, and ecological relations. When focusing on data based in material sites, I identify less with ethnography than with other forms of qualitative research, such as discourse analysis.

In response to different approaches to ethnographic definition, which themselves reflect the multiple forms of ethnography, I have come to identify this work as an ethnography-informed qualitative study of rhetoric, a definition that ultimately privileges rhetoric over ethnography. My choice, made in the process of analysis, to organize my interview-based chapters around analytic categories (such as topics or methods of speaking) rather than around particular regions or informants (such as one ranch or organization per chapter) further removes this work from standard ethnographic practice (that is, writing about people). This organization instead emphasizes rhetorical analysis by shifting focus onto language in an approach more closely aligned with discourse studies. My claims are about ways of arguing and making meaning, not about the worldviews and culture of persons who happen to make those arguments at a particular place and time.

Methodological classification aside, a few words on sources are in order. I treat both print (and online) texts and interview transcripts as primary sources. I selected texts on the basis of their wide circulation (as is the case with the books by O'Connor and Day, Sheridan, and Rifkin analyzed in chapter 1), or on their centrality to public deliberation (as is the case with many of the documents related to the Sonoran Desert Conservation Plan). I used snowball sampling to identify potential informants. While a snowball method is sometimes faulted for underrepresenting those with few social ties, this actually works in my favor as my primary interest is the most public aspects of debate.

For chapter 2, I rely primarily on Pima County's archives of the Sonoran Desert Conservation Plan, archived online at http://www.pima.gov/cmo/sdcp/. I gained further access to public comment with the assistance of Nicole Fyffe, assistant to the county administrator. I supplemented this archival work with attendance at two public meetings: one of the Science and Technology Advisory Team, and one of the Steering Committee. Though these observations add a bit of life to my account, due to the ad hoc nature of my meeting attendance and the need for a more thorough perspective on these meetings (such as that supplied by archived minutes), my analysis for this chapter is primarily text-based, at times in combination with comments from my informants.

Chapters 3, 4, and 5 are primarily based on tape-recorded interviews combined with observations (such as ranch tours) that arose from these interviews. I ultimately rely on thirteen recorded interviews (out of sixteen conducted), which range from just over thirty minutes long to slightly over two hours, averaging slightly over an hour each, and involving one or two informants per interview. I also use untaped comments of these and other informants recorded in my notes. I interviewed six ranchers (representing three ranches), three environmentalists affiliated with two different organizations (either as staff or as contributors), and a staff member from the

Buenos Aires National Wildlife Refuge who supports the refuge's cattle-free policy. To represent those involved in bureaucratic or advisory capacities, I interviewed a county extension agent, a range scientist, two additional employees of government agencies responsible for leases, and two others who participated in deliberative committees in an official role. One person from this group had previously worked for yet another government office responsible for leases, and another government agent participated in an unrecorded tour. Although on some occasions I identify informants according to their organizational affiliations, each informant participated as an individual, not as a representative of a particular organization. When I judge that that organizational affiliation will significantly compromise confidentiality, I exclude this information even when it may be of interest to readers.

I chose to stop interviewing new informants when I could generally anticipate the arguments I would hear, and when references to particular events and persons had become, on the whole, redundant with other accounts. Environmentalists are less well represented than ranchers or bureaucrats and advisors, in part because I strongly identified with the environmentalist standpoint and preferentially sought out those I could learn more from, and in part because of a large number of unreturned phone calls and e-mails from staff at environmental nonprofits, whereas all ranchers and most others I contacted gave me immediate welcome.

By the time I began systematically analyzing interviews, I had already developed a focus on ecological arguments and identifications, especially about cattle impacts on grass cover and watersheds. After selecting excerpts based on these topics, I found that I had more, and more diverse, excerpts related to grass cover, and I chose to further analyze only these. For chapter 5, I coded all transcripts for identity labels—including "I," "we," "you," "manager," "general public," and others—before settling on environmentalist and rancher identities as those that I had the most data to further analyze. My focus on dialogism and reification in these excerpts arose out of further analysis, informed, clearly, by my disciplinary perspective.

When I quote from interviews, ellipses (". . .") refer to material I have chosen to delete, either because audio quality is poor at that point (for example, as a speaker trails off or momentarily hedges in speech, or because of sudden background noise, as in outdoor interviews near roads), or because I want to make relatively short cuts (i.e., under two sentences) for concision. When I wish to delete long excerpts to be more concise, I typically end a quote and interject before continuing, with the result that several narrative dialogues between my informants and me are significantly shorter in the text than in conversation. When I supply words in brackets ("[rancher]"), I am either guessing at words that are unclear in my recordings or, in some instances, I am replacing specific markers with more generic ones or pseudonyms to protect confidentiality.

[NOTES]

PROLOGUE

1. My use of the term "web" is influenced by Donna Haraway's use of the same metaphor in *Modest_Witness@Second_Millennium*. Haraway describes her analytic method as following connections between multiple sources, sites, and actions. She explains that this method traces a web similar to the Internet (6–7) or a game of cat's cradle (268–71). For example, calling herself a "subtle ethnographer and theorist of the complex, shifting, and nonsystemic geometries of margins and centers in the contemporary world," Haraway notes that her work requires her to "navigate both the imagined Net and the actual net" to trace linkages between communication and other practices (6, 7). The metaphor indicates a systems-oriented analysis. In my case, this analysis traces a system of rhetorical practices and material impacts that, I argue, cannot be fully understood separately from one another. Like Haraway, I stress the importance of connecting margins—such as social movements—to centers—such as legislatures and mainstream politics.

While Haraway is my inspiration, I have since seen the metaphor of a web used by Marilyn Cooper, in language and purpose notably similar to mine ("The Ecology").

2. See my methodological appendix.

3. Pima County maintains an official web site for the Sonoran Desert Conservation Plan at http://www.co.pima.az.us/cmo/sdcp/.

4. Quoted by Tony Davis in "A Pocket-Sized Bird Takes on Sunbelt Subdivisions."

1. THE RANGE OF RHETORIC

1. Many argue that watershed protection and water consumption are the most significant issues at stake in arid land use. Southern Arizona's major urban area, Tucson, is built on an aquifer that, for years, has been depleted at a significantly higher rate than it has been recharged. The rapid growth of the largest Arizona city to the south of Tucson, Sierra Vista, has become an international issue: the city's wells are implicated in the degradation of the San Pedro River that flows north from Mexico to Arizona, supporting a

riparian area that is an essential link in the migration of birds from Canada to Mexico and Central America (Kingsolver). Not surprisingly, then, the impact of cattle on watersheds and riparian areas is a particularly sensitive point of debate that tends to draw passionate responses. Cattle are charged with both historic and contemporary contributions to watershed erosion. Riparian areas draw the most attention in land management plans, frequently with the requirement that cattle be fenced out of those areas. Yet, some argue that ranching limits the rapid development of thirsty urban centers. This book will weave aspects of debates over the interaction between cattle grazing and watershed management through its analysis. Early in my research, however, I made a decision to make arguments about grass a primary focus of my analysis of ecological argument, at the expense of hydrology and other possible topics.

2. There has been an almost logarithmic growth over the last few decades in narrative analysis within the human sciences. Amia Lieblich, Rivka Tuval-Maschiach, and Tamar Zilber briefly review multidisciplinary interest in narrative research and reproduce a figure of its growth in the first chapter of their methods book, *Narrative Research: Reading, Analysis, and Interpretation*. In tandem with this growth in narrative studies is a tendency to broaden definitions of narrative even so far as to include texts such as questions and images. Michael Chandler, Christopher Lalonde, and Ulrich Teucher review many of these broad definitions in "Culture, Continuity, and the Limits of Narrativity," while themselves arguing that a more limited definition of narrative is more analytically useful. I tend to agree, despite recognizing the vulnerabilities of a dichotomous distinction between narrative and nonnarrative. Differentiating between narrative and nonnarrative genres make it possible to understand narrative as just one possibility among many, and to therefore examine the unique rhetorical impacts of narrative.

3. Somers actually proposes four categories. The remaining two, which are "conceptual/analytic/sociological narrativity" and "metanarrativity," call on her academic audience to be conscious of the narrativity of their own theoretical work. Somers argues that her claims about narrative structure apply to all four categories ("Narrativity").

4. Somers provides a slightly different list: "(1) relationality of parts; (2) causal emplotment; (3) selective appropriation; and (4) temporality, sequence, and place" ("Narrativity" 601).

5. Geographer Paul F. Starrs's "An Inescapable Range" is one example of an academic analysis that reproduces this position.

6. For these critiques, see, for example, Kevin DeLuca's *Image Politics*, particularly the final section of chapter 1, and Gerard Hauser's "Civil Society and the Principle of the Public Sphere."

7. Lyotard asks: "Do ends show up right along with genres?" He answers himself: "They certainly do, and they take hold of phrases and the instances they present, especially 'us'" (136). By "take hold of," Lyotard means that genres arrange and constitute the relationships between their users (speakers, hearers, readers, writers). By ordering and reordering relationships, genres direct our actions toward each other and toward the world.

8. In the creation of this table, I relied primarily on several of the contributions to Charles Davis's *Western Public Lands and Environmental Politics*, especially his own two chapters and that of Sandra K. Davis, Jerry Holechek, Rex Pieper, and Carlton Herbel's textbook history of range management also was helpful, as was Karen Merrill's political history.

9. My history is indebted to Karen Merrill, Thomas Sheridan, and Charles Davis, among others.

10. Sheridan's preface explicitly acknowledges that his conservationism points to both nature and culture: "I want to hear Mexican wolves howl once again in the Altar Valley, but I also want . . . ranchers to keep on running their cattle on public lands" (ix).

11. For a series of historical case studies on nature writing's political impact, interpreted through the disciplinary lens of rhetoric, see Daniel Philippon's *Conserving Words: How American Nature Writers Shaped the Environment*.

12. See Lyotard's discussion of the traditional storytelling of the Cashinahua and of the inscription of these stories by ethnographers in *The Differend*. Lyotard first argues that ritual features of Cashinahua address establish continuity between current and past narrators, as well as between narrators and the events of this story (154). Lyotard then extends this argument beyond the ritual setting.

13. Examples of explicit storytelling occur frequently in *Lazy B*: a roundup recounted to readers is also, we are told, the "subject of many a story in the years" that followed it (87); a yarn told in a bar is later retold (implicitly) to the narrators who tell it to their readers (277). The elision of the narrative "I" of O'Connor with a narrative "we" is also common. The only point at which this elision clearly locates O'Connor in a story where she is physically absent, however, is in the roundup story just mentioned.

14. See Slovic for a full discussion of how rhapsody, in addition to jeremiad, functions within environmental rhetoric.

15. Plenty has been said about the pop culture cowboy and its historical referents. *The American Cowboy: The Myth and the Reality*, by Joe Frantz and Julian Choate (1955) is frequently cited as a key work in this area. More contemporary analyses include a collection by Janet Walker, *Westerns: Films through History*, which focuses on generic and narrative analyses of Hollywood westerns. Bonnie S. Jefferson explores the relationship between John Wayne's screen identity and aspects of generalized American culture in "John Wayne: American Icon, Patriotic Zealot and Cold War Ideologue." John Tuska's *The American West in Film* devotes a chapter to plot-oriented narrative analysis, including a brief focus on a type of plot he calls the "Ranch Story" or "Town Western" (27–29). Films in this genre, he argues, "embody a strong endorsement of community spirit" (29), a point that resonates with O'Connor and Day's construction of ranching culture. This list is far from exhaustive.

16. The symbolic nature of these spaces, and the very real connection between place and action, is graphically illustrated by Merrill in a public hearing called by Farrington Carpenter, Harold Ickes's director of grazing. In response to pressure from those present, Carpenter agreeably leaves the hearing so that the meeting room can be instantly transformed into a state grazing board, which then passes several official resolutions. When Carpenter reenters the room, it is once again transformed into the space of a public hearing, allowing him to hear the resolutions in his official capacity as federal agent (153).

17. The "timidity" in Cintron's title points to his advocacy for critical ethnographies, which he defines as ethnographies that significantly challenge institutional arrangements. Although I am enticed by the flag Cintron waves, I do not believe this book fits its call. Nonetheless, I find his metaphor to be widely applicable to systems-oriented ethnographic writing.

18. There is a significant exclusion of Tohono O'odham reservation lands, however, which, though geographically within the county, are not under the county's jurisdiction.

2. OPEN SPACE, CONSERVATION, AND ENDANGERMENT

1. My account relies on an online report of the meeting, published by the Udall Center for Studies in Public Policy, *Digest of the Pygmy Owl Forum*.

2. Later drafts reduced the number of priority vulnerable species from fifty-five to thirty-five.

3. In Gorgias, Plato has Socrates argue for the supremacy of dialectic as a

means of discovering the truth. Although Socrates's own approach to persuasion does begin to take on some of the features that his interlocutor, Callicles, attributes to rhetoric, in the end Socrates vows to return to his solitary search for truth through dialectic. Aristotle paints a more sympathetic portrait of rhetoric in *On Rhetoric*, but he nonetheless distinguishes dialectic from rhetoric by arguing that the former is a way to gain knowledge and the latter is a way to address the public and decide cases involving probability rather than certainty.

4. So, for example, Burke argues that "Sensory representation is, of course, synecdochic in that the senses abstract certain qualities . . . and these qualities can be said 'truly to represent' a tree" ("The Four" 508). That is, the representation is not the tree itself, but it is nonetheless possible to have a valid idea of what a tree really is, based on the persuasions of sensory experience.

5. Decker provides a gloss of different cultural and historical views of the West, ostensibly including Turner's hypothesis though without explicit citation (65). This gloss illustrates Decker's critical distance on ways of imagining the West, and his critique of aspects of Turner's approach; yet, he nonetheless chooses to reproduce some of the environmental determinism and significance of open space evident in Turner's paper.

6. Mark Bassin, for example, argues that Turner reproduces a common trope amongst nineteenth century historians: that is, both nationalism and historical evolution are determined by geography and environment (476). In other words, for Turner, man is a product of his environment; society is caused by geography. Wilbur Jacobs also remarks on Turner's environmental determinism (xvi).

7. The idea of "deliberative dialogue" is developed by Heidi McKee out of her analysis of student interactions in online communities. McKee defines deliberative dialogue "as discourse characterized by individuals' explicit engagement with multiple perspectives on an issue in a way that reflects listening to and consideration of others' views (although not necessarily agreement) and that demonstrates receptiveness to movement—or to the possibility of movement—in one's own thinking" (3). This definition, which McKee bases in deliberative democracy theory, shares many of the values underlying my own argument. McKee's analysis of online discussion forums especially emphasizes the role of listening (or, in print, "textual listening") to the development of deliberative dialogues.

8. My description of events relies primarily on journalist Mitch Tobin's

reports for the *Arizona Daily Star* ("Wildlife"). I also depend on an Internet-published statement about the events, written by Wayne Shifflett, and a similarly published response by Sue Chilton.

9. In this description, I am reminded of Bruno Latour's discussion of the "links and knots" that help to create stable knowledge, with additional human and nonhuman links adding additional stability (*Pandora's* 100). While Latour's ideas and my own are only loosely analogous here, I wish to acknowledge his long-standing influence on my thought. My thought is also influenced by a metaphoric extension of the value of biodiversity to my argument that diverse human and nonhuman voices can together create healthier socioecologies.

3. FROM BATTLE LINES TO COLLABORATIVE SPACE

1. A point made too frequently elsewhere (famously but not exclusively by Derrida) to elaborate upon here.

2. In a later Steering Committee meeting (February 2, 2002), some committee members did intervene successfully in the construction of knowledge by asking STAT to include one more option in the draft environmental impact statement (EIS), specifically an alternative based on conserving between twenty-five and thirty-five species, to be compared alongside the legally-required no change alternative, an eight or nine species alternative already planned for the EIS, and the fifty-five species alternative STAT was focussing on at that point. At the same time, the members acknowledged STAT's expertise by agreeing that the details of the third option would be left to STAT. The third (2006) draft of the Multi-Species Habitat Conservation Plan now privileges an alternative based on thirty-five species, justifying this choice on the basis of scientific judgments and jurisdiction (Huckleberry "Re: Draft" 2).

3. In my epilogue, I discuss more fully the problem of judgment in plural societies, an issue raised pointedly by many critics of Jürgen Habermas, including, preeminently, the postmodernist philosopher Jean-François Lyotard, to whose influence I am indebted. In my epilogue, however, I draw more explicitly on Nancy Fraser's critique of Habermas, whose concept of counterpublics has expanded scholars' understanding of deliberation.

4. As already mentioned, Hermagoras's texts have been lost. Antoine Braet is my primary contemporary source for stasis theory, though I draw also on Charles Davis, Michael Carter, and Sharon Crowley and Debra Hawhee. I base my paraphrase of Hermagoras's four stases on a synthesis of these four sources.

5. In the preface to his second edition of *The Rhetoric of Science*, echoing Dilip Goankar's critique of Prelli, Gross critiques his own application of stasis theory to science because he ultimately finds stasis less useful for interpreting arguments than for developing them, and his task is ultimately an explanatory form of rhetorical criticism. Here, my purpose for rhetorical criticism is different: in finding a way to classify and sort through routinely invented types of public (science-based, not scientific) argument, I wish to critique some of the effects of arguments that are produced in the same closure-oriented form as arguments systematically developed with recourse to stasis theory.

6. Here, I invoke Alan Gross's more colloquial forms of the stasis questions. Following Richard McKeon, Gross, in a science-adapted approach to stasis, paraphrases the first question as "Is it?" the second as "What is it?" the third as "What properties does it have?" and the fourth as "Why?" ("Why Hermagoras" 141).

7. As an example, Laura Jackson and Patricia Comus spent years trying to determine how agriculture (primarily irrigation agriculture, with scattered ranching) changed plant communities in the lower Santa Cruz River valley between Tucson and Phoenix. Jackson and Comus explain the need for a baseline for restorationist work: "Without a historic model, we do not know whether successional processes are returning the valley to what it once was or to some new state. If changes to the old ecosystem are understood, ecological restoration techniques might be used to help repair the damage" (217). To address this knowledge gap, Jackson and Comus studied historic aerial photos, historic maps, and soil surveys. They conducted interviews aimed at understanding alterations to surface hydrology. Finally, they examined historic accounts and descriptions to attempt to learn about the vegetation of the area (217). Their research underscores the difficulty of establishing a baseline. Nonetheless, in a move typical in nonspecialist forums as well, Jackson and Comus follow up their recognition that it is difficult to establish a baseline by claiming that baselines are important enough to warrant a best guess or, in their case, a scholarly project to use all available sources to create the best possible model. From this model, they create a platform to recommend a restorative management plan.

8. These partners typically divide work by having the woman address paperwork and care for horses while the man takes primary responsibility for the cattle ranch operations. When I speak of the two together, I refer to

them as ranchers, but, for the sake of clarity, I also distinguish between the male "primary cattle rancher" and his female partner.

9. Lyotard influences how I form my question here.

4. SOCIOECOLOGY AND THE FUTURE OF THE LAND

1. In 1971, the *Journal of Range Management* attempted to appeal to a mixed audience of scientists and ranchers. It chose to increase its professional credibility in 1979 by redirecting less academic members of its audience to the newly created *Rangelands*.

2. Cable's conclusions are cited authoritatively, over time, in a wide range of journals, for example: the *Journal Grassland Society South Africa* (Cox and Ruyle, in 1986); the *Journal of Range Management* (Ruyle, Roundy, and Cox, in 1988; Roundy, Taylorson, and Sumrall, in 1992); *Biological Conservation* (Anable, McClaran, and Ruyle, in 1992); the *Journal of Applied Ecology* (McClaran and Anable, in 1992). The later articles illustrate less favorable attitudes toward the spread of Lehmann lovegrass than does Cable's, due to shifting understandings as well as different audiences.

3. There are, of course, exceptions, such as Bruce Roundy, Raymond Taylorson, and Lee Sumrall's 1992 seed germination experiments.

4. I discuss more fully the application of this concept to my work and, more generally, to qualitative research and writing in "Debating Ecology: Ethnographic Writing that 'Makes a Difference.'"

5. See also Nathan Sayre, who endorses a model of "nature as the interface of environment, ideas, and human activities: the nature of human and social ecology" (xvii).

6. Still Rhodesia during Savory's tenure there.

7. See Savory's examples in his 1988 edition of *Holistic Resource Management*.

5. FROM IDENTITY POLITICS TO DIALOGIC IDENTITIES

1. David Snow and Leon Anderson and, later, Snow and Doug McAdam use the term "identity work" to refer to, respectively, ways that homeless create positive identities and ways that social movement members manage the meanings of collective and personal identities. These uses point primarily to the attributions actors give themselves. These sources offer basic definitions of identity work, however, that are compatible with analyses of antagonist identities. For example, Snow and Anderson's definition of identity work as "the range of activities individuals engage in to create, present, and sustain

personal identities that are congruent with and supportive of the self-concept" is easily reworked to point to activities that "create, present, and sustain" attributions or representations of others' identities "that are congruent with" antagonist identity constructions (1348).

2. Timothy Ingalsbee, in a footnote to his analysis of Earth First! identification processes, reports on scholarship that empirically addresses this stereotype. Ingalsbee's report is mixed: some surveys, he notes, confirm the race and class base of environmentalism, but others "claim that environmental concerns and activism are now so diverse and widespread that the movement defies neat sociological categorization, particularly identification with one socioeconomic class" (273).

3. For his part, Phil (the SUV and sticker's owner) has continued to contribute as funds allow to the Southwest Center for Biological Diversity, but he also has remarked, for the record, that ranchers such as the one from Lazy T-Bar should be given the freedom and trust to see if their plans for reclaiming ecosystems can hold true in practice. Though his level of concern about ranch-related damage has not lessened, this skeptical openness to giving attentive managers a chance on public lands is a marked change from his earlier widespread hostility to the industry he holds accountable for much of the destruction of his deeply loved desert home.

4. The concept of "becoming," adapted from Bakhtin, is critically assessed by Hirschkop, whose view informs my language here. In *An Aesthetic for Democracy*, Hirschkop argues that, although "Bakhtin did not want intersubjectivity to be negotiable" in terms of roles and identities "within the intersecting networks of social life," Bakhtin's understanding of becoming must nonetheless be understood in just this type of social and historical context, a context that presumes democratic politics and judgment (295).

Abbey, Edward. "Even the Bad Guys Wear White Hats: Cowboys, Ranchers, and the Ruin of the West." *Harper's* (January 1986): 51–55.

Anable, Michael E., Mitchel P. McClaran, and George B. Ruyle. "Spread of Introduced Lehmann Lovegrass Eragrostis Lehmanniana Nees. in Southern Arizona, USA." *Biological Conservation* 61 (1992): 181–88.

Aristotle. *On Rhetoric: A Theory of Civic Discourse.* George A. Kennedy, trans. New York: Oxford University Press, 1991.

———. "The Poetics." S. H. Butcher, trans. *Aristotle's Theory of Poetry and Fine Art.* S. H. Butcher, ed. 4th ed: Dover, 1951. 5–111.

Awtrey, Janette. "To Whomever It May Concern." Undated. Letter 48 in Huckleberry, Correspondence. 85–88.

Awtrey, Lora. "To Whom It May Concern." December 9, 1998. Letter 47 in Huckleberry, Correspondence. 82–84.

Bahre, Conrad J. "Human Impacts on the Grasslands of Southeastern Arizona." *The Desert Grassland.* Mitchel P. McClaran and T. R. Van Devender, eds. Tucson: University of Arizona Press, 1995. 230–64.

Bakhtin, Mikhail M. "Forms of Time and of the Chronotope in the Novel." Caryl Emerson and Michael Holquist, trans. *The Dialogic Imagination.* Michael Holquist, ed. Austin: University of Texas Press, 1981. 84–258.

———. "From Notes Made in 1970–71." Vern W. McGee, trans. *Speech Genres and Other Late Essays.* Caryl Emerson and Michael Holquist, eds. Austin: University of Texas Press, 1986. 132–58.

———. "The Problem of the Text in Linguistics, Philology, and the Human Sciences: An Experiment in Philosophical Analysis." Vern W. McGee, trans. *Speech Genres and Other Late Essays.* Caryl Emerson and Michael Holquist, eds. Austin: University of Texas Press, 1986. 103–31.

———. "Toward a Methodology for the Human Sciences." Vern W. McGee, trans. *Speech Genres and Other Late Essays.* Caryl Emerson and Michael Holquist, eds. Austin: University of Texas Press, 1986. 159–72.

Bassin, Mark. "Turner, Solov'ev, and the 'Frontier Hypothesis': The Nationalist Signification of Open Spaces." *Journal of Modern History* 65 (1993): 473–511.

Bawarshi, Anis. "The Genre Function." *College English* 62 (2000): 335–60.

Berlin, James. "Rhetoric and Ideology in the Writing Classroom." *College English* 50 (1988): 477–94.

Bijker, Wiebe E. *Of Bicycles, Bakelites, and Bulbs: Toward a Theory of Sociotechnical Change.* Cambridge, Mass.: MIT Press, 1996.

Bingham, Sam, and Allan Savory. *Holistic Resource Management Workbook.* Washington, D.C.: Island Press, 1990.

Bloor, David. "Wittgenstein and Mannheim on the Sociology of Mathematics." *Studies in History and Philosophy of Science* 4 (1973): 173–91.

Bookchin, Murray. *The Philosophy of Social Ecology: Essays on Dialectical Naturalism.* Montréal, Québec: Black Rose Books, 1990.

Braet, Antoine. "The Classical Doctrine of Status and the Rhetorical Theory of Argumentation." *Philosophy and Rhetoric* 20 (1987): 79–92.

Brown, Robert L., and Carl G. Herndl. "Beyond the Realm of Reason: Understanding the Extreme Environmental Rhetoric of the John Birch Society." *Green Culture: Environmental Rhetoric in Contemporary America.* Carl G. Herndl and Stuart C. Brown, eds. Madison: University of Wisconsin Press, 1996. 213–35.

Brummett, Barry. "Communities, Identities, and Politics: What Rhetoric Is Becoming in the Twenty-First Century." *New Approaches to Rhetoric.* Patricia A. Sullivan and Steven R. Goldzwig, eds. Thousand Oaks, Calif.: Sage, 2004. 293–307.

Brunner, Ronald D., et al., eds. *Finding Common Ground: Governance and Natural Resources in the American West.* New Haven, Conn.: Yale University Press, 2002.

Brunner, Ronald. "Problems of Governance." *Finding Common Ground.* Ronald D. Brunner, et al., eds. New Haven, Conn.: Yale University Press, 2002. 1–47.

Bucchi, Massimiano. *Science and the Media: Alternative Routes in Scientific Communication.* London: Routledge, 1998.

Burke, Kenneth. "The Four Master Tropes." *A Grammar of Motives.* Berkeley: University of California Press, 1969. 503–17.

———. *A Grammar of Motives.* Berkeley: University of California Press, 1969.

———. "I, Eye, Ay—Concerning Emerson's Early Essay on 'Nature' and the Machinery of Transcendence." *Language as Symbolic Action: Essays on Life, Literature, and Method.* Berkeley: University of California Press, 1968. 186–200.

———. *Language as Symbolic Action*. Berkeley: University of California Press, 1966.

———. *A Rhetoric of Motives*. Berkeley: University of California Press, 1969.

Cable, Dwight R. "Lehmann Lovegrass on the Santa Rita Experimental Range, 1937–68." *Journal of Range Management* 24 (1971): 17–21.

Carey, James. *Communication as Culture*. New York: Routledge, 1989.

Carr, David. "Narrative and the Real World: An Argument for Continuity." *Memory, Identity, Community: The Idea of Narrative in the Human Sciences.* Lewis P. Hinchman and Sandra K. Hinchman, eds. New York: SUNY Press, 1997. 7–25.

Carroll, Jeffery. "Essence, Stasis, and Dialectic: Ways That Key Terms Can Mean." *Rhetoric Review* 23 (2004): 156–70.

Carson, Rachel. *Silent Spring*. New York: Fawcett Crest, 1962.

Carter, Michael. "*Stasis* and *Kairos*: Principles of Social Construction in Classical Rhetoric." *Rhetoric Review* 7 (1998): 97–112.

CBS. "Wild Wolves." *60 Minutes*. March 5, 2001.

CBSNews.com. "Wild Wolves." *60 Minutes.* http://www.cbsnews.com/stories/2000/03/20/60II/main174111.shtml (accessed July 1, 2004).

Chandler, Michael J., Christopher E. Lalonde, and Ulrich Teucher. "Culture, Continuity, and the Limits of Narrativity: A Comparison of the Self-Narratives of Native and Non-Native Youth." *Narrative Analysis: Studying the Development of Individuals in Society.* Colette Dauite and Cynthia Lightfoot, eds. Thousand Oaks, Calif.: Sage, 2004. 245–66.

Chiavello, Anthony. "Anarchy in Range Science: Allan Savory and the Rhetoric of Holistic Resource Management." *Technical Communication, Deliberative Rhetoric, and Environmental Discourse: Connections and Directions.* Nancy W. Coppola and Bill Karis, eds. Stamford, Conn.: Ablex, 2000. 301–20.

Chilton, Sue. "To Mitch Tobin." March 15, 2004. *Arizona Daily Star.* http://www.azstarnet.com/pdf/chilton_letter.pdf (accessed March 8, 2005).

Cicero. *De Inventione*. H. M. Hubbell, trans. Cambridge, Mass.: Harvard University Press, 1949.

Cintron, Ralph. *Angels' Town: Chero Ways, Gang Life, and Rhetorics of the Everyday*. Boston: Beacon Press, 1997.

———. "The Timidities of Ethnography: A Response to Bruce Horner." *JAC: A Journal of Composition Theory*. 22 (2002): 934–43.

Coalition for Sonoran Desert Protection. *Livestock Grazing and the Sonoran*

Desert Conservation Plan. March 17, 2001. http://www.sonorandesert.org/
pdfs/grazingreport.pdf (accessed January 24, 2005).

Cooper, Marilyn. "The Ecology of Writing." *College English* 48 (1986):
364–75.

———. "Environmental Rhetoric in the Age of Hegemonic Politics: Earth
First! And the Nature Conservancy." *Green Culture: Environmental Rhetoric
in Contemporary America.* Carl G. Herndl and Stuart C. Brown, eds.
Madison: University of Wisconsin Press, 1996. 236–60.

Cox, Jerry R. "Lehmann Lovegrass Live Component Biomass and
Chemical Composition." *Journal of Range Management* 45 (1992):
523–27.

Cox, Jerry R., et al. "Lehmann Lovegrass: Central South Africa and
Arizona, USA." *Rangelands* 10 (1988): 53–55.

Cox, Jerry R., and George B. Ruyle. "Influence of Climactic and Edaphic
Factors on the Distribution of Eragrostis Lehmanniana Nees in
Arizona, USA." *Journal Grassland Society of South Africa* 3 (1986): 25–29.

Crites, Stephen. "Storytime: Recollecting the Past and Projecting the
Future." *Narrative Psychology: The Storied Nature of Human Conduct.*
Theodore R. Sarbin, ed. New York: Praeger, 1986. 152–73.

Crowley, Sharon, and Debra Hawhee. "Stasis Theory: Asking the Right
Questions." *Ancient Rhetorics for Contemporary Students.* 2nd ed. Boston:
Allyn and Bacon, 1999. 44–74.

Dauite, Colette, and Cynthia Lightfoot. "Theory and Craft in Narrative
Inquiry." *Narrative Analysis: Studying the Development of Individuals in
Society.* Colette Dauite and Cynthia Lightfoot, eds. Thousand Oaks,
Calif.: Sage, 2004. vii–xviii.

Davis, Charles. "Introduction: The Context of Public Lands Policy
Change." *Western Public Lands and Environmental Politics.* Charles Davis,
ed. 2nd ed. Boulder, Colo.: Westview Press, 2001. 1–8.

———. "Politics and Public Rangeland Policy." *Western Public Lands and
Environmental Politics.* Charles Davis, ed. 2nd ed. Boulder, Colo.:
Westview Press, 2001. 74–94.

———, ed. *Western Public Lands and Environmental Politics.* 2nd ed. Boulder,
Colo.: Westview Press, 2001.

Davis, Janet B. "Stasis Theory." *Encyclopedia of Rhetoric and Composition:
Communication from Ancient Times to the Information Age.* Theresa Enos, ed.
New York: Garland, 1996. 693–96.

Davis, Kathleen M., John M. Englert, and Jennifer L. Kujawski. "Improved

Conservation Plant Materials Released by NRCS and Cooperators through September 2002." U.S. Department of Agriculture, Natural Resources Conservation Service. Beltsville, Md.: National Plant Material Center, 2002. http://plant-materials.nrcs.usda.gov/pubs/ mdpmcpure12002.pdf (accessed March 11, 2003).

Davis, Sandra K. "Fighting over Public Lands: Interest Groups, States, and the Federal Government." *Western Public Lands and Environmental Politics*. Charles Davis, ed. Boulder, Colo.: Westview Press, 2001. 11–31.

Davis, Tony. "A Pocket-Sized Bird Takes on Sunbelt Subdivisions." *High Country News* (August 30, 1999). http://www.hcn.org/servlets/ hcn.Article?article_id=5218 (accessed March 31, 2004).

Decker, Peter R. "The Death of John Wayne and the Rebirth of the Code of the West." *Across the Great Divide*. Philip Brick, Donald Snow, and Sarah Van De Wetering, eds. Washington, D.C.: Island Press, 2001. 64–70.

DeLuca, Kevin. *Image Politics: The New Rhetoric of Environmental Activism*. New York: Guilford Press, 1999.

Depper, Fred. "To C. H. Huckleberry." Undated. Letter 59 in Huckleberry, Correspondence. 103.

Derrida, Jacques. "Structure, Sign, and Play in the Discourse of the Human Sciences." *The Structuralist Controversy: The Languages of Criticism and the Science of Man*. Richard A. Macksey and Eugenio Donato, eds. Baltimore, Md.: Johns Hopkins University Press, 1972. 247–72.

DeVoto, Bernard. "The West against Itself." *The Western Paradox: A Conservation Reader*. Douglass Brinkley and Patricia Nelson Limerick, eds. New Haven, Conn.: Yale University Press, 2000. 45–73.

Duerkesen, Christopher, and Cara Snyder. *Nature-Friendly Communities: Habitat Protection and Land Use Planning*. Washington, D.C.: Island Press, 2005.

Ellis, Carolyn, and Arthur P. Bochner. "Autoethnography, Personal Narrative, Reflexivity: Researcher as Subject." *Handbook of Qualitative Research*. Norman K. Denzin and Yvonna S. Lincoln, eds. 2nd ed. Thousand Oaks, Calif.: Sage, 2000. 733–68.

Emerson, Ralph Waldo. "Nature." *The Selected Writings of Ralph Waldo Emerson*. Brooks Atkinson, ed. New York: Random House, 1950. 3–42.

Epstein, Steven. *Impure Science: Aids, Activism, and the Politics of Knowledge*. Berkeley: University of California Press, 1996.

Fausto-Sterling, Anne. *Sexing the Body: Gender Politics and the Construction of Sexuality*. New York: Basic Books, 2000.

Fleck, Ludwik. *Genesis and Development of a Scientific Fact*. Chicago: University of Chicago Press, 1979.

Fontana, Andrea, and James H. Frey. "The Interview: From Structured Questions to Negotiated Text." *Handbook of Qualitative Research*. Norman K. Denzin and Yvonna S. Lincoln, eds. 2nd ed. Thousand Oaks, Calif.: Sage, 2000. 645–72.

Foss, Sonja K. *Rhetorical Criticism: Exploration and Practice*. 2nd ed. Prospect Heights, Ill.: Waveland Press, 1996.

Frantz, Joe, and Julian Choate. *The American Cowboy: The Myth and Reality*. Norman: University of Oklahoma Press, 1955.

Fraser, Nancy. "Rethinking the Public Sphere: A Contribution to the Critique of Actually Existing Democracy." *Habermas and the Public Sphere*. Craig Calhoun, ed. Cambridge, Mass.: MIT Press, 1992. 109–42.

Friends of the Sonoran Desert. Mailing. You Can Bank on Question #1. 2004.

Futrell, Robert. "Technical Adversarialism and Participatory Collaboration in the U.S. Chemical Weapons Disposal Program." *Science, Technology, and Human Values* 23 (2003): 451–82.

Gaonkar, Dilip Parameshwar. "The Idea of Rhetoric in the Rhetoric of Science." *Southern Communication Journal* 58 (1993): 258–95.

Gardner, Robert, et al. "Colorado Growth-Related Environmental Conflicts." *Making Sense of Intractable Environmental Disputes: Concepts and Cases*. Roy J. Lewicki, Barbara Gray, and Michael Elliott, eds. Washington, D.C.: Island Press, 2003. 355–86.

Geertz, Clifford. *The Interpretation of Cultures*. New York: Basic Books, 1973.

Gergen, Mary M., and Kenneth J. Gergen. "Qualitative Inquiry: Tensions and Transformations." *Handbook of Qualitative Research*. Norman K. Denzin and Yvonna S. Lincoln, eds. 2nd ed. Thousand Oaks, Calif.: Sage, 2000. 1025–46.

Gieryn, Thomas. *Cultural Boundaries of Science: Credibility on the Line*. Chicago: University of Chicago Press, 1999.

Grissino-Mayer, Henri D., and Thomas W. Swetnam. "Multi-Century History of Wildfire in the Ponderosa Pine Forests of El Malpais National Monument." *New Mexico Bureau of Mines and Mineral Resources Bulletin* 156 (1997): 163–72.

Gross, Alan G. *The Rhetoric of Science*. 2nd ed. Cambridge, Mass.: Harvard University Press, 1996.

———. "Why Hermagoras Still Matters: The Fourth Stasis and Interdisciplinarity." *Rhetoric Review* 23 (2004): 141–55.

Habermas, Jürgen. "Discourse Ethics: Notes on a Program of Philosophical Justification." Christian Lenhardtt and Shierry Weber Nicholsen, trans. *Moral Consciousness and Communicative Action*. Cambridge, Mass.: MIT Press, 1990. 43–115.

———. *The Structural Transformation of the Public Sphere: An Inquiry into a Category of Bourgeois Society*. Thomas Burger with Frederick Lawrence, trans. Cambridge, Mass.: MIT Press, 1991.

Haines, Herbert. "Black Radicalization and the Funding of Civil Rights: 1957–1970." *Social Problems* 32 (1984): 31–43.

Haraway, Donna J. *Modest_Witness@Second_Millennium.Femaleman©_Meets Oncomouse™*. New York: Routledge, 1997.

Harris, Lynn, Gary Fox, and David Harris. "To C. H. Huckleberry." December 16, 1998. Letter 58 in Huckleberry, Correspondence. 101–2.

Hauser, Gerard. "Civil Society and the Principle of the Public Sphere." *Philosophy and Rhetoric* 31 (1998): 19–40.

———. *Vernacular Voices: The Rhetoric of Publics and Public Spheres*. Columbia: University of South Carolina Press, 1999.

Hirschkop, Ken. *Mikhail Bakhtin: An Aesthetic for Democracy*. Oxford: Oxford University Press, 1999.

Holecheck, Jerry L., Rex D. Pieper, and Carlton H. Herbel. *Range Management: Principles and Practices*. 5th ed. Upper Saddle River, N.J.: Pearson, 2004.

Horner, Bruce. "Critical Ethnography, Ethics, and Work: Rearticulating Labor." *JAC: A Journal of Composition Theory* 22 (2002): 561–84.

Huckleberry, Chuck H. "Re: Correspondence Received in Response to the Sonoran Desert Conservation Plan." Draft Memo to the Chair and Pima County Board of Supervisors, Arizona. January 19, 1999. CD-ROM. SDCP Reports Disk 1. #4. 004COR.PDF.

———. "Re: Draft Multi Species Conservation Plan." Memo to the Honorable Chair and Members Pima County Board of Supervisors, Arizona. January 3, 2006. http://www.pima.gov/cmo/sdcp/reports/ SDCP.MSCP.III.pdf (accessed April 7, 2006).

———. "Report on Public Comment, Update and Recommendations on the Draft Sonoran Desert Conservation Plan." Draft Memo to the Pima

County Board of Supervisors, Arizona. March 2, 1999. CD-ROM. SDCP Reports Disk 1. #5. 005REP.PDF.

Hunt, Scott, Robert Benford, and David Snow. "Identity Fields: Framing Processes and the Social Construction of Movement Identities." *New Social Movements: From Ideology to Identity.* Hank Johnston, Enrique Laraña, and Joseph R. Gusfield, eds. Philadelphia: Temple University Press, 1994. 185–208.

Ingalsbee, Timothy. "Earth First! Activism: Ecological Postmodern Praxis in Radical Environmental Identities." *Sociological Perspectives* 39 (1996): 263–76.

Ingham, Zita. "Landscape, Drama, and Dissensus: The Rhetorical Education of Red Lodge, Montana." *Green Culture: Environmental Rhetoric in Contemporary America.* Carl G. Herndl and Stuart C. Brown, eds. Madison: University of Wisconsin Press, 1996. 195–212.

Jackson, Laura, and Patricia Comus. "Ecological Consequences of Agricultural Development in a Sonoran Desert Valley." *Ecology of Sonoran Desert Plants and Plant Communities.* Robert Robichaux, ed. Tucson: University of Arizona Press, 1999. 215–54.

Jacobs, Lynn. *Waste of the West: Public Lands Ranching.* Tucson, Ariz.: Lynn Jacobs, 1991.

Jacobs, Wilbur R. "Foreword." *The Frontier in American History* by Frederick Jackson Turner. Tucson: University of Arizona Press, 1986. ix–xx.

Jefferson, Bonnie S. "John Wayne: American Icon, Patriotic Zealot and Cold War Ideologue." *War and Film in America: Historical and Critical Essays.* Marilyn Matelski and Lynch Street Nancy, eds. Jefferson, N.C.: McFarland, 2003. 25–42.

Killingsworth, M. Jimmie, and Jacqueline Palmer. *Ecospeak: Rhetoric and Environmental Politics in America.* Carbondale: Southern Illinois University Press, 1992.

Kingsolver, Barbara. "San Pedro River." *National Geographic* (April 2000): 84+.

Kuhn, Thomas S. *The Structure of Scientific Revolutions.* 3rd ed. Chicago: University of Chicago Press, 1996.

Latour, Bruno. *Pandora's Hope: Essays on the Reality of Science Studies.* London: Harvard University Press, 1999.

———. *Politics of Nature.* Cambridge, Mass.: Harvard University Press, 2004.

Leopold, Aldo. "Thinking Like a Mountain." *A Sand County Almanac*. New York: Ballantine Books, 1966. 137–41.

Lewicki, Roy J., Barbara Gray, and Michael Elliott, eds. *Making Sense of Intractable Environmental Conflicts: Concepts and Cases*. Washington, D.C.: Island Press, 2003.

Lieblich, Amia, Rivka Tuval-Maschiach, and Tamar Zilber. *Narrative Research: Reading, Analysis, and Interpretation*. Thousand Oaks, Calif.: Sage, 1998.

Lyotard, Jean-François. *The Differend: Phrases in Dispute*. Georges Van Den Abbeele, trans. Minneapolis: University of Minnesota Press, 1988.

Marcus, George. "Ethnography in/of the World System: The Emergence of Multi-Sited Ethnography." *Annual Review of Anthropology* 24 (1995): 95–117.

Marcus, George, and Michael Fischer. *Anthropology as Cultural Critique: An Experimental Moment in the Human Sciences*. Chicago: University of Chicago Press, 1986.

McClaran, Mitchel P., and Michael E. Anable. "Spread of Introduced Lehmann Lovegrass along a Grazing Intensity Gradient." *Journal of Applied Ecology* 29 (1992): 92–98.

McKee, Heidi. "Deliberative Dialogue and Online Communication across Differences." Dissertation. University of Massachusetts, Amherst, 2005.

McKenney, Bruce. "Vacant Land Sales Economic Activity Following Critical Habitat Designation for the Cactus Ferruginous Pygmy Owl (Critical Habitat Units 3 and 4): A Review of Key Economic Indicators." The Coalition for Sonoran Desert Protection. October 2000. http://www.sonorandesert.org/content/reports/economic-impacts.html (accessed December 30, 2004).

McKeon, Richard. *Rhetoric: Essays in Invention and Discovery*. Mark Backman, ed. Woodbridge, Conn.: Ox Bow Press, 1987.

Merrill, Karen. *Public Lands and Political Meaning: Ranching, the Government, and the Property between Them*. Berkeley: University of California Press, 2002.

Merton, Robert K. "The Normative Structure of Science." *The Sociology of Science: Theoretical and Empirical Investigations*. Norman W. Storer, ed. Chicago: University of Chicago Press, 1973. 267–78.

———. *The Sociology of Science: Theoretical and Empirical Investigations*. Norman W. Storer, ed. Chicago: University of Chicago Press, 1973.

Miller, Carolyn R. "Genre as Social Action." *Quarterly Journal of Speech* 70 (1984): 151–67.

Moore, Mark P. "Constructing Irreconcilable Conflict: The Function of Synecdoche in the Spotted Owl Controversy." *Communication Monographs* 60 (1993): 271–300.

Nelkin, Dorothy. *Science Textbook Controversies and the Politics of Equal Time.* Cambridge, Mass.: MIT Press, 1977.

———. *Selling Science: How the Press Covers Science and Technology.* New York: W. H. Freeman, 1995.

O'Connor, Sandra Day, and H. Alan Day. *Lazy B: Growing Up on a Cattle Ranch in the American Southwest.* New York: Random House, 2002.

Papa, Lee, and Luke Eric Lassiter. "The Muncie Race Riots of 1967, Representing Community Memory through Public Performance, and Collaborative Ethnography between Faculty, Students, and the Local Community." *Journal of Contemporary Ethnography* 32 (2003): 147–66.

Peterson, Tarla Rai. *Sharing the Earth: The Rhetoric of Sustainable Development.* Columbia: University of South Carolina Press, 1997.

Phillipon, Daniel. *Conserving Words: How American Nature Writers Shaped the Environmental Movement.* Athens, Ga.: University of Georgia Press, 2004.

Pima County, Arizona. Science and Technical Advisory Team, Sonoran Desert Conservation Plan. Personal observation of public meeting. January 16, 2002.

Pima County, Arizona. Steering Committee, Sonoran Desert Conservation Plan. Personal observation of public meeting. Feb. 2, 2002.

———. "The Cactus Ferruginous Pygmy-Owl." Sonoran Desert Conservation Plan. http://www.co.pima.az.us/cmo/sdcp/sdcp2/PO/pygmy.html (accessed March 23, 2005).

———. "Draft Pima County Multiple Species Conservation Plan." January 13, 2004. http://www.co.pima.az.us/cmo/sdcp/MSCP/MSCP.pdf (accessed January 24, 2005).

———. "Draft Sonoran Desert Conservation Concepts: Report on Issues Related to Public Planning Process, Liability, Incentive Options, and Study Series." February 1999. CD-ROM SDCP Reports Disk 1. #5. 005REP.PDF.

———. "Draft Sonoran Desert Conservation Plan." October 21, 1998.

———. "Our Common Ground: Ranch Lands in Pima County: A Conservation Objective of the Sonoran Desert Conservation

Plan/Ranch Conservation Element." October 12, 2000. http://
www.co.pima.az.us/cmo/sdcp/reports/d1/002OUR.pdf (accessed
January 24, 2005).

Plato. "Gorgias." W. R. M. Lamb, trans. *The Rhetorical Tradition: Readings
from Classical Times to the Present*. Patricia Bizzell and Bruce Herzberg,
eds. Boston: Bedford, 1990. 61–112.

Plummer, Ken. "The 'Ethnographic Society' at Century's End: Clarifying
the Role of Public Ethnography." *Journal of Contemporary Ethnography* 28
(1999): 641–49.

Pollack, Elliot D. and Company. "The Economic and Fiscal Impact of the
Designation of 60,060 Acres of Privately Owned Land in Pima County,
Arizona, as Critical Habitat for the Cactus Ferruginous Pygmy-Owl."
For Southern Arizona Home Builders Association. February 25, 1999.

Polletta, Francesca. "Culture and Its Discontents: Recent Theorizing on
the Cultural Dimensions of Protest." *Sociological Inquiry* 67 (1997):
431–50.

———. "Snarls, Quacks, and Quarrels: Culture and Structure in Political
Process Theory." *Sociological Forum* 14 (1999): 63–70.

Prelli, Lawrence J. *A Rhetoric of Science: Inventing Scientific Discourse*. Columbia:
University of South Carolina Press, 1989.

———. "The Rhetorical Construction of Scientific Ethos." *Landmark
Essays on Rhetoric of Science: Case Studies*. Randy Allen Harris, ed. Mahwah,
N.J.: Hermagoras Press, 1997. 87–104.

———. "Topical Analysis and the Problem of Judgment in Environmental
Disputes: The Case of Sustainable Forestry in New Hampshire." *Green
Talk in the White House: The Rhetorical Presidency Encounters Ecology*. Tarla
Rai Peterson, ed. College Station: Texas A&M University Press, 2004.
233–57.

Richards, Evelleen. "(Un)Boxing the Monster." *Social Studies of Science* 26
(1996): 323–56.

Richards, Rebecca T., Jeanne C. Chambers, and Christopher Ross. "Use of
Native Plants on Federal Lands: Policy and Practice." *Journal of Range
Management* 51 (1998): 625–32.

Rifkin, Jeremy. *Beyond Beef: The Rise and Fall of the Cattle Culture*. New York:
Plume, 1992.

Rosaldo, Renato. *Culture and Truth: The Remaking of Social Analysis*. Boston:
Beacon Press, 1989.

Roundy, Bruce A., Raymond B. Taylorson, and Lee B. Sumrall.

"Germination Responses of Lehmann Lovegrass to Light." *Journal of Range Management* 41 (1992): 81–84.

Ruyle, George B., Bruce A. Roundy, and Jerry R. Cox. "Effects of Burning on Germinability of Lehmann Lovegrass." *Journal of Range Management* 41 (1988): 404–6.

Savory, Allan. *Holistic Resource Management.* Washington, D.C.: Island Press, 1988.

Sayre, Nathan. *Ranching, Endangered Species, and Urbanization in the Southwest: Species of Capital.* Tucson: University of Arizona Press, 2002.

Sheridan, Thomas E. *Arizona: A History.* Tucson: University of Arizona Press, 1995.

———. "Cows, Condos, and the Contested Commons: The Political Ecology of Ranching in the Arizona-Sonora Borderlands." *Human Organization* 60 (2001): 141–52.

Shifflett, Wayne A. "Statement." 2004. http://www.peer.org/docs/az/2005_21_2_shifflett_statement.pdf (accessed March 8, 2005).

Slovic, Scott. "Epistemology and Politics in American Nature Writing: Embedded Rhetoric and Discrete Rhetoric." *Green Culture: Environmental Rhetoric in Contemporary America.* Carl G. Herndl and Stuart C. Brown, eds. Madison: University of Wisconsin Press, 1996. 82–110.

Snow, David A., and Leon Anderson. "Identity Work among the Homeless: The Verbal Construction and Avowal of Personal Identities." *American Journal of Sociology* 92 (1987): 1336–71.

Snow, David A., and Robert D. Benford. "Ideology, Frame Resonance, and Participant Mobilization." *International Social Movement Research* 1 (1988): 197–217.

Snow, David A., and Doug McAdam. "Identity Work Processes in the Context of Social Movements: Clarifying the Identity/Movement Nexus." *Self, Identity, and Social Movements.* Sheldon Stryker, Timothy J. Owens, and Robert W. White, eds. Minneapolis: University of Minnesota Press, 2000. 41–67.

Somers, Margaret R. "The Narrative Constitution of Identity: A Relational and Network Approach." *Theory and Society* 23 (1994): 605–49.

———. "Narrativity, Narrative Identity, and Social Action: Rethinking English Working-Class Formation." *Social Science History* 16 (1992): 591–630.

Stacey, Judith. "Virtual Social Science and the Politics of Family Values."

Critical Anthropology Now. George Marcus, ed. Santa Fe: School of American Research Press, 1999. 29–54.

Starrs, Paul F. "An Inescapable Range, or the Ranch as Everywhere." *Western Places, American Myths.* Gary J. Hausladen, ed. Reno: University of Nevada Press, 2003. 57–84.

Stegner, Wallace. "Wilderness Letter." *Marking the Sparrow's Fall: The Making of the American West.* Page Stegner, ed. New York: Henry Holt, 1998.

Stevens, Sharon McKenzie. "Activist Rhetorics and the Struggle for Meaning: The Case of 'Sustainability' in the Reticulate Public Sphere." *Rhetoric Review* 25 (2006): 297–315.

———. "Debating Ecology: Ethnographic Writing That 'Makes a Difference.'" *Ethnography Unbound: From Theory Shock to Critical Praxis.* Stephen Gilbert Brown and Sidney I. Dobrin, eds. New York: SUNY Press, 2004. 157–82.

Szerszynski, Bronislaw. "On Knowing What to Do: Environmentalism and the Modern Problematic." *Risk, Environment and Modernity: Towards a New Ecology.* Scott Lash, Bronislaw Szerszynski, and Brian Wynne, eds. London: Sage, 1996. 84–103.

Tell, David. "Burke's Encounter with Ransom: Rhetoric and Epistemology in 'Four Master Tropes.'" *Rhetoric Society Quarterly* 34 (2004): 33–54.

Thomas, Craig. *Bureaucratic Landscapes: Interagency Cooperation and the Preservation of Biodiversity.* Cambridge, Mass.: MIT Press, 2003.

Tobin, Mitch. "Cattle to Be Removed: Enviro Group Buys South Arizona Grazing Lease." *Arizona Daily Star.* May 29, 2003. http://www.citizenreviewonline.org/may_2003.htm (accessed January 27, 2006).

———. "Wildlife Manager Moved Tadpoles, Will Pay $3,500." *Arizona Daily Star.* February 22, 2005. http://azstarnet.com/dailystar/printSN/62511.php (accessed March 8, 2005).

Turner, Frederick Jackson. *The Frontier in American History.* Tucson: University of Arizona Press, 1997.

Tuska, Jon. *The American West in Film: Critical Approaches to the Western.* Westport, Conn.: Greenwood Press, 1985.

Udall Center for Studies in Public Policy, University of Arizona. "Digest of the Pygmy Owl Forum Facilitated by Congressman Jim Kolbe: A Public Meeting, Held January 7, 1998, to Discuss Issues Surrounding the Cactus Ferruginous Pygmy-Owl in Pima County, Arizona." February 1,

1998. http://wwww.udallcenter.arizona.edu/programs/
enrp/publications/pygmyowl/owldigest.pdf (accessed March 11, 2005).

Ulman, H. Lewis. "'Thinking Like a Mountain': Persona, Ethos, and
Judgment in American Nature Writing." *Green Culture: Environmental
Rhetoric in Contemporary America.* Carl G. Herndl and Stuart C. Brown,
eds. Madison: University of Wisconsin Press, 1996. 46–81.

United Nations, World Commission on Economic Development. *Our
Common Future.* Oxford: Oxford University Press, 1987.

United States Fish and Wildlife Service. *Buenos Aires National Wildlife Refuge:
Draft Comprehensive Conservation Plan and Environmental Assessment.*
Albuquerque: 2000.

Van Nattan, Steve. "The Nature Conservancy: Are These People the Mafia
of the Greens?" http://www.blessedquietness.com/journal/prophecy/
naturcon.htm (accessed July 1, 2004).

Waddell, Craig. "Defining Sustainable Development: A Case Study in
Environmental Communication." *Technical Communication, Deliberative
Rhetoric, and Environmental Discourse: Connections and Directions.* Nancy W.
Coppola and Bill Karis, eds. Stamford, Conn.: Ablex, 2000. 3–20.

Walker, Gregg B., and Steven E. Daniels. "Dialogue and Deliberation in
Environmental Conflict: Enacting Civic Science." *The Environmental
Communication Yearbook.* Susan L. Senecah, ed., vol. 1. Mahwah, N.J.:
Lawrence Erlbaum, 2004. 135–52.

Walker, Janet. *Westerns: Films through History.* New York: Routledge, 2001.

Weber, Edward P. *Bringing Society Back In: Grassroots Ecosystem Management,
Accountability, and Sustainable Communities.* Cambridge, Mass.: MIT
Press, 2002.

White, Hayden. "Literary Theory and Historical Writing." *Figural Realism:
Studies in the Mimesis Effect.* Baltimore, Md.: Johns Hopkins University
Press, 1999. 1–26.

———. "The Value of Narrativity in the Representation of Reality." *The
Content of the Form: Narrative Discourse and Historical Representation.*
Baltimore, Md.: Johns Hopkins University Press, 1987. 1–25.

Winkel, Von K., and Bruce A. Roundy. "Effects of Cattle Trampling and
Mechanical Seedbed Preparation on Grass Seedling Emergence."
Journal of Range Management 44 (1991): 176–80.

Winkel, Von K., Bruce A. Roundy, and David K. Blough. "Effects of
Seedbed Preparation and Cattle Trampling on Burial of Grass Seeds."
Journal of Range Management 44 (1991): 171–75.

Wuerthner, George, and Mollie Matteson. *Welfare Ranching: The Subsidized Destruction of the American West.* Covelo, Calif.: Island Press, 2002.

Zappen, James P. *The Rebirth of Dialogue: Bakhtin, Socrates, and the Rhetorical Tradition.* New York: SUNY Press, 2004.

[INDEX]

Abbey, Edward, 33, 141, 142
aesthetics: in Bakhtin, 179; of landscapes, 26, 67, 80, 144
allotments. See grazing leases
Amphi School Board, 45
antagonist identity fields, 68, 140–41, 179, 196–97n1
anthropocentrism, 63–64, 66
antigrazing activists, 27, 133, 147, 173
applied ecologist, 6, 133, 165
archaeological preservation, 10, 36, 74, 96
Aristotle: on dialectic, 55, 193n3; on division, 53; on epideictic, 28; on genre, 22, 28; on metaphor, 58; on science, 78; on stasis, 84; on topic analysis, 20
Arizona: A History, 25, 28, 31–33, 34, 35, 37, 191n10
Arizona State Constitution, 48
Arizona State Game and Fish, 68, 69
ATVs, 152, 166
Audubon Society, 71, 154
autobiography, 28

Babbitt, Bruce, 5
Bakhtin: and becoming, 164, 179, 197n4; on chronotopes, 17, 34; on clowns, 180; on dialogism, 73, 138, 149, 155, 163–64, 179–80; on heteroglossia, 138; on monologism, 163–64; on personification, 164; on reification, 163–64
baselines, 89–91, 94, 125, 195n7; in Marcus, 162
becoming, 164, 179, 181, 197n4
Berlin, James, 2–3, 12, 59
Beyond Beef, 20, 25, 30–33, 35, 37
biocentrism, 63–64, 66
biodiversity, 124, 132, 147; and core reserve and corridor system, 63–64, 67; in socioecologies, 67, 194n9

Bookchin, Murray, 65
boundary work, 76, 80–81, 82
Brundtland Commission Report, 21
Buenos Aires National Wildlife Refuge: burn program, 105–6, 110, 124–25; and Chiricahua leopard frog controversy, 67–70; Draft Comprehensive Conservation Plan, 96, 106, 123, 124–25; as example of restoration, 123–26
Bureau of Land Management, 33, 68, 153
Burke, Kenneth, 2, 54–60, 155, 159, 193n4
burns. See fire

cactus ferruginous pygmy owl, 42, 45–47, 54, 70, 87
Carson, Rachel, 31, 65
cattle rotation, 27, 97–98, 119, 121, 127, 129, 130, 131, 143
cattlemen's associations, 30–31, 33
Chilton, Sue, 68–69
Chiricahua leopard frog, 46–47, 67–70
chronotope, 17–20, 33–34
Cicero, 84
Cintron, Ralph, 34–35
coalition-building, 57–58, 62–63, 177
Coalition for Sonoran Desert Protection, 52–53, 63
collaboration, 57–58
Common Ground Roundtable, 13
Congress, 22, 33; and appropriations for land purchases, 68, 105
consensus: as ideal in public forums, 5, 174–75, 178; and science in public, 73, 78, 86, 106; in scientific community, 74, 78; and skew argument, 104; in Sonoran Desert Conservation Plan, 5, 41; and stasis theory, 86, 104; and trust-building, 69, 172
conservation easements, 52, 63, 142

conservationism: 26–28, 32–33, 173

conservative ranching, 32, 37

core reserve and corridor system: compared to urbanization, 40; as concept contributing to socioecology, 67; in dramatic analysis, 49–50, 54; in maps, 38, 47; as metaphor, 59, 63–64

counterpublics, 175, 176, 194n3

Court of Appeals, 54

courts, 54; and power struggles, 6, 10, 54; and rulings for environmentalists, 87, 176; and self-protection, 70; and stasis theory, 85–86

cowboy: as lifestyle aspiration, 142, 167; as myth, 32, 142; in popular culture, 33, 192n15; as ranch hand, 68; as sign of the West, 60, 71; stereotype, 139, 142, 144

coyotes, 9, 18

critical habitat, 42, 48, 54, 63. *See also* habitat conservation plans

cultural logics, 162

cultural preservation, 18. *See also* tradition

Defenders of Wildlife, 46

deliberative dialogue, 65, 193n7

deliberative rhetoric, 85–86

Department of Justice, 67

development: and erosion, 111–12, 130; as growth industry, 10, 42; and impact on fire policies, 134; as motive for cooperation and coalition-building, 57, 62–63, 176; in opposition to biocentric cores, 64; and plans for McGee Ranch, 40, 41; and pygmy owl, 41–42, 45–48; and ranching, 10, 18, 32, 33, 48–49, 51–53, 63, 80, 132, 142, 151, 165, 190n1; and Sonoran Desert Conservation Plan, 5, 35, 49, 51–53, 57, 74; and state land sales, 48; and water consumption, 51, 132, 189–90n1

DeVoto, Bernard, 33, 140–41, 142

diachronous argument, 143–44, 147–49

dialectic, 54–55, 56–60, 64, 81, 192–93n3

dialogism: compared to dialogue, 73, 144, 149, 154–55, 169; compared to dramatic

discussion, 175; compared to monologism, 3, 163–64; and conflict, 14; in science-based argument, 73; and socioecologies, 65, 169; and stasis theory, 86

diffraction, 122

District Court, 54

drama, 42, 49–54, 56–58, 64, 140, 175

Earth First!, 11, 14, 145, 168, 173, 197n

ecohumanism, 65

ecospeak, 171

Emerson, Ralph Waldo, 55–56, 61, 66, 71

emplotment, 15–16, 20, 27, 29, 32, 190n4

Enabling Act of 1910, 48

endangered and threatened species, 33, 84, 96, 114, 147; cactus ferruginous pygmy owl, 42, 45–47, 54, 70, 87; Chiricahua leopard frog, 46–47, 67–70; in conflict with resource users, 69–71, 79, 132–33; fish, 89; masked bobwhite quail, 105, 123, 124; southwestern willow flycatcher, 35, 70–71; spotted owl, 70; wolf, 12–13, 191. *See also* critical habitat; Endangered Species Act; National Environmental Policy Act

Endangered Species Act, 46, 70, 79, 87. *See also* habitat conservation plans; Section 10 permit

environmental determinism, 62, 193n5, 193n6

environmental impact statements, 21, 164, 194n2; Buenos Aires National Wildlife Refuge Draft *Comprehensive Conservation Plan*, 96, 106, 123, 124–25

epistemic: rhetoric as, 56, 59, 118, 161, 163; and science, 108, 114–15; social, 2–3, 12, 59

epistemology: in Burke, 56, 59, 118; in Kuhn, 108; in Latour, 3; and ontology, 118, 120

erosion: and ATVs, 166; baselines, 89–90; causes, 1, 84, 91, 99, 100, 122, 147, 190; control of, 9; and development, 130; and drought, 89; and seeding grass, 129–30; and stock management, 27; and stop-check dams, 158

ethnography, 189n1, 191n12; critical, 161–62, 192n17; and mapping, 35

eulogy, 28

facts. *See* Bruno Latour

fenceline photographs, 83–84, 85, 89, 119

fences, 2, 9, 96, 140; destroying, 145; for experimental exclosure, 84; for permanent exclosure, 123, 125, 190n1; for rest and rotation management, 27, 35–37, 129, 130, 131, 164; used figuratively, 22, 35, 138. *See also* Taylor Grazing Act

fire: cycle, 124, 132, 134; as disturbance, 75, 121, 127; let-it-burn policies, 92, 132, 134, 158; prescribed, 105–6, 110, 124, 158; substitutes for, 84, 92, 134; suppression, 132, 134, 165; and vegetation change, 11, 106, 110, 116, 121, 124–25, 132, 134

Fish and Wildlife Service, 42, 46, 177. *See also* Buenos Aires National Wildlife Refuge

fishing industry, 95

Fleck, Ludwik, 108

flycatcher, 35, 70–71

forensic rhetoric, 84–86, 104

Forest Guardians, 176

Forest Reserve Act, 62

framing strategies: in media, 12–13; in rhetorical instruction, 53; and social movement, 68, 140, 147, 179; in Sonoran Desert Conservation Plan, 41, 47–48, 50–52, 63; in stasis theory, 85

Fraser, Nancy, 174–75, 176, 177, 194n3

frontier, 32, 61–62

Galvin, Peter, 114

generic hybridization, 22, 25, 28, 31

genre: autobiography, 28; eulogy, 28; Hollywood western, 192n15; memoir, 25, 28–30, 31, 61; nature writing, 25–26, 55–56, 191n11; oral history, 28, 30;

polemic, 31–32; and rhetorical action, 21–22, 191n7. *See also* narrative analysis; narratives

Gieryn, Thomas, 80–81, 82, 115

grassroots ecosystem management, 14, 172, 175

Grazing Adjudication Board, 29

grazing: and bureaucratic management, 1, 93–94, 98, 178; critiqued as below real cost, 79, 140; and endangered species, 69; fees, 22, 26, 30, 140–41; leases, 10, 102, 176; and state land, 40, 48; and stocking numbers, 93–94, 98, 127; and Taylor Grazing Act, 4, 22, 26–30

Growing Smarter Initiative, 57

Habermas, Jürgen, 174–75, 176, 179, 194n3

habitat conservation plans, 46–47, 64. *See also* Section 10 permit; Multi-Species Habitat Conservation Plan

Haraway, Donna, 122, 189n1

herd effect. *See* hoof action

Hermagoras, 84–85, 194n4

heteroglossia, 138

Hinduism, 20

Hirschkop, Ken, 179–80, 197n4

Hispanic ranchers, 146

Holistic Resource Management, 11, 119, 131, 156–57, 196n6–7; and cattle's impact on grasslands, 121, 127–30, 134–35

home builders' associations, 54; Southern Arizona Home Builders Association, 42, 46

hoof action, 97, 99, 111–12, 127–29, 131, 134

horses, 7, 28, 90, 125, 195–96n8; clubs, 152–53

Huckleberry, Chuck, 38–41, 54, 177

hunting, 7, 8, 10, 125, 181

idealism, 55–56

identification: and dialogism, 169; and differentiation, 12, 155, 159–60; in drama and dialectic, 57–58, 175; with land, 80, 127; of readers, 28, 31, 61, 161 identities, 12, 137–70; antagonist 6, 68, 140–41, 171, 179, 196–97n1; dialogism and invention of, 6, 149, 153–55, 164–65, 169–70; of environments, 14, 47, 62–64; reification of, 138–139, 141, 143, 144, 148–49, 154; of West and nation, 22, 26, 60–61, 71. *See also* applied ecologist; narrative identities; stakeholder; stereotypes

identity politics, 6, 57, 151, 164

identity work, 145, 196n1

indicator species, 42, 70, 75

interviews, 155

introduced species, 5, 49, 106, 114, 117, 122, 123–25, 135, 181

invention: in Aristotle, 20; and dialogism, 87, 138, 149, 154, 162–64, 166, 170; and grassland (re)construction, 122; in skew rhetoric, 104, 107

Ironwood Forest National Monument, 62

irony, 56, 59, 180

Jacobs, Lynn, 119, 141, 142

jeremiad, 26, 31, 191n14

Journal of Range Management, 116–17, 121, 196n1, 196n2

Kolbe, Jim, 45

Kuhn, Thomas, 108–10, 112, 114–15

Latour, Bruno: on epistemology and ontology, 118; on facts, reference, and the mobilization of the world, 3, 73, 115–18, 163, 194n9; on historicity, 118; on nature and politics, 72–73, 78, 108, 118

Lazy B, 25, 28–30, 31–33, 35, 37, 61, 191n1, 192n15

Leopold, Aldo, 25, 34, 65

let-it-burn policies, 92, 132, 134, 158

litter, 99, 103

logging. *See* wood products industry

Lyotard, Jean-François, 191n7, 191n12, 194n3, 196n9

Malpai Borderlands Group, 13

maps: compared to socioecologies, 66, 71, 74–75, 78; developed as part of Sonoran Desert Conservation Plan, 37, 38, 41, 47, 64, 67, 177; for ranch management, 36, 149; rhetorical, 20, 33, 34–35, 36–37, 47, 64, 102, 137

Marcus, George, 59, 161–63

masked bobwhite quail, 105, 123, 124

McGee Ranch, 38–41, 57

memoir, 25, 28–30, 31, 61

Merrill, Karen, 30, 33–34, 140, 173, 191n8, 192n16

Merton, Robert, 81, 108

metaphor, 58–60, 161; in analysis, 59–64, 66; as place, 139, 184; and socioecology, 66

Mexican ranching, 94, 99, 123, 125

Mexico, 123, 125, 189–90n1, 191n10

mining, 8, 38, 121, 135, 157; Sierrita Mining and Ranching Company, 39–40

mobilization: for fact construction, 115–18; for social movement politics, 13–14, 31, 140; and socioecology, 120

monitoring, 93, 124–25, 153. *See also* vegetation transects

monologism, 3, 86,163–64

morality, 2, 71, 159; in histories, 17, 137; in *Lazy B*, 28–29, 31, 32, 61; in narrative, 16, 19, 20, 25; and scientific objectivity, 79

movement: environmental, 79, 146, 156, 168, 173, 197n2; participatory forums as, 175; rhetorical, 6, 56, 176, 193n7; social and collective, 1, 6, 13, 17, 31, 115, 133, 140, 160, 176, 179, 189n1, 196–97n1; in systems, 2, 64, 66, 67–70, 125, 162, 180; westward, 61

Muir, John, 26, 173

Muleshoe Ranch, 13

Multi-Species Habitat Conservation Plan, 47, 54, 63, 177, 194n2

narrative: analysis, 14–17, 20, 21, 161, 190n2–4; closure, 16–18, 26, 30, 31; iden-

tities, 14–20, 22, 26, 137, 138. *See also*
chronotope; emplotment; Hayden White
narratives: 7, 10, 17–20, 22, 24–33, 35, 37,
84, 143, 160, 165, 191n13
National Environmental Policy Act, 87, 88.
See also environmental impact statements
National Resources Conservation Service,
130. *See also* Soil Conservation Service
Native Americans, 10, 177. *See also* Navajo
ranching; Tohono O'odham.
native grass, 99, 106, 110, 116–17, 121–22,
123–25, 129, 135, 161
Nature Conservancy, 13, 14, 20, 68, 154, 173
nature: in dichotomies, 47–51, 72, 78, 89,
126; writing, 25–26, 55, 191n11
Navajo ranching, 99
non-native species. *See* introduced species

objectivity, 79, 81, 108
O'Connor, Sandra Day, 25, 28, 30, 31–33,
61, 191n13, 192n15
open range, 22, 62, 88
open space: as component of West, 2, 22; as
a metaphor, 59–64, 66–67, 193n5;
preservation of, 5, 32, 51, 53
open space bonds, 5, 54, 62, 178
oral history, 28, 30
orality, 28, 191n12–13
Our Common Ground, 51–52

paradigms, 108–14
parks, 38–41, 49, 54, 63, 79
personification, 164
pest species, 49, 64
Pima County. *See* Sonoran Desert Conservation Plan
Pinchot, Gifford, 26, 27, 173
Plato, 54–55, 78, 192n3
polarization, 3, 13, 14, 176; in science-based
argument, 77, 81–82
population vulnerability analyses, 74–75,
77
preservation, 18. *See also* tradition
preservationism, 26–28, 32–33, 37, 173

priority vulnerable species, 47, 75–76,
192n2, 194n2
pronghorn, 36, 48, 84, 91, 105–6, 134
property rights, 8–9, 29–30, 32, 33, 74, 76
public sphere, 173–76, 179
public understanding, 82
purchase of development rights, 52
pygmy owl, 42, 45–47, 54, 70, 87

qualitative research, 155, 162, 173, 196n4
questions: as rhetorical form, 10–11, 21, 109
Quivira Coalition, 13

radical flank effect, 133, 173, 176
Ranch Conservation Technical Advisory
Team: 35, 50, 51–53, 57
ranch economy, 18, 27, 79, 96, 112, 113, 151,
167. *See also* rural economies; welfare
ranchers
ranchettes, 48
range science, 116–17, 120, 121
RECON, 49–50
(re)construction, 122, 126, 129–32, 135–36
recreation, 2, 10, 67, 146; in a multiuse context, 4, 5, 65, 80, 123, 125, 126, 153; and
negative impacts, 40, 85, 166; in Sonoran
Desert Conservation Plan, 65, 80
reference, 84; in Burke, 56, 59–60; in science, 3, 107, 115–18, 125; worlds, 176
rehabilitation, 122, 126–29, 132, 135–36
reification, 3, 53, 57; of identities, 138–39,
141, 143, 144, 148–49, 154; as opposed to
personification, 164; of science-based
argument, 81–82, 108, 135, 163. *See also*
stereotypes
restoration, 122–26, 131, 133–36
reticulate public sphere, 176
rhapsody, 55, 191n14
rhetorical analysis, 2–6, 12; compared to
rhetoric, 12, 59; of genre, 21; and narrative analysis, 14–15; and socioecology,
106, 137, 162; topic analysis, 20
Rifkin, Jeremy, 20, 25, 30–33, 35, 37
riparian areas, 89, 96; and erosion, 9, 119,

rhetorical analysis (*continued*)
158, 189–90n1; and tree regeneration, 92, 98, 131–32; and wildlife habitat, 35, 84, 189–90n1
Roosevelt, Franklin Delano, 30
Roosevelt, Teddy, 26
rural: economies, 10, 18, 70; lifestyle, 18, 28, 32, 79, 157. *See also* ranch economy

Safe Harbor permits, 67, 69
sagebrush rebels, 8
San Pedro River, 189–90n1
Santa Rita Experimental Range, 116, 143
Schwalbe, Cecil, 67
science studies, 3, 82, 107–8, 114–15
Science Technical Advisory Team, 49–50, 74–78, 194n2. *See also* Multi-Species Habitat Conservation Plan
Section 10 permits, 46–47, 54, 63, 71, 178
self-interest, 31, 69, 79–81, 83, 97, 104
Shaw, Bill, 45–46
Sheridan, Thomas: and *Arizona*, 25, 28, 31–33, 34, 35, 37, 191n10; used as source, 89, 126, 191n9
Shifflett, Wayne, 67–69, 106, 193–94n8
Sierra Club, 153, 154
Sierra Vista, 189n1
Sierrita Mining and Ranching, 39, 41
Sierrita Ranch Conservation area, 38–41, 49, 54
Silent Spring, 31, 65
60 Minutes, 12–13
skew rhetorics, 101–4, 107, 135
social ecology, 65
social epistemic, 2–3, 12, 59
social movement scholarship, 115, 160, 184, 189n1; and environmental studies, 13–14, 173, 197n2; identity fields and framing, 68, 140–41, 147, 179; identity work, 145, 196–97n1; radical flank effect, 133, 173, 176. *See also* counterpublics
socioecology: compared to cultural logics, 162; compared to social ecology, 65–66; and contingency, 122, 135, 138, 151, 161,

171; definitions of, 2, 11, 65, 66, 72; language and symbol as constituents of, 2–3, 12, 37, 65, 71; as metaphor, 66–67; in narratives, 16–18, 22, 25–26, 32–33; and need for dialogue, 151, 154, 159, 169, 171; in primatology, 65; and processes of change, 180–81; and science-based argument, 72–74, 80, 107, 115, 120, 136, 161, 194n9
Soil Conservation Service, 123. *See also* Natural Resources Conservation Service
Sonoita, 48
Sonoran Desert Conservation Plan, 37–64; cactus ferruginous pygmy owl in, 42, 45–47, 54, 70–71; Draft Plan, 38–41, 47, 50; as example of participatory forum, 13, 171–72, 177, 179; open space bond, 5, 54, 62–63, 178; Multi-Species Habitat Conservation Plan, 47, 49, 54, 63, 177, 194n2; *Our Common Ground*, 51–52; Pima County Administrator Chuck Huckleberry, 38–41, 54, 177; public comment, 39–41; Ranch Conservation Technical Advisory Team, 35, 50, 51–53, 57; Science Technical Advisory Team, 49–50, 74–78, 194n2; Steering Committee, 64–65, 74, 77–78, 139; web site, 180, 189n3
Southern Arizona Home Builders Association (SAHBA), 42, 46
Southwest Center for Biological Diversity, 12, 45–46, 90, 114, 147, 156, 160, 167, 197n3
species recovery plans, 46
stakeholder, 2, 74; as fixed role, 57–58, 71, 172, 175; science, 77
stasis, 179; applied to grazing, 85, 87, 90, 95, 100; contrasted with skew argument, 100–2, 104; described, 73, 84–86, 88, 194n4, 195n5–6
Stegner, Wallace, 25, 34
stereotypes, 138–53, 158, 164, 197n2
stockmen's associations, 30–31, 33
subsidies, 140–42

Suckling, Kieran, 12, 46
sustainability: and Hispanic ranching, 146; impediments to, 132, 151; management, 80, 93–94, 100, 113, 122, 127, 130–32, 143, 157, 168; and need for agriculture, 92, 134, 157–58, 165; in published texts, 21, 26–28, 32–33, 51; as topic of interview questions, 21, 98, 120, 171
SUVs, 157, 158–59, 197n3
symmetrical analysis, 83–84, 88, 106–7, 121–22, 138
synchronous argument and challenging stereotypes, 143, 144, 149–50, 166
synecdoche, 56

Taylor Grazing Act, 22, 24–33, 62
textbooks, 75, 82, 112
third party, 73, 86–88, 178
third term, 51–53, 57–58
threatened species. See endangered and threatened species
Tohono O'odham, 105, 177, 192n18
topic analysis, 10, 11, 20–21, 139, 196n4,
tourism, 10, 40
tradition, 18, 113, 114, 146, 165; in Lazy B, 25, 28, 32; in Sonoran Desert Conservation Plan, 50, 51–52, 74
transcendence, 55–58, 60, 61, 66, 71
transects. See vegetation transects
transmission model of communication, 137–38
tropes, 55–60. See also metaphor
Tucson, 62, 189–90n1; and development, 37, 472, 48

Turner, Frederick Jackson, 61–62, 66, 193n5–6

Udall Center Common Ground Roundtable, 13
Udall Center for Studies in Public Policy, 45–46, 192n1
urban boundary, 50–51, 52–53, 59, 62–63, 66
urbanization. See development

vegetation transects, 85, 93–94, 110, 116–17, 125. See also monitoring

Waste of the West, 119, 141, 142
watersheds, 10, 96, 160, 165, 189–90n1; and cattle impact, 84, 89, 99, 100, 122, 132; and stop-check dams, 1, 158
Watts, James, 79–80
web as metaphor, 2, 11, 189n1
welfare ranchers, 139–42, 146, 147, 158, 164
Western identity, 2, 22, 26, 60–62, 193n5
White, Hayden, 15–17, 25
wildness, 33, 64, 66–67
wilderness areas, 22, 25, 105
wood products industry, 8, 70, 177, 178
woody plant control methods: burns, 106, 124; chaining or spraying, 116–17, 119, 158; harvest, 177; spread, 84, 165

zoning, 5, 37, 41, 48, 177

[AMERICAN LAND AND LIFE SERIES]

Bachelor Bess: The Homesteading Letters of Elizabeth Corey, 1909–1919
Edited by Philip L. Gerber

Botanical Companions: A Memoir of Plants and Place
By Frieda Knobloch

Circling Back: Chronicle of a Texas River Valley
By Joe C. Truett

Edge Effects: Notes from an Oregon Forest
By Chris Anderson

Exploring the Beloved Country: Geographic Forays into American Society and Culture
By Wilbur Zelinsky

Father Nature: Fathers as Guides to the Natural World
Edited by Paul S. Piper and Stan Tag

The Follinglo Dog Book: From Milla to Chip the Third
By Peder Gustav Tjernagel

Great Lakes Lumber on the Great Plains:
The Laird, Norton Lumber Company in South Dakota
By John N. Vogel

Hard Places: Reading the Landscape of America's Historic Mining Districts
By Richard V. Francaviglia

Landscape with Figures: Scenes of Nature and Culture in New England
By Kent C. Ryden

Living in the Depot: The Two-Story Railroad Station
By H. Roger Grant

Main Street Revisited: Time, Space, and Image Building in Small-Town America
By Richard V. Francaviglia

Mapping American Culture
Edited by Wayne Franklin and Michael C. Steiner

Mapping the Invisible Landscape: Folklore, Writing, and the Sense of Place
By Kent C. Ryden

Mountains of Memory: A Fire Lookout's Life in the River of No Return Wilderness
By Don Scheese

The People's Forests
By *Robert Marshall*

Pilots' Directions: The Transcontinental Airway and Its History
Edited by *William M. Leary*

A Place for Dialogue: Language, Land Use, and Politics in Southern Arizona
By *Sharon McKenzie Stevens*

Places of Quiet Beauty: Parks, Preserves, and Environmentalism
By *Rebecca Conard*

Reflecting a Prairie Town: A Year in Peterson
Text and photographs by Drake Hokanson

Rooted: Seven Midwest Writers of Place
By *David R. Pichaske*

A Rural Carpenter's World: The Craft in a Nineteenth-Century New York Township
By *Wayne Franklin*

Salt Lantern: Traces of an American Family
By *William Towner Morgan*

Signs in America's Auto Age: Signatures of Landscape and Place
By *John A. Jakle and Keith A. Sculle*

This Vast Book of Nature:
Writing the Landscape of New Hampshire's White Mountains, 1784–1911
By *Pavel Cenkl*

Thoreau's Sense of Place: Essays in American Environmental Writing
Edited by *Richard J. Schneider*